Priscila Uppal is a Toronto poet, fiction writer, and York University professor. Among her publications are eight collections of poetry, most recently, *Ontological Necessities* (2006; shortlisted for the $50,000 Griffin Poetry Prize), *Traumatology* (2010), *Successful Tragedies: Poems 1998–2010* (Bloodaxe Books, U.K.), and *Winter Sport: Poems* (2010); the critically acclaimed novels *The Divine Economy of Salvation* (2002) and *To Whom It May Concern* (2009); and the study *We Are What We Mourn: The Contemporary English-Canadian Elegy* (2009). Her work has been published internationally and translated into Croatian, Dutch, French, Greek, Italian, Korean, and Latvian. She is also the editor of several anthologies, including *The Best Canadian Poetry in English 2001*, *The Exile Book of Poetry in Translation: 20 Canadian Poets Take on the World*, and *The Exile Book of Canadian Sports Stories*. She was the first-ever poet-in-residence for Canadian Athletes Now during the 2010 Vancouver Olympic and Paralympic Games and the 2012 London Olympic and Paralympic Games, as well as the Roger's Cup Tennis Tournament in 2011. *Time Out London* recently dubbed her "Canada's coolest poet." For more information, visit *priscilauppal.ca*.

projection

projection

encounters with my
runaway mother

PRISCILA UPPAL

DUNDURN
TORONTO

Library and Archives Canada Cataloguing in Publication

Uppal, Priscila, author
Projection : encounters with my runaway mother / Priscila Uppal.

Issued in print and electronic formats.
ISBN 978-1-77102-274-3 (pbk.).—ISBN 978-1-77102-320-7 (epub).—
ISBN 978-1-77102-321-4 (mobi)

1. Uppal, Priscila.   2. Uppal, Priscila—Family.   3. Mothers and daughters—Biography.
4. Poets, Canadian (English)—20th century—Biography.   I. Title.

PS8591.P62Z53 2013   C811'.54   C2013-902857-9
C2013-902858-7

Editor: Janice Zawerbny
Cover design: Michel Vrana
Cover image: ostill/shutterstock.com

2 3 4 5   17 16 15 14 13

Conseil des Arts Canada Council
du Canada for the Arts

ONTARIO ARTS COUNCIL
CONSEIL DES ARTS DE L'ONTARIO

We acknowledge the support of the **Canada Council for the Arts** and the **Ontario
Arts Council** for our publishing program. We also acknowledge the financial support
of the **Government of Canada** through the **Canada Book Fund** and **Livres Canada
Books**, and the **Government of Ontario** through the **Ontario Book Publishing
Tax Credit** and the **Ontario Media Development Corporation**.

Care has been taken to trace the ownership of copyright material used in
this book. The author and the publisher welcome any information enabling
them to rectify any references or credits in subsequent editions.

J. Kirk Howard, President

The publisher is not responsible for websites or their
content unless they are owned by the publisher.

Printed and bound in Canada.

Visit us at
Dundurn.com | @dundurnpress | Facebook.com/dundurnpress |
Pinterest.com/dundurnpress

Dundurn
3 Church Street, Suite 500
Toronto, Ontario, Canada
M5E 1M2

Gazelle Book Services Limited
White Cross Mills
High Town, Lancaster, England
LA1 4XS

Dundurn
2250 Military Road
Tonawanda, NY
U.S.A. 14150

For my surrogate mothers
and for evenings at home with popcorn and two videos

main menu

OPENING CREDITS:
Blade Runner 1

ONE
Maid in Manhattan 19

TWO
The Big Blue 45

THREE
Mommie Dearest 75

FOUR
Ladyhawke 97

FIVE
God Is Brazilian (Dues É Brasileiro) 109

SIX
Stella Dallas 127

SEVEN
Freaky Friday 153

EIGHT
Throw Momma from the Train 169

NINE
Alien Resurrection/Happy Easter, Felice Pasqua 187

TEN
The Myth of Fingerprints 213

ELEVEN
The Purple Rose of Cairo 237

END CREDITS
Bye Bye Brasil 251

EPILOGUE
Blade Runner, The Director's Cut 259

ACKNOWLEDGEMENTS
The Red Carpet 267

Movie Credits 269

lobby cards

Photograph from My Mother's Website of
Herself, Jit, and Me (circa 1976) 17

The Day I Arrive: My Mother and Me in Front of a Bookstore 43

My Mother and Me at the Italian Restaurant 73

Mother at the Breakfast Table in São Paulo 95

Museum of Precious Stones 107

Soares 126

Encontro e Desencontro 151

Postcard of Guilt 168

Postcard of Essential Questions 168

Family at Airport upon Arrival in Brasilia 185

My Grandmother Therezinha at the Church of Dom Bosco 212

Uncle Fernando at the University of Brasilia 236

The Painting of Mother Goddess
and Her Two Children 250

The Women of the Family—(left to right) Fernanda,
Victoria, Therezinha, Priscila, Theresa 258

My Brother's Wedding Day: (left to right) Chris,
Priscila, Avtar, Jit, Jennifer 265

---

blade runner

Holden (Interviewer): They're just questions, Leon. . . . It's
a test designed to provoke an emotional response. . . .
Describe, in single words, only the good things that come
into your mind about your mother.
Leon Kowalski (Replicant): My mother?
Holden: Yeah.
Leon Kowalski: Let me tell you about my mother.
(Leon shoots Holden.)

I HAVE ALWAYS AVOIDED talking about my mother. Mostly
because when people ask "What did your mother say?" or
"What does your mother do for a living?" or "When will I
meet your mother?" they assume I have one. And not only that
I have one, but also that answers to these questions about my
mother will be quick, clear, and simple. And yet, who has a simple relationship with one's mother, even if that mother did raise
you and support you and is still an integral part of your life? Nevertheless, when people innocently ask about my mother, they
don't realize they are unlatching a gate to a house I have kept
closed for years. It's not fit for living in. There's no one hiding out

in the attic or rotting in the basement, no bones buried under the floorboards or secret wills tucked into pantry tiles; in fact, quite the opposite. The house is empty, swept clean, sanitized. No furniture, no gardens, not even a box of baking soda in the fridge. And I like it that way. I can acknowledge the address (*yes, yes, I used to live there, a long time ago now*), when necessary, but keep on moving. No upkeep required. It wasn't always this easy. The house used to call out to me sometimes—a reverse break and enter, forcing its way into my imagination to rummage about. But I didn't know what the burglars were looking for. And I didn't expect to find myself, later on, knocking at the door.

I hated being the girl in school without a mother. Growing up in Ottawa in the 1980s, I didn't encounter a single other schoolmate without a mother. Some had two mothers—remarriage or adoption. Some had alcoholic or depressed mothers. Some had mothers with rare diseases who revolved in and out of hospital. But all had mothers. I didn't even know anyone, at that point, with a dead mother, a special brand of martyr enabling motherhood, however faulty, to glow enshrined in eternal love. Fairy tales thrive on this notion, which is why all stepmothers are evil; no new woman can possibly compare to the idealized dead mother. The daughter is left unprotected, vulnerable to the trickery of witches and trolls. She must either find a new saviour—fairy godmother or brave prince—or learn to outwit her enemies. I didn't know it at the time, but growing up, my main test would be to figure out which fate was going to befall me. And I had no role models. No one I knew had a "runaway mother": a mother who had abandoned her family without a trace, and without securing a new mother for the children before disappearing off the map. It wasn't a story you could tell quickly, clearly, or simply to people who wanted to know why your mother didn't materialize on parent-teacher interview day, or at Girl Guides camp, or why no one ever picked you up from basketball practice or a birthday party. Of course, after an appropriate time spent at a given school or as part of any club or organization, teachers, coaches, administrators, parents, and schoolmates would eventually discover I was the girl without a mother, a discovery I both loathed and that brought some relief. I didn't need to avoid the topic any longer. Others would now gladly avoid it for me. No one wants to remind the motherless girl that she's motherless. Motherlessness in my situation was far too closely equated with lovelessness. To be this young and this loveless was pitiful. I knew it, and so did the adults. Kids my own age just thought I was weird.

But I still avoided talking about my mother. What was there to say? I couldn't describe in single words the good things I remembered about her. I couldn't remember good things. The bulk of my memories of her had packed up and left inside her luggage and were lost on the other side of the planet. I used to imagine this faceless woman picking up the memories and holding them to her chest. Like I imagined a mother would. And if I remembered bad things, I tried to shoo them away like wasps at a picnic. What was the point of remembering if it only stung? What could I say about my mother? Her name: Theresa. Her place of birth: Rio de Janeiro. Her favourite movie: no clue.

Not that I didn't have a father. I did. And still do. But to talk about my father opened up another set of difficult, sometimes embarrassing, questions. My father, Avtar Uppal, an Indian immigrant, was once an up-and-comer, a tall-dark-and-handsome intelligent civil servant, a junior project manager for the Canadian International Development Agency (CIDA), responsible for overseeing the building of infrastructure projects on eight Caribbean commonwealth islands, until, on January 13, 1977 (a Friday the 13 no less), he swallowed contaminated water during a sailboat accident in Antigua. That water mercilessly attacked his immune system in the form of transverse myelitis (a neurological

disorder caused by an inflammatory process of the spinal cord):
within forty-eight hours my strong, ambitious father was a quadriplegic. He was thirty-seven with two children, a boy and a girl,
Amerjit and Priscila, ages three and two. At the time, my mother
was basically a middle-class housewife living in a three-bedroom
bungalow with an outdoor swimming pool. Overnight, she was
cruelly cast in a new role: no longer the beaming wife in a the-
sky's-the-limit immigrant mixed-race love story, but the suffering heroine of a tragic family melodrama, required to attend to
the relentless needs of an invalid day and night.

I'm not sure when I became conscious of the fact that my
mother deserved some pity for her situation. Probably not as a
child, since I likely accepted my father's condition and everything it entailed—hoists in and out of bed and into a wheelchair,
elaborate pill boxes, a washroom commode, wooden ramps, and
a shaky grey platform attached to electric pulleys that served
as an elevator—as a normal part of our lives, and my mother's
stress and subsequent violent mood swings as irritating factors
that kept her from playing dolls or board games with me. Like
most children, my love for my mother probably existed without me even trying because she was my mother and I wanted
her attention, approval, comfort, hugs, kisses, gifts, bedtime stories. I probably thought she was a good mother, maybe the best
mommy in the whole world, because she was mine. I'm sure I
never thought too hard about how difficult it must have been to
be married to a disabled man, to try to keep up a decent lifestyle
on a small pension and with skyrocketing health care costs (my
father's income took as big a blow as his body), to find oneself
still a young woman but now one forced to say goodbye to sex
and travel and to accept a life of constant emotional suffering.
She disappeared shortly after my eighth birthday, so I hadn't yet
developed such intellectual complexity. But later on, as an ado-
lescent and young teenager, as I became a caregiver for the man

my mother found impossible to withstand, amidst all my own anger and resentment, I did feel something akin to pity for her.

But I always felt more sorry for my father. Even when my mother lived with us. His medically adjusted motorized bed with the steel guardrails and the triangle hoist was a source of constant sorrow but also of reliability. While my overwhelmed mother busied herself around us, cooking separate meals to account for my father's new low-calorie diet, sewing clothes and cutting endless grocery and drugstore coupons, flying into fits of tears and glass-shattering screams, my father would quiz me on my times tables or sing silly nursery rhymes with me. Eventually, my mother couldn't stand it anymore (I use the expression purposefully). The charmed life of happy domesticity and bourgeois luxury she had once imagined for herself banged futilely against wheelchairs and suppositories and spitting tubs. As I said, eventually I ended up feeling sorry for her. Part of me still does. As Hardev Dange, the quadriplegic protagonist of my novel *To Whom It May Concern*, explains to his daughter Birendra before her wedding, *In sickness and in health* might slip eloquently off the tongue as poetry, but is not an easy vow to keep. *Marriage is a written contract, but also a contract of the imagination. . . . In sickness and in health.* Hardev asks, *Who can imagine this? Really imagine it? Very few.* For my mother, the contract was an impossible one to fulfill. The voyage of my father's life had reached an impassable border. His passport had been stamped: sickness. Health would no longer issue him a visa.

In late November 1982, my mother fled, draining all the money from the bank accounts, including the small savings my brother and I had painstakingly deposited in our silver piggy banks. She was thirty-six years old; we were eight and nine. She had purchased three plane tickets for Brazil. One afternoon she tried to pull my bony brother into a beige car I didn't recognize. As his lanky limbs writhed in her grip, I screamed with all the lung power I could muster until she let him go. My brother and I whipped open the screen and front doors and tore inside the house and upstairs, latching ourselves onto my father's bed like animals to tree branches in a storm. Afraid (of what exactly, I didn't know—of tomorrow, the future, the realization that if my mother had been able to shove my brother inside the car we might have been split apart forever), we locked the front and back doors. But there was no need for locks. She didn't want in. She wanted out. And she was already gone.

My father needed help. On all kinds of medication and requiring continuous support to manage basic daily tasks such as shaving, using the toilet, bathing, cooking soup for lunch, he was not equipped to raise young children on his own. As we clung anxiously to his bed, watching episodes of *Happy Days* and *The Facts of Life*, then falling asleep exhausted against his steel guard-rail (I still find rectangular medical rails—stomach pressed to metal, a hand or elbow peeking out—strangely reassuring), my father made phone calls. The next afternoon, a tall man with a warm brown face and mild speech, an uncle I'd met only once before, arrived in a tiny red Toyota, quickly and efficiently piled us all in, folding my father into the front seat like a dress shirt and the two of us in the back like shoe boxes, and drove us over the border. We made no fuss, as if we knew our lives were now placed in other people's hands and we needed to be able to say goodbye, not just to the idea of a mother but to all the things we associated with home. Although I was only in grade three, I was to sing the lead in the Christmas choir pageant, which included not one but two solos I had been practising nonstop for weeks. I had prepared a presentation on monarch butterflies, including dozens of specimens painstakingly copied and coloured-in from our *Encyclopedia Britannica*. My brother must have had hockey practice, a science quiz, a friend's birthday party at the McDonald's caboose. But we didn't tell our teachers we were leaving. We didn't have the chance to tell a single friend. Within twenty-four hours, our Ottawa house, 2134 Erinbrook Crescent, once painfully alive with wounds and despair and skinny energetic siblings playing in the basement with trains, battling at Ping-Pong or belting out *The Wizard of Oz* records, blinked into emptiness as we filed into place on the highway, our own form of purgatory, awaiting our fate.

That night, after the clouds became blacker and the traffic lights fuzzier, we checked into a roadside motel with worn brown carpets and curtains, and a funny odour like moist towels. My unfamiliar uncle, whose skin smelled of sweet spice, wheeled my father into the room, unzipped a beige luggage bag, and handed my brother and me two packages wrapped in glossy red Christmas paper.

"An early present," he offered, his white teeth, like my father's, a sharp contrast to his dark brown skin. "You've had a hard day."

He was probably right, but I honestly don't remember it being a hard day. We had no idea where we were going or for how long, but we packed very little—my brother and I an army-green canvas backpack each with T-shirts and underwear, colouring and puzzle books—mine with a plush lamb toy as well as a pink skipping rope for pit stops. Plus: a day off from school! What a rarity! Usually only gifted on blisteringly cold snow days. We sang along to Top 40 pop music the whole ride: Toni Basil's "Mickey," Olivia Newton-John's "Physical," Billy Idol's "White Wedding." Like a vacation, although I'd never been on vacation. New York? I had never been to New York. I wanted to see the Empire State Building and the Statue of Liberty. I wanted to taste a New York hotdog, like I'd seen on television cop shows. We're off to New York!

"Cool!" my brother exclaimed, punching his left hand into the pocket of the baseball glove, beaming a buck-toothed smile. This uncle knew he was left-handed. A real soft brown leather Wilson baseball glove!

For me: Barbie. A real Barbie, with silky blond hair and blue eyes and a frilly white sundress. Not a fake plastic copy with rough broom hair you could buy for $1.99 at Boot's Pharmacy or Dominion. What was happening was something from the movies, like *Miracle on 34th Street* or *Cinderella*. Our family couldn't afford name-brand baseball gloves or Barbie dolls. We played with these things at our friends' houses, but they remained in other bedrooms and play bins, on greener lawns. I now knew something was very, very wrong. I stared at my new blond playmate and I didn't want to give her back, but I did want some sort of explanation. Like my mother, she already seemed unreal, a plastic substitute for something essential we were being deprived. Why were these two small childish dreams coming true? What larger dream had disappeared into that anonymous beige car?

Dreams are resilient. Like down-and-out street fighters, or single moms challenging the legal system. Dreams are also dangerous. My mother's heart was stuffed to the brim with dreams, and after my father's accident she watched them poke out like pillow feathers and fly away. I can't claim to know the specific content of her dreams, but I do know she was a passionate and visceral dreamer. Everyone in my family is. My father dreamed big dreams too. Eight Caribbean islands: Antigua, St. Kitts, Nevis, St. Lucia, Grenada, St. Vincent, Montserrat, Dominica. A three-bedroom house with a green yard lined with pines and a large maple tree in front for his kids to climb and swing from, vegetable gardens and strawberry bushes, and, of course, a swimming pool. Plans for a farm in the country where, for a hobby, he might breed German shepherds or border collies. And I know he still carries those dreams with him. My father is the most resilient person I've ever met. I just don't know if he still recognizes himself in those dreams, of if they belong to another time and place, like old film reels of a young man who had travelled the world before coming to Canada as part of his job on British Airways, who had swept the Brazilian military attaché's daughter off her feet and into a sari to marry him, who had stood beside prime ministers to christen airports and power plants. A young man who little resembles the distressed and balding man, legs shaking uncontrollably in his wheelchair, white linen with blue stripes draped over his lap supporting a tray he uses as a surface to sign cheques and write out lists of medical supplies and doctor's appointments. My father avoids talking about his dreams. He'd rather talk NHL hockey scores, health care cuts, or Dirty Harry movies. Not dreams. And certainly not about my mother.

Neither will my brother. He pretends she is dead. That fantasy suits his own dream life. My brother is practical, and confronting an unchangeable past is simply impractical. It interferes with his enjoyment and quality of life. The lie places my mother not on the other side of the world eating and sleeping but on another plane of existence without movement or substance, no possibility of interaction. He's thrown his fistful of dirt on the coffin. His memories have run like hell, no intention of returning. I wish I were able to believe she were dead.

Tell me about your mother.
Tell me about your mother.
Tell me about your mother.

Writers' psyches are a tad perverse. Ever since I was eighteen and had started writing seriously at university, I entertained the idea of embarking on a trip to find my runaway mother, and to write a book about the journey even if I didn't find her (and for some reason I actually believed I wouldn't—as if she were an elusive fairy-tale villain who lived under a mystic bridge or a sci-fi monster hibernating in a cave on another planet, and not a flesh-and-blood human being who predictably ran back to the land of her birth and to the nest of her immediate family). I've always been fascinated by how we mourn people and places that still exist, are still very much alive but are dead or unattainable to us. When someone disappears, we create and re-create that person in our imaginations, shaping them to suit what we think of ourselves at this particular stage in our lives, a specific time and place in our personal history. To come up face to face against the real person—whose face will never appear to you as you envisioned it—is to come up against and interrogate your own imagination and discover through cross-examination how true or how false you've been to this person, to the past, and to yourself. The ramifications are serious, no matter how elusive. Perhaps, more truthfully, I hoped I wouldn't actually find her and force her to become real once again. Who you imagine others to be reflects on who you imagine yourself to be.

Exposed as inhuman because he has no mother, the replicant in *Blade Runner* resorts to brutal violence. That uncomfortable opening scene always makes me laugh. And I laugh even harder since I've discovered *Blade Runner* is my mother's all-time favourite movie. She's seen it over a hundred times. *In the theatre.* I'm pleased that her favourite movie is, I think, a great movie, a cinematic classic, the epitome of sci-fi, which I know is snobbish on my part, but I can't help it. At least in this, my mother has good taste.

Directed by Ridley Scott in 1982 and set in future Los Angeles, in the year 2019, the film is a dizzying spectrum of industrial waste, neon strip clubs, smoke-filled interrogation rooms, eerie toy-filled hotel suites, and advanced biological labs. Through a tough-talking, alcoholic hit man, Rick Deckard (played by Harrison Ford), and a tragically beautiful disillusioned android, Rachael (played by Sean Young), the film exposes a dirty, greedy, racist, and irresponsible civilization imploding. (Sound familiar?) It is also a movie about exile and homelessness, suffering and survival, and the horror and vitality of dreams. It doesn't escape me any longer that the seductive porcelain replicant, who wants to rewrite her fate and that of her lover Roy (played by Rutger Hauer) as doomed machines programmed to live only a few years, the role that star-rocketed Daryl Hannah's career, is named Priscilla. Secretly, I've imagined, it's one of the reasons my mother watches that movie over and over again. Does my mother envision her daughter as a weary traveller wandering through alleyways and Dumpsters masquerading as a mannequin, hoping for a longer lease on life, hoping for a future? I certainly must not live in *this* world to her. I must be jumping from one devastated planet to another.

What I find most interesting about *Blade Runner*'s human-machine-mixed society is how fake memories serve the androids to convince them they're human. The pain of discovering that the memories are false is too much for some of the disillusioned to bear. Probably the most heartbreaking scene in an otherwise thrilling disaster movie occurs when the impeccably groomed and controlled Rachael, off-kilter at the suggestion that she is a replicant, thrusts forward a photograph of a dark-haired woman she believes to be her mother as irrefutable evidence of her human biology. Deckard proves the photograph is a fake. Rachael has no mother, no family, no human blood. The most pressing question at the end of the film is: Does Deckard know that he too is likely inhuman? Yet being inhuman doesn't stop them from suffering, loving, hating, caring, running, or dreaming.

What does it mean to have a mother? Is it the necessary condition of humanity? If you don't have a mother (or have no contact with her), what is the value of your invented memories or projections of this person over the years? Does this change how you suffer, love, hate, care, run, or dream? Does it change how the humans with mothers interact with you? Like Rachael, I have sometimes insisted to skeptics my story is a human one after all.

Like Rachael, I have sometimes gone home with tears in my eyes and a hopelessly ineffectual photograph shoved in my pocket.

I found my mother by accident on the internet on a sunny September afternoon in 2002. I wasn't looking for her. I was searching for online reviews of my first novel to print out and catalogue for my professorial tenure file. Scrolling down the hits that popped up after typing in my name, I halted at a link that included my brother's name alongside my own. Amerjit Uppal. That's what caught my eye. My partner, Chris, was sitting beside me in our cramped home office.

"What do you think this is?" I gestured.

"Probably a genealogical site," he quickly replied. "The internet is full of them."

Never know when you might need a family tree, I thought rather innocently and clicked.

My story, my dreams, my sense of who I am as a daughter: permanently altered. There, in front of my stunned eyes, in full colour, as if by a magician's wand, appeared the personal website of my runaway mother, a person I hadn't seen or heard from and whose name I hadn't spoken aloud in twenty years: Theresa Catharina de Góes Campos. Alarmed by both familiarity and strangeness, my eyes flitted all over the site, a jigsaw puzzle of my buried past and an unknown present. I immediately recognized her large dark eyes and jet-black hair, her first name, but not her short afro-like curls, her pudgy, powdered-white face with startling red lipstick, the words *jornalista, conferencista, escritora, professora, universitária e productora cultural* underneath her headshot. When I was a child, she'd always worn her hair straight, parted in the middle, a uniform inward curl at the ends; and she was thin, not bone thin, but a slim woman with an angular face with a hint of tan. Then my eyes centred underneath the banner heading *Sobre minha família e meus amigos*: where I discovered my childhood self, and my brother—two and three years old. She'd posted a photograph of us in clothes I recognized as ones she had made—my brother in a red-and-white-checkered cowboy-style shirt and navy blue pants, me in a pink dress covered up with a white poncho-style jacket and a pink bonnet, our choppily cut short hair sticking out—nestled in front of my mother with her signature 70s-style wide orange hairband setting her black shoulder-length hair in place, orange-and-white-striped cardigan open over a white shirt. A fake fall landscape backdrop. All smiles, Sears portrait. I recognized the photograph immediately, uncannily, because my father keeps one from the same studio session; us in the same clothes, my father in his best navy blue suit and tie perched on the same sitting block, film tinted with the same slight pink hue. I know there must be a photograph somewhere of all four of us from this same day, before my father's accident, but I've never seen it. Maybe at some point it too rested on the mantel, but those days are long gone. My mother does not appear in my father's photograph. My father does not appear in hers. But there we are on her website.

I believe my first words were: "What the fuck is this? What the fuck is this?" And then, for clarification: "That's me. That's me and Jit!"

Accustomed to few words and fewer certainties on the subject of my mother, Chris immediately adopted the role of detective and protector, as well as curious spectator. "Is that *your mother*? Is this *your mother's* website? Yes, this is your mother's website. Why are *you* on her website? It's all in Portuguese. We'll need to use the translation function. Go back. Go back."

Go back. Go back. I didn't want to go back. Our basement apartment in Toronto's Annex, crammed to the rafters with books and racks of clothing, now seemed even smaller to me. An unwanted, unwelcome intruder had just entered the premises, dropped her luggage, and taken up residence without so much as an alarm bell or a knock at the door as I flipped back to the search engine to click that seemingly innocuous phrase: "Translate this page."

It was a function I'd never used before. Translate this page. The promise of understanding. But I didn't understand. My brother and I were still there, like clones, living an alternative existence in cyberspace, our infant selves kidnapped for an as yet unknown ransom. And there she was again, my mother, my runaway mother, with her white pudgy cheeks, now smiling at me in strange, broken, ungrammatical English as I examined the various columns and messages and images—in our tiny yellow office, a colour I specifically chose to keep me alert during long nights of writing or studying—informing me that she is a journalist, head of the ethics board ("You've got to be kidding me!" I cried), a professor, a writer, and a prolific movie reviewer. And a woman riddled with cancer—a special section of her website dedicated to thanking and acknowledging the many doctors who have kept her alive.

"Fuck," I said again. "Oh, fuck." I knew what the cancer message meant. What it meant to me. It hit me as hard as the fateful click of that mouse. "I'm being told to go. To go see her. *Meet her.* If I wait any longer, I might not get the chance."

Chris was holding my hand like you would that of a shock victim, gently caressing it, and listening to me, but he was also scanning, reading and rereading the website with keen interest and disbelief. He'd never seen a picture of my mother. I'd not even glanced at one in over ten years. For a time after my mother's disappearance, I used to trudge guiltily down to the basement to sequester myself at the foot of a cardboard box of photo albums, like a pilgrim at the base of some oracle, intensely poring over the collection of esoteric images for clues as to why my family had been singled out by the gods for tragedy. The white album with silver embossing and lettering, *Our Wedding Album*, held special fascination for me: my father in an imposing dark turban (I'd never seen him in one before; he'd cut his hair when he moved to England and only wore the turban at his wedding for ceremonial purposes) and suit, my mother in a lacy red sari and then white princess wedding gown complete with veil, both exuding strength, confidence, happiness, and if I'd known how to recognize it perhaps something we call "love." I studied those albums page by unforthcoming page. Sometimes I would cry, without knowing exactly why, my mother and father frozen in a dance or cutting their wedding cake. The black-and-white ones affected me the most, as if the past was being drained of all its colour and would soon be nothing but a grey haze. I know I missed my mother, as any child would regardless of whatever resentments I also carried with me, but I also missed my father, the man I felt was supposed to raise me, a strong man who could command an entire room full of people with his stature alone, a happy man who winked at the camera with anticipation of the joys life had in store for him. When I cried, I would sometimes say softly to myself, reminiscent of Dorothy from *The Wizard of Oz*: *There's no place like home. There's no place like home.* I desperately wanted to go home, even though I didn't know where home was. I just knew I hadn't found it yet, because home would be a place where pain ends, where one believes again in *I do* and *forever*. Then, one day, no further along in discovering the answers I sought than the day my mother left, I dried my tears, put the photo albums away, and washed my hands of them. So whenever Chris's family would pass family album after family album around on holidays, rehashing ordinary moments from a collective past over cookies and tea, I'd have nothing to show from my side. And this state of affairs pleased me. I found their desire to relive the same memories over and over again pointless. I liked the fact that my past, my family, was off limits to everyone except me. My imaginative territory alone. Able to change if needed, at a moment's notice.

But now my past was uploaded on a public website. In the collective photograph, my mother's presence was not so much that of a person of flesh and blood but more architectural, like a cottage where you once spent the summer. I could smell her the way one remembers the smell of campfire smoke. The recent photograph of her with at least forty extra pounds, a wave of dark curls framing a cartoonish, large-lipped smile, I wouldn't have picked out of a police lineup.

Chris turned to me and then back to the screen, his hand still stroking mine. This was the first time I registered I was shaking involuntarily from my waist down, just like my father. "Do you think you're ready?"

"I don't know. But I have to go, don't I?"

Writers' psyches are a tad perverse. If a story presents itself, we are sometimes loyal to the story at the expense of ourselves.

It's a test designed to provoke an emotional response. . . .
Describe, in single words, only the good things that come into
your mind about your mother.

Chris and I spent the entire night searching the website for more clues. My name and my brother's name were not tagged under the photograph but on her c.v. Apparently, in Brazil, you are legally required to list all your known children on your resumé. She'd also listed her phone number and email address. I decided on the phone.

Calendars were consulted. Tickets purchased. Items packed.

This is a story about mothers and daughters, disappearances and reunions, family bonds and family secrets, travel, trauma, grief, art, and the nature of the imagination. And movies. This is the story of how I became a blade runner.

While I am writing this, there is a good 75 percent chance my mother is ensconced in a plush movie theatre seat, a bag of popcorn tucked in her lap. Right now. She screens anywhere from one to eight movies *per day*. Her dream world has fully and firmly supplanted itself in the simulacrum of Movieland. Not a rare condition. One of the ways I've come to understand my relationship with my mother has been through the lens of movies: movies she loves, movies about Brazil, and many, many movies about mothers and daughters. Projecting thoughts and emotions onto mother and daughter characters in film. I imagine I'm not the only one.

So feel free to grab a warm blanket, heat up some popcorn, and join me in the tragicomic adventure section of your video store. Here's your ticket. Feel free to project.

Photograph from My Mother's Website of Herself, Jit, and Me
(circa 1976; this photo has since disappeared from the website.)

1

maid in manhattan

Chris Marshall: Can we start over? Second chance, second date? You as you, me as me. No secrets. What do you think?

Take One

APRIL 8, 2003: Late afternoon. Orange and green Beck taxi pulls in front of our apartment on Brunswick Avenue. I throw two large black suitcases, one full of clothes (even though my mother has insisted she wants me to bring no clothing whatsoever so that she can buy me a brand new Brazilian wardrobe), toiletries, and books to read (including Portuguese phrase books and poetry and prose by Brazilian authors: Moacyr Scliar, Carlos Drummond de Andrade, Clarice Lispector), and one empty, in anticipation of the gifts and souvenirs I might bring home, into the trunk. Although Chris is nervous about sending me off on my prodigal journey while he waits anxiously for news at home, he understands why I insist on embarking alone. This is a once-in-a-lifetime reunion, decades in the making, between me and this wide-faced, fuzzy-haired woman on the internet. While this virtual woman did extend

an invitation to "my husband" to join me, she expressed no surprise—at least online—at his polite decline. After almost seven
years of living and writing together, Chris trusts my gut instincts
when it comes to art and people. *Yes, I'll admit I'm a little scared
to be alone with a complete stranger on the other side of the planet,
but you'd be a barrier between us. Brazil is a machismo culture.
I know she'll alter how she acts, what she says, because you're a
man. And she'll always be worried about what you actually know
of the past, what you think, if you're influencing me. She'll assume
I brought you for protection. I don't want her to think I'm afraid
of her. I want her to know I come in peace. At least I think I come
in peace.* I kiss our cats: Professor, my pudgy black-and-white
tuxedo, who knows how to open the fridge and kitchen drawers to extract treats and has sat by my computer on a black fold-
out chair during the writing of every term paper and book; and
Junior, a confident marmalade with a fluffy squirrel tail and
"puffy pants" legs, who likes to sprawl out on manuscript pages
and bat pens about. Chris tucks a yellow beanbag duck I've
named Quark into my carry-on to remind me of home, gives me
a long, forceful hug, several kisses about my face and neck, and
wishes me luck.

   And I'm off, looking rather spritely in a stylish black jumpsuit
with a jaunty yellow and orange pleated neck scarf. At Toronto's
Pearson airport, I buy a bar of dark chocolate and a pink neck
pillow (at nine hours this will be the longest flight I have taken
thus far in my life) and file into the check-in line. I flash the Air
Canada attendant, a middle-aged woman with brown wavy hair,
a huge smile, the same smile I flashed the taxi driver, the confec-
tionery attendant, and the store clerk. I am on a mysterious and
exciting adventure after all, and I have the feeling that everyone
I encounter is a co-conspirator in the tale about to unfold. At
the airline counter, I feel restlessness brewing in every muscle. I
tell myself to calm down, yet as I slide over my passport and my

ticket, I am nearly giggling with anticipation. I'm about to board a plane and travel nine hours to meet a woman that I haven't seen or heard from in nearly twenty years who happens to be my mother; I am going stay with her in São Paulo in a hotel and then later on Easter weekend in her condominium in the capital city of Brasilia. Finally, I'm going to come face to face with her, discover what she's like, what she's been doing these last twenty years, who we will be now to each other instead of runaway mother and abandoned daughter. I am so brave.

The Air Canada attendant flips through my passport.

"Where's your visa?"

"I've already paid for the ticket." Still smiling, I point to the paper, resume clenching and unclenching my toes.

"No. Your traveller's visa. Canadians need a visa to visit Brazil."

I might not yet be a world traveller, but I am responsible. This woman is confused. "I asked my travel agent. He said I didn't need one. I don't need one."

She shakes her head, sliding my documents back to me. "You can't trust travel agents. Always check the customs website. You can't travel to Brazil without a visa."

My smile drops, along with my courage. I am now a scared, ignorant girl. "But I'm Canadian."

"We don't need visas for most countries, but Brazil got upset when Canada put a restriction on Brazilians travelling to Canada. Tit for tat thing. Every country has the right to set its own customs laws." She shrugs.

I make no motion to leave the counter. It finally dawns on me. "Does that mean I can't go?"

The attendant nods sympathetically. "You need to go to the Brazilian consulate and apply for a visa. Air Canada will transfer your ticket, no problem."

"I can't go?" Even as I ask the question, I'm hopeless. Unexpectedly and quite uncontrollably, I start to cry, passport in hand in the bustling terminal. Not the first or the last person to do so, I realize, even as it's happening, but I never thought that lost soul bawling her eyes out amid steel carts and luggage belts and gate signs would be me. What I want to say is, *That stupid travel agent should be fired,* but what I actually say rises from a long-buried pain in my chest: "I'm going to see my mother. She's sick . . . . I haven't seen her in . . . years . . ."

"It's going to be okay," the attendant assures, lightly caressing my shoulder as we walk over to the Air Canada ticket booth. "Normally it takes two weeks to get a visa, but if you're visiting family and mention your mother is ill, you should have a visa by our next flight, exactly forty-eight hours from now."

"Forty-eight hours? But . . ." But I'm ready to go now. I want to confess: I might not be ready again in forty-eight hours. I'm a twenty-eight-year-old woman with a stuffed toy in her carry-on who reads and writes poetry for a living—not exactly the blueprint for a fearless explorer. I only have so much bravery, and I might have used it all up today. You have no idea what you're preventing me from doing. You're interfering with my story. I didn't write a visa complication into the script.

"Be patient at the consulate. They'll give you your visa, but they'll probably give you a hard time and make you wait until the very last possible minute. It's not a friendly consulate. I hate going there. I'm Brazilian too." She hands me an address: 55 Bloor Street West. At least it's downtown, not far from where I live.

I am still crying openly among those who are flying out today, sniffling all over the receiver when I talk to Chris from an airport pay phone, fiddling with my scarf as I explain, between sobs, that I'm coming home in another expensive cab ride, my two disappointed suitcases, one full and one empty, flung like deflated wishes back in the trunk.

Take Two

Pacing outside the Brazilian consulate the next morning before it opens, application in hand.

The Air Canada attendant was right. The Brazilian consulate is a cold, unfriendly place with a stocky and dour woman in a matronly blue blazer working the window.

"If you're Brazilian, you should have a Brazilian passport," she grunts.

"I'm not Brazilian. I'm Canadian. My mother is Brazilian."

"If your mother is Brazilian, then you're Brazilian."

The logic eludes me. I am told to come back tomorrow.

The next day proceeds much like the first, me pacing outside the consulate in the morning before it opens, the same stocky and dour woman, this time in a matronly purple blazer, working the window. *Sit and wait.* Even through lunch hour when they close the wicket, I am told not to leave or I will lose my spot. What spot? I'm beginning to wonder if it's worth it. If I can't even manage to get myself a visa and onto a flight without a massive hassle, how will I navigate a foreign culture and language in one of the most dangerous countries in the world on top of whatever my mysterious runaway mother will throw at me? Maybe my missing visa is an omen, a sign? As a writer and literary scholar, my eyes and ears should be attuned to such blatant foreshadowing.

"Excuse me, I won't make my flight if I can't get the visa by four o'clock."

"I know," she snarls as she points for me to resume my post on the uncomfortable bench, periodically shooting me dirty looks until it's five to four before calling my number out to a waiting room of one. *I've already lost control of this story,* I admit to myself as I tear out of the building and rush home to phone another taxi.

The taxi, the suitcases, the hugs and kisses, the airport, all déjà vu, except that my Air Canada attendant is on the lookout for me in the crowd and waves me to the front of the line.

"You must be anxious to see your mother," she whispers.

"I am." Though this time, I don't feel giddy or brave, only scared.

"I hope she'll be well soon."

"Me too," I offer, though I don't know what I wish as I step back from the counter admiring my travel visa like it's a certificate of achievement.

On the flight, I am seated beside a woman named Dalva with gorgeous olive skin and friendly eyes. She introduces herself, telling me her name means morning star. She points to my phrasebook.

"First time to Brazil?"

"Yes."

"You look Brazilian. Are you visiting family?"

"Sort of."

I note that this beautiful Dalva is acting motherly toward me. Do I look like a need a mother? I'm not sure that's a look I should be going for.

"You'll be fine. Just relax. You're from Ottawa, aren't you?"

"How did you know? My accent?"

"I work at the Brazilian consulate. Not at the booth, but in the office. I saw you today. I saw your application. I knew your mother and father. It's a coincidence that we're on this flight together, but I know your story. It's a sad story. You haven't seen your mother for some time."

I'm not as shocked by her words as I imagine I should be. Although I'm not altogether convinced the designation of "coincidence" is accurate, I don't feel threatened by this woman with wavy black shoulder-length hair in a flowery pantsuit eating slices of green apple beside me. In fact, she is oddly comforting. Plus,

the fact that she has some knowledge of my parents matches my
original vision of my trip as epic voyage. Every epic hero or heroine is watched over by sympathetic gods who send wise advisors
down to earth for aid. Dalva strikes me as one of these special
characters. Of course she is disguised in government garb: my
father was a successful civil servant, my mother the daughter of
a high-ranked diplomat. The tragic tale of my father's accident
and my mother's subsequent flight to Brazil circulated among
government office water coolers in Ottawa, why not Toronto?

The plane conspicuously empty, I lower the back of my chair.
"Twenty years."

"Now I feel old," she laughs, pressing her lever to follow suit.

The pilot warns us of turbulence, which lasts for eight hours
of the nine-hour flight (not ideal for a nervous traveller who suf-
fers from motion sickness—another sign from the gods?) and
delays the serving of dinner until well after midnight. Dalva
closes her eyes and sleeps, never moving a muscle. I cannot join
her. Nor can I watch the movies—it's funny, now that I am much
more travelled, I still can't enjoy movies on an airplane; the size
of the screen offends me—not that I want to, as they are showing *Harry Potter and the Chamber of Secrets* and *The Hurricane*.
Why a children's movie after midnight? I wonder. When I scan
the seats, there are no children on this flight. Just some business-
men, Dalva, and me.

Before we land, Dalva asks over a tray of tasteless scrambled
eggs, "What are you hoping for with your mother? Forgiveness,
reunion, a new start?"

She doesn't apologize for her bluntness or curiosity. I like this
Dalva that I will never see again, who fits nicely into the role I
have assigned her in my narrative. She exudes good will. I know
I'm projecting, but I suddenly wish I could leave the plane and
go off with her rather than the woman from the website who

when I phoned from the airport swore retribution to those who wouldn't let me on that original Toronto–São Paulo flight. Without a visa I would be detained in São Paulo, I told her, to calm her down. Either that or jailed. I was lucky the attendant refused to issue me a boarding pass. But she was inconsolable. Although I was somewhat alarmed by the force of her anger, at least it proved she's as invested in this reunion as I am.

"No. Not forgiveness. I was raised Catholic, but I'm an atheist. I don't understand their obsession with forgiveness. I don't care about forgiveness. I don't believe in it."

"Once a Catholic, always a Catholic," Dalva laughs, poking her orange juice open with the plastic fork. I've heard it before. I've even said it before. But I don't mean it. And now I'm visiting one of the most Catholic countries on the planet, a people who built one of the world's largest statues of Christ to watch over the country day and night. "What do you care about then?"

"I want to fill in the blanks of the story, you know?"

"Your mother's not going to like being a character. I can tell you that straight off."

I'm about to interrupt, but she gives me a friendly wave to stay my protest and piles my breakfast containers inside her own.

"I understand you. You have a book with half the pages ripped out and you think you're going to find those pages and place them back in the spine, shut the cover, and start another book. You're a writer, I know. But when you find those pages, you're going to discover you didn't have the pages in the right order to begin with and you're going to spend a lot of time rearranging things and in the meantime the book is going to get written in ways you can't even imagine."

As we fold our trays and prepare our seats for landing, the blinding light of sunrise forces me to turn away. Although I can no longer see her, I feel her kind eyes upon me, like a silent blessing. "Who are you?"

"Dalva. Morning star. I'm the woman who sat beside you on the plane, wishing you good luck."

Flashback

"Angel, my angel, your voice is music to my ears, most amazing earthly choir, oh my beautiful lady, beautiful girl, my angel, intelligent, amazing, wondrous angel, just to hear your voice sent me, your mother, into ecstasies, such happiness to hear you, I cannot tell you, such happiness, I am overjoyed, oh my angel of course you are welcome to join me in Brazil, we will go to museums, and art exhibits, and music nights, and you must come with no luggage, no clothes, oh my angel, what a voice you have, I have saved your voice on the machine and I listen to it over and over, my angel you will bring no clothes, none, we will buy you a new wardrobe, a new Brazilian wardrobe, in bright beautiful colours, my wondrous angel, we have the best shopping malls in the world in Brazil, the best designer clothes, the best shoes and purses and jewellery, I will buy you all new things, me, your mother, we will be together again and eat ice cream and shop and go to the theatre and the movies . . ."

"Okay."

That's all I managed to say our first telephone conversation. I'd left her a message, October 3, 2002, two weeks after discovering her website. *This is your daughter, Priscila.* Did I need to say that? My name? My relation? I don't know. This is the rest of the message, word for word, as I wrote myself a little script to avoid the phone equivalent of stage fright: *I found you on the internet by accident. I've seen your resumé and the pictures of me and Amerjit.* (I used my brother's old name here—he legally changed his name to Jit—because I didn't want to confuse her above and beyond the shock of hearing from me. My brother, as first-born male, received an Indian name, and I received a Portuguese one. Priscila in Portuguese has one L.) *I've also seen on your resumé that you retired because you were sick and I want to know if you are still unwell. I'm living in Toronto and my number is _____. Good-*bye. Not Oscar-worthy writing, I know, but practical, concise, straightforward English. Confronted with the reality that no matter how many times I might have imagined conversations between us, invented monologues or dialogues between our two selves, I really didn't know a single thing about her or her life in Brazil, I didn't know what other information to offer. I fretted over whether or not to admit my discovery was an accident, and decided I wanted to start on a truthful foot.

A week later, she called back. She'd been working in São Paulo. That's what she said. Who was I to disbelieve her? This woman calling me angel over and over again in such a loud, passionate, saccharine voice? This woman who would later write to me in faulty grammar in an email, in anticipation of my arrival, *Your voice is like music of angels. And it reminds me the scent of roses and lilies of the valley.*

Cut Back to Airport

I've landed in Brazil, the land of my mother's birth, a place I have only seen on world maps and in movies—a place I only vaguely associate as relevant to my life, like a kindergarten teacher whose name I can't recall or a vacation trinket given to me by a co-worker—and am immediately accosted by security guards in hospital masks handing out forms due to new precautions in light of the global SARS (severe acute respiratory syndrome) epidemic, a virus with flu-like symptoms that the World Health Organization put on Code Orange Alert and which has already resulted in several deaths in China (where it is believed to have originated), France, and in Canada in Toronto where hospitals are under quarantine in an attempt to contain the outbreak. Flights from Toronto require extra forms. My mother warned me: *You'll be tired from your flight, but try to look healthy. Don't sneeze, or you might be questioned.* I shuffle forward in a haze, a healthy haze, but a haze nonetheless, as I extract my luggage from the turnstile.

Sliding doors. Slap of immediate heat. Signs. Buses. Palm trees. Pockets of people. I am breathing shallowly, scanning the crowd for a face I am not accustomed to look for—only in the sludge of dreams where my mother surfaces now and then like a porpoise in dark waters. It doesn't take long to identify her though, as she is wearing a bright orange blouse and a 70s orange-and-yellow square-pattern skirt, a long strand of costume jewellery and matching thin hairband (*she still wears hairbands*, I note), and is waving wildly at me, like a teenage girl at a pop concert, jumping a little on her toes. I step forward. *Oh God, there is no turning back.*

My mother recognizes me. At least I think she does. We each had the benefit of photographs—me of her website, and her of a few photographs I sent in anticipation of my arrival—but photographs are not live people and the fact that she spots me right off the bat comforts me somewhat, evidence that even if she abandoned us as children, she didn't erase our features from her psyche, that some connection remains. When I have pulled my bags past the barriers and present myself in front of her—I am much taller than she is, a good six inches in my heels; I didn't know that—she says warmly, "Priscila," then kisses me European style on both cheeks, and in booming accented English: *Did they treat you all right? You are so beautiful.... Did they treat you well at the consulate? You are so beautiful.* She kisses me again—I smell the wax of her lipstick, a scent that triggers a flash of time spent at her vanity—then a large hug. I am aware that this woman is touching me, touching me rather intimately for a perfect stranger, and that she likely expects reciprocal motions, but I'm ironically frozen by the heat of the foreign climate and the novelty of the exchange. It's as if I am watching my mother through a camera lens—framing her at a safe distance, mesmerized by her large red lips and creased white forehead and bloated cheeks. I simply nod in response to her questions, having also lost, it seems, the ability to speak.

I follow her the way I would a security guard directing me to the exit, obediently and a couple of paces behind. This doesn't seem to bother my mother, who eagerly leads us out in her orange attire (did she wear such bright clothes so I wouldn't lose her in a crowd?), assuming control of one of the luggage bags, making a beeline for the street exit. As we weave through the people, I think of all the times over the years I've felt my heart race—speed up and then drop to a dull throb—when I've caught a glimpse of a woman purchasing a handbag in a clothing store, or sitting on a city-park bench, or pacing outside my campus office door, who, somewhere deep down in the recesses of my childhood, reminds me mournfully of my mother—my pulse literally crying out for powerful, ineffable motherly love. But here, my elusive runaway mother actually in front of me, her hips cutting side to side as she ploughs us through passengers and greeters, my heart is virtually still. Funny how it doesn't recognize her—the similarity between my memories of my mother, thousands of conscious and unconscious invocations over time, and the real living person, is lost on the heart's unscientific logic. And yet, there are hundreds of women with dark hair, the scent of waxy lipstick, the hint of a hairband, going about their day-to-day business, eating sandwiches and salads, shopping for books or toothpaste or a silk scarf, with a piece of my heart clinging to their sleeves.

A white van taxi awaits us. We ride rather comfortably even in the blistering heat—no one would suspect our fraught history as we stare out the window side by side on a cushioned bench to Caesar Park, a luxury hotel with a glass elevator and towering palm trees in what appears to be the middle of nowhere but I learn is northeast of the city centre to cater to travellers who wish to stay near the international airport. My mother's mouth zips along like a monorail, a stream of questions about the flight mixed with compliments about my appearance. Although I have defrosted enough to offer partial answers, I can't wave her down; my mother's train is an express, making few stops. Her voice is muscular but rhythmic, the linguistic equivalent of a tumbler. If she were a singer, she would be a bass soprano. Both her English and her Portuguese are punchy, the nasal quality of the Portuguese accent only minimally dulling the syllables into a hum like that of a roomful of data inputters on keyboards. My mother's voice is not a good thing I remember about her. I wonder if living back in her homeland all these years has altered her voice. For whatever reason, I can't place it, my brain makes no connections between it and semblances of motherhood, no flashes of nursery rhymes or afternoon puzzles or admonishments about wasted food or time for sleep. And it occurs to me that while I've imagined extensive conversations with my mother over the years, I've never given her voice an oral character—staged by me, both voices have reflected my own internal speech patterns and tonal qualities. I've never heard my mother's voice saying, "I'm so proud of you" after winning a scholarship or sports prize; or "That man is all wrong for you" when I've suspected it to be true. What did I do with her voice? Did I crumple it up like a piece of paper and swallow it? Did I grind it to a pulp and sprinkle it like pepper on pasta? Inside my body somewhere, but obviously so deeply hidden that this whirlwind of live syllables unearths no twins from the past. If she had been the one to leave a message on my answering machine without declaring *Theresa, your mother,* I would never have known. Likely, I would have erased the message as a wrong number.

The hotel staff, dressed in crisp white linen shirts, pants, and skirts, know about me because of the visa delay. My mother had returned a mess of tears. I'm welcomed with warm smiles and exaggerated "Good mornings" and "Welcome to Brazils" as bags are carted to our room, and we're directed to the lunch buffet.

You will eat a lot of beans and rice and seafood here. The best beans and rice and seafood in the world is in Brazil. My mother has a wide toothy smile, like I do, and the staff respond to her the way you do to an eccentric aunt. *She's sort of charming,* I think, with her compliments and excitable questions and effusions of appreciation as she hands me a cold plate and starts piling food from each steel dish on it, without bothering to ask what I might want. By the end of the line, I'm holding a smorgasbord of white fish and shrimp, multicoloured beans, broccoli, and beef stew.

I can eat anything at anytime, she declares once we are seated at our wooden table on brown wicker chairs. *I like this about myself. I never lose my appetite. Not even chemo touched my appetite. The doctors were so proud of me. Eat, eat, they told me. And I ate, ate. I am such a good patient.*

She is true to her word. Three towering plates. And still, she never stops talking—everything from fashion to politics to health to family gossip. Like a skilled ventriloquist, she can scoop a forkful or spoonful of beans and rice or salmon or lamb into her mouth and let it pool over to one cheek and slide down her throat without missing a syllable. I'm relieved I don't have to carry the conversation, that I can just listen and enjoy a plate of fresh food. I'm compelled to concentrate on nothing but her voice. Maybe she's not a ventriloquist but a hypnotist.

Ten Things I Learn

1. She wears only bright clothing and feels naked without earrings on.
2. Her father was a pilot in the Brazilian Air Force. Then military attaché (how they ended up in Canada).
3. My first cousins are also in the Brazilian Air Force (one is a dentist, one is in public relations), and my Uncle Wilhelm, their father, is head of the Air Force.
4. She thinks her mother (my grandmother? I don't even know her name) is "the bossiest person in the world."
5. She's had surgery on all ten of her fingers for carpal tunnel syndrome. Excessive typing.
6. There is no curfew for liquor here and the shopping centre turns into a nightclub and amusement park after the stores close.
7. She has ten different email addresses. (I don't know why.)
8. In Brasilia there are more trees for every person than in any other city in the world.
9. She voted for the current president, Luiz Inácio da Silva, otherwise known as Lula, even though her taxes will go up. "It's better than all these people without jobs."
10. She lives for the movies. Likes to sit right in front so she can "live inside the movie." Some movies she's seen over a hundred times in the theatre. She calls this pinnacle her 100 Club: *Blade Runner*, *The Big Blue*, *Ladyhawke*, *The Mirror Has Two Faces*, *The Last of the Mohicans*. Theatres are second and third and fourth homes. She views at least one movie per day at an actual movie house. Usually more. Her father and mother went to the movies every day. It's a family habit, but no one goes more than my mother. "We must go to the movies to laugh too, not only to cry."

Is it possible for me to take a quick nap? I ask. Do I need permission? I'm an adult after all, but I suppose a part of me wants to test out the dialogue of parent and child, see how it feels on my lips.

Of course, of course, angel, I was going to recommend it. You see, I knew you would be hungry and then tired. Me, I do not sleep. Too much to do. No sleep. Time to sleep when you're dead. But you should nap, yes, so you do not get sick. You are allowed to do whatever you like here. Whatever you like. Except run away! That you are not allowed to do!

Run away! I am taken aback by the reference then realize her words contain no intended irony. I file this away under "disconcerting." Nevertheless, genuinely tired, I decide to postpone semiotic analysis to surrender to an air-conditioned room and hotel bed. I have always loved hotels, and none more than luxury hotel beds with big fluffy pillows and comforters, as if sleep itself were your destination. As my mother sits making notes at the mahogany desk and I pull the cozy white comforter over my exhausted body, I can't believe I'm actually here, in Brazil, with *my mother*, and at first I think disbelief will keep me up as I try to adjust my old memories to the new reality, the bulges of her frame, the white powder on her cheeks—has chemo ruined her skin?—but, hugging the queen-sized feather pillow, my thoughts dissolve like salt in water and I sink into the serenity pool of sleep.

After my nap, which my mother has used to crank out a glowing review of the film *The Quiet American*—I must get my prolificness from her—I put on the same clothes I wore to the airport (I haven't yet unpacked) and we head out in a taxi to the Internacional Guarulhos shopping plaza. Though Guarulhos is designated a suburb of São Paulo, with its litany of skyscrapers cramped like fistfuls of straws, its tyranny of grey and blue among a smidgen of green and orange, its population of over one million people, it reeks of bustling city life rather than tranquil suburbia. I read in my tourist book that Guarulhos means "eaters, big-bellied people." What food courts they must have!

At the mall, we take our first photograph together—a young couple aimlessly window-shopping offer to do the honours— outside the bookstore, after my mother has helped me pick out Portuguese poetry books, plucking them naturally off the shelf like papayas off a tree and placing them in my plastic shopping basket without a query as to how I will read them when I have no knowledge of Portuguese let alone the sophistication necessary for Portuguese poetry. We don't tell the couple we are mother and daughter. They don't ask. Taking photographs is more common than taking a bus. Because we're speaking English together, I'm sure they assume we're on vacation, and people on vacation take photographs of everything, even bookstores. But as I thank the couple for the trouble, I'm aware of how monumental this innocuous photograph actually is. The first irrefutable document of our reunion. Evidence of its reality. Not a filmic projection, a revisable fantasy, repeating on a loop in our minds. My mother's colourful outfit and my bright scarf blend in with the crammed storefront, rows and rows of books against glass. My mother's arm lightly touches my back, either proudly or protectively; it's difficult to ascertain which. We look like we've known each other for some time, and in some ways I suppose we have, but our limbs are stiff, like colleagues unused to body contact. As if the photograph has alerted my mother to the potential of an audience for our reunion story, she now tells every person we encounter on our stroll to the Cineplex, from store managers to clerks to janitors, that I am her Canadian daughter and she is very happy I am visiting Brazil. "It is so nice her husband let her come." With such little, yet such charged, information (why wouldn't your daughter be permitted to visit?), god knows what these people think our story is. Likely our complicated situation has flitted in front of their eyes, a brief interlude, like a commercial for a product you will never buy. The clerks keep tapping on their cash registers and ripping paper receipts, the janitors keep sweeping dirt and soda pop off the floor. But I register that this is a public display of pride. Even if she doesn't know me, she's proud I'm here.

I am not a feminist, she announces outside the theatre. *I'm a traditionalist. My friends think I'm a feminist, but I'm not. We are both writers. We are alike.*

"I'm a feminist." I'm not embarrassed to say this the way a lot of writers now are, as if the term is outdated and identifies not a group of reasonable political activists but angry man-haters. I'm also uncomfortable with the idea that my mother wants, from the beginning of this trip, to see us as alike. I decide I will need to stand my ground, as politely as possible, but allow our differences to emerge like friendly rivalries between sports fans—me in one jersey, my mother in another. But this is Brazil, I remind myself, where rival fans kill each other and where soccer players who make mistakes on the field arrive home in body bags.

What does that mean? You like being a woman, and you would have come to Brazil even if your husband said no. But isn't it nice he said yes? Be careful with your purse. Even in the shopping mall. I've been mugged four times. That's why I carry this big purse now. No one wants to run away with such a heavy thing. My purse is a little organized factory. Like yours, I see. We are the same. I only pay for what I can afford. I resent sleep. There is too much to do. There are hundreds of interesting things to do in Brazil. Museums, galleries, concerts, all the highest quality, you'll see.

Okay, I agree with that. I don't say which part I'm agreeing with, but she assumes I'm agreeing with everything. As my father's bookkeeping helper I, too, learned early on that it's important to buy only what you can afford. Since debt became a debilitating issue only after my father's accident, I associate credit with the breaking of my father's back. I've never let a credit card balance go unpaid at the end of the month. Aside from student loans, I have never taken a loan or line of credit from the bank. Offers to "raise my credit limit" turn my stomach. I don't like the idea of owing. Neither, it seems, does my mother. I just wonder how far this extends beyond money. The conversation is enlightening, in a number of ways. I now know something about what deters a purse snatcher. I also know she has seen the inside of my purse. When—at the airport? While I was sleeping? Was she snooping through my things?

Here, touch this, my mother orders before entering the line. She is pointing to her chest, and I do what I'm told even though I haven't touched my mother of my own volition—I've let her hug me at the airport and touch my back for the photograph, but I've made no motions to touch her—in over twenty years. The flesh is hard, a dense bump. *That's my chemo tube.* She lifts her blouse an inch or two to reveal stitches on her white flabby stomach. *There's a skating rink in this mall. Did you know there are skating rinks in Brazil?*

I didn't know that. I didn't know it was relevant to chemo tubes. I haven't experienced her enough yet to track her verbal habits, but it occurs to me that maybe my mother, as a teacher, is of the "happy sandwich" school—those who follow up every negative comment with a positive comment so as to lessen the emotional impact of the negativity. And then I do have a flash of my mother speaking to me as a child: I am drawing a flower of some sort, with red and green crayons, writing the words "I Love You Mommy" underneath. A crude drawing—I've never been gifted in sketching or painting—and I know I mean the words as I write them, but my mother is watching me make the card, maybe she even asked me to (*Angel, why don't you make Mommy a Valentine's card?*), and so with the love I feel something else: anxiousness, worry, fear. The childhood memory arrives with discomfort, a familiar feeling: I love making cards and picking perfect presents for friends and loved ones, and I might be one of the last people on the planet to still send out over a hundred holiday cards to friends and colleagues, but each bow or envelope seal includes a tiny dose of fear along with the good wishes. I worry about losing touch, about people drifting away, and all those good feelings no longer having a place to land. When my mother lived with us, I now remember, I used to write her letters, cards, poems, stories, fake postcards from magical lands. After she left, I never wrote to her or about her again, not until I was skilled enough to transform her into an unrecognizable presence in various poems and fictions—mother and daughter characters built on the pain of separation but whose personalities and fates differ starkly from our own. I was not one of those children who kept a special diary dedicated to her or wrote her a birthday card every year, stuffing them unstamped under a pile of T-shirts in my dresser drawers. When she left, I stopped writing to her. I have no clue whether or not she's been writing to me. If she has, they've been returned to sender. Now, I suppose, we are catching up for lost time. Purse snatching to museums and galleries. Chemo surgeries to ice skating rinks. Uncomfortable childhood memories to . . . movies.

We decide on *Maid in Manhattan*, or *Encontro de Amor* in Portuguese, because it will screen in English with Portuguese subtitles and because it is debuting tonight so my mother has not seen it yet. In the last two days, waiting for me to land, she has seen *all* the other films. And as I scan movie posters for *Catch Me If You Can*, *Two Weeks Notice*, *My Big Fat Greek Wedding*, *The Quiet American*, and the Brazilian film *City of God*, I wonder how easy or difficult it was for her to forget her anxiety and disappointment through car chases and unexpected love connections and political bombings and drug lord murders. And then I remember that I too rented movies after returning home from the airport. We watched *Spider-Man* and *Solaris* to pass away the time between filling out the visa application and waiting at the consulate. For me, unfortunately, distractions are usually met with mixed success—I can forget for a small stretch of time, ten or twenty minutes at the most, and then my mind wanders back to the trouble at hand and I have to either rewind or simply accept what I've missed and move on. It's the same with reading, except that if I'm trying to distract myself with a novel I will at times need to reread the same page over and over again. But I'm beginning to suspect my mother has more practice escaping her worries through art.

Falling in love with a movie star is the best thing for you, she spontaneously instructs the young popcorn server, whose perky breasts are peeking out over her T-shirt. *You'll never get hurt. You can have all the romance and romantic feelings you want, and then just leave them in the dark theatre.*

All the young female cinema employees smile warmly at my mother, and the twenty-something female manager sporting tinted sunglasses personally escorts us to our seats.

As the lights dim, I feel relieved to be given a break from all the incoming information—I too have something of the family movie bug and adore the plush seats and buttery popcorn and ice-cold Cokes of the theatre, rarer for me than renting videos—but I also feel guilty. I can only remember going to three movies with my brother: once in high school on an awkward double date, and twice in childhood, *Ghostbusters* in an Ottawa theatre and *E.T.* at a Michigan drive-in when we were living with another one of my father's brothers after my mother left. We rented movies every week growing up: Eddie Murphy, Clint Eastwood, and Bill Murray some of our favourites. But I have never gone to the movies, or to a buffet lunch, or shopping, with my father. I have done all three with my runaway mother within twenty-four hours of landing on her turf. We don't do what we can't afford. Financial, or otherwise. My father had the burden of raising us; she has the luxury of leisure time. Why has her mysterious existence accorded her more indulgence? A part of me desperately wants these kinds of mother-daughter experiences, but another part equally wants to reject them as betrayal. What will these surreal excursions, so separate from my actual family life with my father, cost me?

Normally, I adore Ralph Fiennes. I first fell in love with him in the film based on the Peter Carey novel *Oscar and Lucinda*. As he burned and drowned in his floating church, I wept on my couch, enraptured by the poetic sensibility. A glass church floating on a river.

I hated *Maid in Manhattan*. Absolutely hated it. And Ralph Fiennes as Mr. Christopher Marshall, a smarmy New Yorker running for senator, repulsed me. Any feminist or Marxist analysis of the film would relegate the proofs to a bonfire. The premise: Marisa Ventura, played by Jennifer Lopez, a sexy maid in a five-star Manhattan hotel and a single mother can't be bought by an upper-class, unethical, and callous politician. Marisa possesses moral integrity and proletarian passions, which will protect her from his onslaught of sexual interest. Predictably, the two end up falling in love, and in the end she becomes his political partner in his successful senatorial race. While the whole rags-to-riches dimension of the movie is forgivable fantastical convention, what is truly horrific about this film is that the screenwriters have made Ralph Fiennes's character so despicable that his transformation is not Scrooge-scared-to-death-and-of-death-to-correct-the-error-of-his-ways, but a plot twist so unlikely that the only motivation, no matter what the movie's claims, is lust. The worst part is that Marisa Ventura keeps giving this man access to her time, her thoughts, her son, and later her lips and other body parts, for no other reason than that he is rich and powerful and has condescended to spend a little time with her precocious son. By the end of the film, he has barely revealed a single good quality, but the audience is expected to applaud her for bagging a bank account.

As we vacate the theatre, my mother is beaming. *What a beautiful film—such a nice love story, with very good values: greed is not everything. Very realistic. You can't find love if you are greedy. The head butler gives up his job because of his ethics. Ethics is everything.*

Although overweight, my mother walks briskly when she is excited, and I'm having a hard time catching up as she talks and walks and waves wildly to all the cinema employees.

But that's what I found so unrealistic, I reply. *Who would give up his job after all those years to make a point that will be forgotten by the time the next labourer is hired?*

You're right, of course, my mother concedes, not slowing down for a second, *but that is why the point is made in a movie.* And not for the first time, I wish we could actually devise a test for assessing whether or not people learn lessons from films and novels and other art forms, and what conditions are necessary for translating understanding into behaviour. *The movie is optimistic. We should applaud that Mr. Marshall chose a common person for his wife. She is no longer a slave, but a public servant. This way we can imagine a better world. Art should educate the masses, and this movie educates. I will give this movie a very positive review.*

Dismayed by her artistic judgment and by the fact that she plans to set it all down in print, I voice my own review. *What does it teach? Why should Marisa be interested in him? Because he is rich and powerful and famous? He has no moral qualities.*

He has no good qualities until Marisa gives them to him. This is the history of romance film. You must accept the premise.

The premise is ridiculous, I counter. I won't accept such an excuse for an offensive script so easily, but then relent somewhat on the basis of genre. *I guess I'm not a fan of romance films.* Which is true. I have a soft spot for teenage comedies with romance structures, as long as there's lots of cringe-worthy coming-of-age embarrassment, classics from my own teen years like *The Breakfast Club* (which I will admit I have seen not a hundred but thirty or forty times), *Pretty in Pink*, *Sixteen Candles*, and the more recent American Pie series and *Napoleon Dynamite*, but I don't go in for the standard why-can't-she-find-the-perfect-man-and-then-she-does variety of Meg Ryan, Julia Roberts, Jennifer Aniston, and Jennifer Lopez. I have sympathy for the misguided and misplaced affections of clueless teenagers trying out love for size, but little for self-centred adults who ought to know better.

I love romance films, my mother announces to the street as she hails a cab. *Romance should only exist in film, then there would be no pain, no pain anywhere. Don't you see? Films should be idealistic. Not realistic. Why go to relive misery? Love stories only last on film.*

And while I know my mother is expressing her own desire for freedom from the pain of love—which left her with a broken husband and a broken heart—her disappointment in love extends, apparently, to all. Does she assume I, too, have a broken heart? That I've never experienced true romance? That my relationship with Chris must be a sham, a recipe for misery? Doesn't she realize that my fears in love always centre on abandonment, love withdrawn at a moment's notice because loving is too hard in an imperfect world? That I learned this, profoundly, from her?

Or is she warning me that she is incapable of love? Even for her own daughter, dropping into her life out of the blue like a convenient plot trigger?

To counter, I quote Marisa: *Letting someone believe something's true when it's not is just as much a lie as a lie is.*

As the words leave my mouth, I know this adage will haunt me. Haunt us as the trip progresses. Shallow films sometimes contain profound lines. This one reverberates as premonition.

Haven't we been forced to encourage lies for the better part of our lives?

As the taxi weaves its way through the dark streets of Guarulhos, throngs of young men in jeans and T-shirts tapping their feet anxiously on the street corners, I am suddenly aware that my mother and I, notwithstanding shared blood and eight years living together at the same Ottawa address, come from vastly different worlds, both culturally and artistically. *It's as if we watched entirely different films,* I think, my mother chattering in Portuguese with the taxi driver, recommending the movie. I might as well be strolling Manhattan while she bustles about São Paulo. I replay the movie in my mind, try to figure out why my mother and I diverge in opinion on nearly every aspect of the film, what this says about us. Head butler Lionel's words stake a challenge: *What we do, Miss Ventura, does not define who we are. What defines us is how well we rise after falling.* But I think what defines us is what we would identify as a "rise" or a "fall." Fall. Rise. *Queda. Ascensão.* We're not even speaking the same language.

The Day I Arrive: My Mother and Me in Front of a Bookstore

2

the big blue

Enzo: So between Mamma, Roberto, and Alfredo, we yell
and scream all day long. Except with Angelica. She just cries.
And then, finally, we all end up kissing. Can you explain
that to me? Huh? Because that's what love is all about.

*

Jacques (showing his lover a photograph of a dolphin he
keeps in his wallet): That's my family. What kind of a man
has such a family?

THE OCEAN has always terrified me. Even now as I antic-
ipate my eighth trip to Barbados in over three years and
the utter delight I will experience on the beach reading
books I've set aside for such pleasure, intricate Victorian plots
or snappy postmodern dialogue interrupted as soon as skin
graduates from warm tingling to unbearable sweat for the joys
of swimming in blue-green salt water, I am still uneasy about
the unfathomable depth and width of the ocean waters and the
entire cities of alien life housed within those currents.

I do not stray too far from shore, I do not go in search of
secluded beaches, I do not snorkel without a good deal of urging

(even in St. Lucia, which boasts some of the best snorkelling in the world, my friend David Layton, who introduced me to the beauties of the Caribbean islands, had to shove the flippers on my feet before sending me floating into reams of barracuda). As awed as I am by schools of neon tropical fish shimmering by my flittering legs and outstretched arms or the translucent mushroom bodies of squid languidly bouncing up and down, slow-motion acrobats trailing shiny boas, I would rather experience such wonder behind the safety of glass.

I'm a show-me-the-full-horror kind of person; then, at least, I can plan my escape. My brother is the opposite. He'd rather enjoy himself, blissfully unaware of what might be lurking under a rock or in the coral reef, and take his chances. Both are survival strategies; each has served us well. Me, I'm convinced unpredictable danger exists everywhere. Look at what happened to my father. *I guess this was my fate,* my father sometimes shrugs, his wheelchair a permanent sidekick. I am brave if danger can be controlled or overcome through my own talents or reserves, but am a hopeless coward if I have no information or experience in handling my adversary. Therefore, I am vindicated by the morbid predictability of classical and Shakespearean tragedies, confessional poets, Russian and Polish modernists, dysfunctional family dramas, horror movies, Lars von Trier and Ingmar Bergman films. My brother prefers underdogs and go-getters, feel-good sports films and animated adventures, the triumphs of lovable losers like Zach Galifianakis, Homer Simpson, and Adam Sandler. No tragedies, no satires. Only comedies and inspirational films with happy endings. Preferably with a catchy soundtrack you can dance to. Deep down, I'm convinced the universe is cruel and antagonistic; my brother, that if you keep your head up and believe, it might be benevolent.

My first night in Brazil, in a four-star hotel furnished with two queen-sized beds with high thread-count white sheets, the marble and granite washroom impeccably scrubbed, double locks on the doors, ends up a painful and exhausting one. Anticipating that once we are dressed in our nightgowns (pink and black satin pajamas for me, a blue cotton sleep-dress for my mother) I will soon be able to surrender to the comfort of the bed, where I can close my eyes and assess the day's thoughts to gain more solid footing on this pebbly, sand-shifting beach, before allowing myself to be swept away into sleep, I am rudely countered from my purpose, as if by a violent tropical storm.

My mother is a snorer. She snores like a predator, a loud, rumbly intake like the igniting roar of a lawn mower, the exhale an even louder high-pitched whistle. *Oh no,* I panic, but then reassure myself her body cannot sustain such a spirited performance forever. Either that or jet lag will inevitably overwhelm me. Be an optimist. Like my brother. Like my mother wishes me to be. I put on the eye mask we were given on the plane, the first time I've ever worn one, convinced I will wake up a new person.

But the human calliope never shuts down. Not once over seven hours. I try to bury myself under the feather pillows; I try to whisper to her unconscious to cool it for just ten minutes so I can pass through the sleep wall to the other side; at one point I even poke her fleshy white arms and then, having grown desperate, I place my pillow over her mouth to see if I can stop the snoring by altering the air flow. Lack of sleep I know can cause terrible thoughts and actions to blossom from the otherwise tame, which is why sleep deprivation is such a successful form of torture. Anxious about this trip, I haven't slept well in weeks. This isn't good. I need to be alert for whatever dangers may arise.

Over the course of the night, in an effort to escape the circus, I conjure up the two recurring dreams I have had about my mother since her disappearance. Both are elemental, one in water and one in the sky.

Dream Sequence

In the water dream, I am swimming without scuba gear deep in the ocean, doing my best to ignore the colourful schools of fish as I approach a shipwrecked boat at the bottom of the sea. I am carrying a pack of some sort and, once within reach of the wreckage, I stuff my sack with treasures: coins, pearls, tools, books. As I move from cabin to cabin, each full sack is replaced by a new empty one. My motions are calm, repetitive, natural; until my mother appears, bobbing up and down in the water like a tired mermaid, long hair tendrils clutching the legs of furniture. I attempt to claim her treasures of pearls and feather hats and makeup cases, but every time I reach out my hand, an unseen creature bites it. Eventually fed up, I slowly swim away, sad and defeated. I wake as I'm rising back to shore.

In the sky dream, my mother is young. Younger than I ever remember her, maybe late teens, early twenties—cheeks rosy, body lithe—and she's sitting in the upper branches of the maple tree in our yard, the same maple I would climb in defiance of my father's warnings, dozens of bright red apples stashed in the lap of her skirt. The lower branches I usually use to hoist myself up are cut off. I jump up and down in futile frustration. My mother laughs, tenderly at first, then more forcefully, until thunder shakes the tree and a streak of lightning flies out her mouth. Then she starts pelting me with apples. *Why? Why?* I scream. *I am made of sheet lightning,* my mother replies. (I implement a variation of this line in a poem in my first book: *I was made/ of sheet lightning/which is why my life/was shockingly short.*) The length of time between when she says this and how many more times I am pelted with apples before I wake varies, but her answer never does.

Suddenly I am struck by the fact that I have, over the years in my dreams, pictured my mother running, screaming, eating, laughing, driving, bleeding, swimming, even shooting a gun; I have never imagined her sleeping.

Finally my mother wakes. Instantly. No morning yawn or yoga stretch or lounging in bed—she is wide awake, extricating herself from her sheets like the sun from the horizon, grabbing her notebook and eagerly planning our day. I close my eyes, hoping I might get away with an hour or two if she thinks I'm too tired to register her stirring, but she hovers over me and booms:

"It's morning in Brazil! I'm starving!"

Disappears. Shower flips on and off. Re-emergence in blue. Yesterday, orange. Today, blue. Blue blouse, blue skirt, blue scarf, blue costume jewellery. The over-coordination exudes the opposite effect: unevenness, unawareness, a woman so lacking in an organizing principle that a superficial one must be imposed to contain the chaos.

Her mouth opens. It begins.

She talks while I'm showering, while I'm using the toilet, while I'm changing, while I'm brushing my teeth, while I'm applying my makeup. Sometimes she forgets that I only speak English and French and flings streams of Portuguese. A language littered with "ao" sounds, long nasal vowels equivalent to an English "ow" as in "cow" or "wow" and stretched into a long melancholic whine, her commentary seems linguistically littered with hurt: ow, ow, ow, ow. Word wounds. The relentless picking of a scab. (Later on, when prodded to describe the Portuguese language to a friend, I will claim: Portuguese is the language of sorrow.)

I'm happy you are so feminine. Like me. I feel more secure when people are predictable and the same. I am always the same. The most predictable person of my friends and family. Everyone always knows where to find me, any time of day, I am that predictable. I do not like unexpected things, changed personalities. If I don't like reality, I go into another dimension. I go to the movies or some-where else in my head. I left work once without my umbrella, coat, and sunglasses, but I refused to return to the elevator. I bought a new umbrella, coat, and sunglasses because I'd already left work in my mind and did not wish to return. I don't own a single suit. I do not like to look severe. I am always nice to people. It's fair for some-one to say, Theresa is always nice to me, but still I don't like her. I only hurt someone when I can't help it. I do not like to fight; only if I absolutely have to fight will I fight. The rest of the family, they love fighting. My mother loves fighting. Me, I leave the place where the fighting is. That's why I spend so much time in São Paolo. Let my mother fight with my brother. She never fights with my sister, but my brother also likes to fight. I am always cold. My father used to say, Theresa would be happy in the freezer. It's warmer in the freezer. I've had five surgeries for the cancer . . .

Declarations and contradictions flutter about me like swarm-ing butterflies and I try to catch them, putting one in a jar labelled "True" and one in a jar labelled "False" from what I know so far, telling myself I can transfer a butterfly from one jar to another once I have more information about its species. My mother thinks she's predictable. *False.* That she can always be found. *False.* That she lives in another dimension when she can't handle reality. *True.* That she doesn't own a suit. *True.* That she doesn't like to fight. *True.* That she is eternally cold. *True.* That she hurts people only when she can't help it. *Don't know.* This butterfly I will pin to my collar. This butterfly is precious, and potentially poisonous.

It is at breakfast when I realize that aside from questions about my flight, my mother has not asked me a single question about my life since I've landed. Whenever I interject to respond to some-thing she has said, or to offer my own opinion, aside from our discussion of *Maid in Manhattan*, she cuts me off. I wonder if she's worried about what I will say or ask in return or if this is merely nervous energy that will dissipate as we grow more comfortable with each other's habits. She asks only polite social questions. *Would you like this?* Or, *Is this seat okay?* Or, *Would you like more?* She allows no time for silence. Or reflection. Or contemplation. Our schedule is packed with words. And food. We eat a lot for breakfast. I too have a very healthy appetite and am a sucker for a buffet. I blame it on growing up poor, worrying that one day there might be nothing good to eat in the fridge or pantry so load up while you can, even though my father was adamant that we would always have food on the table. And the fact that food is a reliable source of pleasure and comfort, unlike the other unpredictabilities of our lives.

Montage from childhood

While my father ate for the purpose of fuel an uninspiring daily diet of flaked tuna, cream of mushroom soup, Shake'n Bake chicken, Green Giant frozen peas and carrots, and a hot pot of cranberry juice to help soothe recurring bladder infections, my brother and I fought over food: pepperoni sticks, tangerine oranges, Pop-Tarts, Lucky Charms, mint chocolate chip ice cream. We would sneak behind each other's backs to snatch the last Chips Ahoy cookie or to wolf down the end of a brick of mozzarella cheese. Now, though my tastes are more refined and I've lost my sweet tooth, I still associate the enjoyment of food with a brief sojourn from sadness and worry. I know my brother does too. And this is why my father rarely yelled at us for our gorging. Also, as I have no food allergies, very few food dislikes, and fewer intolerances (only coffee and green tea, for some reason— my stomach bottoms out if I drink coffee and I pass out if I drink green tea), I try everything in sight. In our show-me-the-full-horror versus what-has-worked-in-the-past-will-work-again-in-the-present personalities, my brother, although an opulent eater, has highly restrictive food preferences (staples like pasta, pizza, cheese, steak, ordinary fruits; but no vegetables or fish or seafood, no "foreign" foods like Indian curries or Thai noodles or soy, and such an extreme dislike of cream sauces of any sort that his friends, playing off his name, now call sour cream "Jitronite").

I haven't shared any of this commonplace information with my mother because she hasn't asked. She informs me she is on a strict diet, but what she is capable of eating, she eats by the pound. I look everywhere among the dozens of coffee pots for "English tea"—caffeinated tea—and can't find any, so I ask my mother where to find some. She takes it as a personal offence.

Coffee upsets my stomach, I tell her.

Many things upset stomachs in this family. Not coffee. Don't expect tea.

Though I am curious, I don't ask about the history of upset stomachs because lack of sleep has rendered me ravenous. In addition to all the fruit and pastries, meat slices and beans, I manage to polish off not one but two omelets. I make a mental note to search for a box of tea in the next shopping mall we visit. I never thought I would be dependent on such a small thing, but I am. Predictable.

Location shift

We will now be setting up camp in my mother's rented flat in the middle of São Paulo, a suite-style hotel geared toward long-term stays for families and business travellers. I know this is cheaper for her, and I don't betray a hint of disappointment, but I must admit I do prefer boutique hotels to suites and apartments. It's not the expense, per se, that defines more desirable accommodation. It's that higher-end hotels are more anonymous; the chandeliers and elevator buttons shimmer in their claimlessness. For me luxury is not defined by the feather comforters and marble sinks and all-night room service menus but by what these items signify: *you don't live here, this is a space of your imagination, do what you will for this limited time. We don't know you. You don't know us. Comfort yourself.* Whereas my mother's rented flat will be filled with *her*. While this is something I'm anticipating, so that I can observe her surroundings and compare them to the statements she has already made about herself—the psycho-analytically informed writer coming out in me who wants her butterfly jars properly labelled—I also fear losing myself in her insistent voice, her routines, her vortex. This will be her set, filled with her lighting, her props, her actors.

Her cast includes her usual taxi driver, who was off yesterday but picks us up today. His name is Soares: a thin black man of about fifty with a salt-and-pepper buzz cut, a few gold teeth, looking refreshed wearing an ironed blue cotton dress shirt, black slacks, and a large, welcoming smile.

I will not use anyone but Soares, even if they were cheaper. Soares likes me. I must know that my driver likes me. If someone doesn't like me, I drop them. I don't wait for them to like me. No. You either like someone or you don't. I don't have a second for people who do not like me. If you don't like me, I won't have a second for you either.

Did she really say that? This makes me nervous. How do I know if I like her after only a day or two? Right now, I just find her overwhelming, as if I'm a kid surrounded by blaring music inside a house of mirrors. I've handed over my ticket and am trying to make my way from one end of the hall to the other while visions of myself and my mother grow thin and rubbery then bloated and ballooned, and I'm at a loss as to which are real and which illusions, which are close and which far away. I'm sure there's one image I will be attracted to more than the others, but I haven't picked it yet. I'm in the middle of the intersection of reflections, blinded by light and teeth and dark hair, dizzy with the abundance of us. Will she ask me if I like her? Does she know if she likes me? It's hard to like someone if you don't know anything about her. Then again, maybe it's easier if you don't. Less refraction. If I say no, will she leave me on a precarious street corner and drive away with Soares into the smog?

One of my mother's 100 Club movies is *The Big Blue*. The oceanic and Mediterranean landscapes, the lush cinematography, the unlikely love story; all these elements enrapture her. Once again, as with *Blade Runner*, I wonder if my mother's subconscious has latched onto these movies; they seem to speak in interesting, sometimes accusatory ways to our situation. She engages the surface spectacle of each, transporting herself to another dimension, a safe place where one can love movie stars and watch them make love to others, and then one can leave the theatre satisfied, contained, safely alone. Except now I'm leaving the theatre with her.

I'd never heard of *The Big Blue* before my mother raved about it, and so rented it upon my return to Toronto, as I rented *all* the movies in my mother's 100 Club. Released in 1988, it is an epic 168 minutes directed by Luc Besson, and features Rosanna Arquette as Johana, Jean-Marc Barr as Jacques, and Jean Reno as Enzo. Two of the main characters of the film, childhood rivals Jacques and Enzo, are extreme divers, meaning that they dive competitively in the ocean without the aid of breathing apparatus. By the end of the film, each has managed to crack four hundred feet below the surface and hold their breath for over five minutes. In actuality what they are searching for are not world records, but the fairy-tale eternal love of mermaids. For the protagonist Jacques, this quest begins in childhood with the death of his sea-exploring father and the disappearance of his mother. Just before his father dies, in the midst of Jacques and his Uncle Louis adjusting the breathing apparatus, Uncle Louis berates Jacques for never asking questions:

> *Uncle Louis: Ask me something, goddammit.*
> *Jacques: Why did mother leave?*
> *Uncle Louis: Pump. Your mother didn't leave. She went back*
>   *to America, that's all. It's her home. Women are like that,*
>   *unpredictable like the sea.*

Jacques spends his life in the ocean, literally swimming with dolphins, searching for a mermaid who will accept his pure love and invite him to live with her in the sea. He falls in love with a real woman, Johana, an insurance agent who gives up everything—job, home, security—for him, but it isn't enough to dissuade him from the mysterious depths of the ocean. The void created by a missing mother's love is deeper than the earth, deeper than any mortal lover can fill, and while Jacques can be loved, he cannot experience love in a satisfying way. He is left with two choices: surrender to fantasy or die. He chooses both. Diving into the blue after a love that has passed him by, as irrecoverable as my mother's treasures in my watery dream.

The Big Blue is a unique, tragic, and funny film that introduced me to a competitive world I had no clue existed. But more than that, it's a film that asks the question How deep are you willing to go to find out the truth about yourself? How many more feet?

Penetrating the city limits, we are smack in the middle of the ear-splitting chaos of São Paulo, population eleven million plus,

the largest city in Brazil, as well as one of the most diverse, infil-
trated by masses of European immigrants following the abolition
of slavery in 1888, and one that managed a fairly successful switch
from an industrial to a service and finance economy, now housing
the highest number of billionaires in Latin America. More skyscrapers than stars; more vehicles than flowers; more graffiti than
street signs; more poison than air; boasting the largest fleet of
helicopters in the world. I pop an imaginary kernel in my mouth:
let the show begin. We lurch forward then halt, then crawl, then
stop, then lurch forward again. As my mother yells over the racket
of São Paulo downtown traffic, I decide, in an effort to make the
trip as pleasant and reconciling as possible, to prepare a mental
list of things I've learned my mother and I have in common.

Ten Things My Mother and I Share

1. We both reapply lipstick after each course of a meal. (Pre-
   dominantly red.)
2. We both possess zero sense of direction.
3. We are both workaholics and resent the physiological
   demands of sleep.
4. We are both blessed with healthy appetites and are free of
   food allergies.
5. We both love books, movies, music, visual art, and theatre.
6. We both gesture with our hands a lot when we talk.
7. We both apologize for little things, not big things.
8. We both sport a no-teeth smile when we're concentrating.
9. We are both charming to strangers.
10. We may both have a thing for Rutger Hauer.

Listing helps momentarily calm my nerves, but the pollution in
São Paulo is thick as maple syrup and makes Toronto look like

a quaint lakeside town. As someone who doesn't drive and ordinarily doesn't spend much time in cars, I turn into a yawner when a vehicular passenger. More than usual, in this heat and filth and sleep deprived, my yawns are endless.

Did you not sleep well? my mother finally asks. *The hotel was the best available. How could you not sleep well? Clean sheets, warm comforter, big bed. Is it your stomach? Are you sick? Should we see a doctor?*

No, no, I'll be fine. I'm sorry.

I don't know how you're going to sleep better at the flat if you couldn't sleep well in the luxury hotel. We should see a doctor.

My mother is adamant that I must be sick. I've seen such mothers on television—who turn a fever into malaria and head-aches into brain tumours—but I've never experienced one. I learned to take care of my illnesses—from colds to flus to sinus infections—on my own. In high school, I was allowed to sign my own sick notes. I remember once, during a particularly angst-ridden time after leaving home at age fifteen for rented rooms, calling the principal and informing him that I was on the verge of a nervous breakdown and needed a week off to collect myself. As I had a near 100 percent average, the principal allowed it. By day four of lying in bed despairing at being alone in the universe, without a proper protector, without someone to fight for and care for me, I woke up in the sweat of a revelation I have adhered to since that singular morning: breakdowns are a luxury I cannot afford. Who would pay my bills if I were incapacitated? No one, that's who. So, I slipped on my skull skirt and skeleton rings and packed my calculus and physics homework, and went right back to homeroom as if I'd never left. The teachers said noth-ing. I think I unnerved them: a straight A+ student and jock who wrote dark poetry and stories about suicide for the school newspaper and worked full-time as a pharmaceutical assistant in addition to her classes. I was like a science experiment set to explode. The teachers stood back to avoid the fallout, but took interest in observing the anomalous results.

As I don't want to spend the day in a doctor's office, particularly a foreign doctor's office, when all I have is jet lag mixed with sleeplessness, I feel cornered into the truth. *It's just . . . just . . . I whisper . . . you were snoring . . . all night . . . it was pretty loud. I'm sure everything will be fine tonight.*

Complete standstill. Fifteen minutes. Stuck between a convenience store and a rundown pharmacy. Soares apologizes as if he is responsible. In São Paulo, rush hour lasts a good eight hours, he informs me, my mother translating between us. That's just traffic then, I reply, and he laughs.

Beautiful kid, I am very happy you are here, but you should know better at your age not to lie. Don't be a liar. I do not snore.

Is *don't be a liar* in Brazilian Portuguese equivalent to *don't be silly* in English? Nevertheless, I'm stunned by her accusation, so contrary to my preference for calming the choppy waters, I attempt to speak my piece. *I'm sorry, but you did snore. You snored loudly all night. I'm not saying this to hurt you, just to explain why I'm tired.*

As if someone has just placed a package with an unpleasant odour in the car, she scrunches her nose and lowers her voice. This is the first flash—unfortunately, not the last—of inexplicable anger my mother lashes at me.

Don't you lie, or I will have no time for you. Do you think you can lie to your mother? Your father never complained about any snoring. Everyone in the hospital could sleep fine with me. Chemo patients, okay? No one ever complained about snoring.

It's the first time she's mentioned my father, and I am taken aback by how quickly she invokes him then sweeps us both aside to keep chattering with Soares about our day's schedule—if we make it through the maze of dense traffic, that is. I've read

before that snoring in animals can be traced back to hibernating, a survival strategy to signal life is nearby if one of the family
wakes too early. Living alone for so long now, throughout her
forties and fifties, I wonder if my mother's developed a louder
snore since her immediate family is a continent away. My father
is also a grand snorer, and I do think as children it comforted
us to hear him, evidence he was alive, that there was a parent,
even an injured parent, down the hallway, looking out for us. My
brother fell from his bed a lot—a guardrail remained fixed to its
side until he was about twelve. And apparently, I was a bit of a
sleepwalker, and am still an active sleep-talker—I would have
all manner of conversations with my father down the hallway,
between walls and our bedroom doors, where I would ask for
pets (I desperately wanted a dog), chatter on about the antics of
my friends, and frequently exclaim that I thought our house was
on fire. My father would talk me down until I went back to sleep,
to mostly silent nightmares. Again, I don't share any of this with
my mother. I keep stumbling upon what she doesn't want to hear
or talk about. Her psyche a minefield, snoring, I note, sets off a
charge.

> *Jacques: The hardest thing is when you're at the bottom.*
> *Johana: Why?*
> *Jacques: 'Cause you have to find a good reason to come back*
>   *up and I have a hard time finding one.*

As Soares drops us off at Mont Clair's black iron gate and green,
leafy walkway, with room keys attached to large plastic circles,
my mother informs me that she will leave me for a couple of
hours while she attends church. *It is the only thing I am not flex-
ible about,* she insists. I guess she knows a little more about me
than I've realized, since she hasn't bothered to ask if I'd like to join

her even though it's because of her we were raised Catholics and attended Catholic schools. (My father, raised a Sikh, approved our Christian upbringing, reasoning that whether Jesus was or was not the son of God was irrelevant: he was "a nice man" and we wouldn't learn anything bad from him. Regardless, Catholic school was a recipe for atheism.) That, or else she'd like some time alone with her thoughts—thoughts she hasn't voiced out loud. Perhaps she wants to consider more deeply how my presence is affecting her. Or maybe she wants to ask God why I'm here. Why I can't digest coffee. Why I'm accusing her of snoring.

We roll our luggage into my mother's "regular" suite: tones of orange and brown, beige and yellow, in the fixtures and carpets, the dressers and sofa cushions; a small kitchenette with a counter adjoining the living room; washroom with shower (no bath); TV/living room with a table desk, a long curved couch and matching armchair; and a separate bedroom. My mother opens the bedroom door.

Since you don't wish to sleep in the same bed as me due to my snoring, you can have the bedroom and I will sleep on the couch in the living room. Okay?

Grateful for the arrangement, I nod—it never occurred to me she would expect us to sleep in the same bed and I'm relieved to be spared the mother-daughter experience.

Since you don't like to pray, would you like to swim? I'm sure you've read enough about Brazil to have packed a bikini?

She is smiling, so I laugh. *I love swimming.* And while my mother holds counsel with God, I change into a modest tank top–style two-piece swimsuit with red and yellow tropical flowers. There is a "piscina" on the rooftop, labelled "indoor" for some reason I can't figure out, and "pool" even though it is whirlpool size, about eight feet by eight feet and four feet deep, ten lawn chairs packed like white teeth surrounding the perimeter. I don't think ten people could fit inside the pool. Maybe four, if no one is splashing.

I wade in and then turn on my back into a star. The water cool and refreshing, my body relaxes as I marvel at the fact that I am actually here on this rooftop in São Paulo, alone in a tiny pool, floating in the dirty heat. I feel oddly elated as I try to analyze more purposefully why my mother hasn't asked me any questions about my childhood in Ottawa or my current life in Toronto. I think it would feel good—like progress, albeit difficult progress—to tell her about my academic and sports achievements in high school, the courses I took in university and the scholarships I earned, how I met Chris and when he confessed he wanted to spend the rest of his life with me, how close I am to finishing my PhD dissertation, my book launches, the book of poetry I'm working on, my favourite films. If she asks about my life, I reason, we won't have to pretend so much. She will learn about me bit by bit, and properly fill in the gaps she must have been avoiding all these years. I need to find a friendly or at least non-threatening way for her to face the fact that she hasn't been in my life; I am who I am regardless of her wishes for me. My mother is like an old building with a deteriorating façade and faulty electrical wiring. I want to break down the layers without causing the foundation to crumble into a pile of rubble. I didn't come here to protect my mother though. I didn't come here to protect myself. Reunion is the opposite of protection; it's confrontation. It's renovation. And we both require helmets and gloves. How to confront my mother so that I can gain some understanding of her and the past without resorting to aggression or direct accusation? This is the challenge.

After the "swim," I unpack my clothes, toiletries, and books, then decide to take a stroll to explore the stores in the immediate area—I noticed a high-end lingerie boutique called Fruit de la

Passion and some pastry shops as Soares inched us closer to
our destination—but am thwarted by Aleshandro, the young
desk clerk with cropped dark hair and gangly arms and legs, who
speaks a smattering of English.

"You *must not* go out."

I am practically bouncing out the door. "Excuse me?"

"You *must not* go out."

"Why?" Extreme pollution alert?

Aleshandro leaves his post behind the counter to block my
way. "Your mother does not wish for you to go out on your own."

"Really? My mother told you I'm not to leave the hotel?" I
laugh and twirl my purse flirtatiously. Why not?

Aleshandro eyes me the way you would a rain cloud. "São
Paulo dangerous. Not Canada. You *must not* get hurt."

"So I must stay inside all day?" You've got to be kidding me.

"Your mother loves you."

I am offended by the idea of a perfect stranger speaking to
me about my mother's love. Especially a man who is practically
a teenager. "Really?" I repeat, twirling my purse a little more as
Aleshandro blushes. "And if I go out, are you supposed to follow
me?"

"Truth, yes."

"How far can I go before you'll stop me?"

"One block, this way that way. Most three blocks."

"I want to go to the lingerie store."

He blushes again, dropping his hands in defeat, unaccustomed
to the severity of the role of security guard. "Okay. One block." He
gestures, pointing down the street.

Chuckling to myself as I turn past the black iron gate toward
the peach storefront of Fruit de la Passion, I skip a bit, amused
by my new role as potential Canadian damsel in distress. That
is until I notice that Aleshandro wasn't kidding. The block of
boutiques is an upper-middle-class oasis plunked in the middle

of a crime-ridden neighbourhood, even if the Mont Clair pamphlet claims: "Privilegiously located in the heart of Jardins, the most noble area of the city." I must keep in mind my guidebook's warning: although Rio de Janeiro is one of the most violent cities in the world, São Paulo is "less safe than Rio." Population estimated to rise to twenty-five million by 2025. Almost the entire population of Canada in one city. Most of the citizens dirt poor and desperate. The minority rich trampling all over their hearts for the latest ten-thousand-dollar alligator handbag.

Six or seven steps behind, Aleshandro sweats nervously as I gaze at the bras and panties and nightgowns in the store window. I can't toy with him any longer. I walk an additional block for good measure, buy an item from the drugstore, and return to the flat like a good scared foreign girl to wait for my mother.

"You English. You kidnapping target," Aleshandro sighs, handing me my room key.

"I used to be," I reply, but he has no context to understand the comment.

The lobby rumbles. Aleshandro points up to the sky. "Helicopters to catch kidnappers."

My father was always afraid my mother would kidnap my brother and me, and he would have little recourse or ability to protect us since he was confined to his bed or chair. My brother and I were, for years, film noir detectives or witness-protection-program clients on the lookout for a woman with thick black hair, dark glasses, and a coloured hairband who might be hunkering in the bushes outside our school, or in the stands of a basketball tournament, or beside the parked cars at a friend's birthday party, calling to us: *I have something for you.*

My father's fears were not unfounded. She did try to kidnap us once more, right after we were shipped to live with my father's affluent brother and his wife and two children in West Bloomfield, Michigan, about eight months after her initial disappearance

that cool November afternoon. A dark limousine had been cir-
cling the area for the better part of the day. We noticed it, but
it faded into the background like a bicycle or a hockey net on
a driveway. My brother was out front tossing a baseball to himself, and I was out back playing with my new sidekick, the family's honey-coloured cocker spaniel, Prince. Next thing I know,
my brother is screaming, running past me through the screen
door and into the kitchen, tearing up the stairs, and Prince, pre-
vented from causing any real damage by his leash, is leaping and
barking at this woman I recognize immediately as my mother,
though I react to as a rabid animal or unstable chemical. My
Aunt Mary, a white woman with cold hands and a colder heart,
was blunt: *Hello, Theresa. I will make us tea and then you will
leave.* As they drank, my brother and I were swiftly smuggled
through the front door to a neighbour's home; three hours later
my efficient Aunt Mary arrived with our clothes and school
books and stuffed toys packed, two plane tickets in her bony
hands. *You can't stay here any longer,* she said with the dismis-
siveness of a mall cop. My cousins, teenagers, older than us by
several years, who treated us warmly and curiously like exotic
pets, sharing their go-carts and mobiles and toy airplanes with
us, looked distraught but also relieved. We were interlopers in
their otherwise normal upper-middle-class suburban life.

We never saw my mother again. In less than twenty-four
hours, we were holed up with a French-Canadian family on farm-
land in a town an hour outside Ottawa. My father still refuses to
admit we were placed in foster care. Instead, he likes us to think
that he'd arranged for "friends" we'd never met, never heard of,
and who barely spoke English, to take us in, no questions asked,
for nearly a year while the house in Ottawa underwent renova-
tions to facilitate his caring for two children on his own. We were
the only people without white skin in that town, and the only
ones whose French was textbook French, not colloquial French,

and we were so advanced in our studies that the teachers gave us perfect marks on all our tests and sent us to their pathetic library to supplement their meagre offerings. We spent a year literally chasing chickens with their heads cut off—a task we were given as part of the yearly slaughter—snowshoeing through the forest and trying to make ourselves as inconspicuous as possible (as brown kids with buckteeth, high IQs, and lots of physical energy, not an easy task).

I wonder if Jit remembers that day in Michigan my mother appeared out of the blue? If I ask him, my brother claims obliviousness, total erasure of memory, then switches the topic to hockey trades. But it's always been unclear what my brother actually remembers, especially since he's older by eighteen months. Does he remember that his panic was so intense he ran right past me—his younger sister who less than a year earlier had screamed her heart out to keep him from being shoved into a strange car—without uttering a word of warning, only the smell and swiftness of his fear? She wanted us: But why? And here I am, awaiting the cause of that fear to escort me out on the town.

While I rest on my stomach on the bed, with almost zero knowledge of Portuguese, I attempt to read the book of Celeste Duarte Baptista poetry purchased at the mall bookstore, translating lines from a short poem entitled "*Chuva Quente*" (Hot Rains) with my two dictionaries: After two hours of intense concentration to translate fifteen lines, I think I understand that the melancholic speaker is watching her father cry for the first time, without knowing what he's done to elicit the tears. She then stares up at the sky and addresses a star, asking "why she is so distant/why my voice never succeeds to reach her there."

I think of my father, whose tears were shed quietly, like drops squeezed from a dried-up lemon, who never wanted us to see more pain than what was obvious by the constant tremors in his right arm, the degeneration of his leg muscles, the blueness of his toes. *I see you cry/without knowing what you've done.* Did my father ever blame himself for my mother's flight? Did he blame bad luck, or did he rack his brain for earlier evidence of my mother's fickleness or mental instability? He could never refer to her without disdain, and we were willing converts to his way of dealing with the loss—don't mention her, try your best not to think about her. One of my biggest fears as I grew older was that I would look too much like my mother and my father would hate me by instinct. In fact, whenever I was in a particularly despairing mood, I would goad him: *She was ugly, wasn't she? How could you marry such an ugly, stupid woman?* My father would look upon me with sorrow, as if sensing my worst fears: *She did the best with what she had.* Or, *You don't need to think about her at all.* Or, *Why worry about a woman you don't need, who doesn't love you like your old dad.* And I would hug my deteriorating father, clinging to him as if he were a life jacket, not a discarded hole-ridden unfixable raft.

As translating from any language is mentally exhausting, but particularly from a language one doesn't know (I experienced this for the first time in an Anglo-Saxon English course during my master's degree, which required us to translate dozens and dozens of lines per night with our glossaries), I quit and write a short letter to Chris about my impressions of São Paulo, rather than of my mother, but am unable to mail it because the hotel has no stamps and the envelopes in the room, no matter how much spit I apply to them, do not seal.

When my mother returns, I announce that I have been attempting to translate a poem by Celeste Duarte Baptista. My mother regards me like a cat who's left a dead mouse at her door. This surprises me, because my mother's c.v. highlights her work as a translator for the Brazilian Senate as well as for publishing houses.

There is so little appreciation for translation, she sighs, shaking her head as if she is picking up the offending rodent with a paper towel. *I got tired of the ingratitude. Better to write your own work. You only have so many years on earth.* I stare at the few lines that have taken me hours to compose, and I'm aware they are faulty and awkward but I suppose I did hope for a favourable response, either as a mother interested in the activities of her daughter—mothers do this, right?—or for my attempt to enter her language, at least. When she scans the sights I've highlighted in my guidebook, she shakes her head some more. Instead of a bridge, we're at a dead end.

Women are like that, as unpredictable as the sea.

Soares pulls up in front of the hotel in his white hatchback to drive us to dinner, and as the orange roofs and grey apartments of the day give way to the samba rhythms and flickering lights of the night, without missing a beat he and my mother delve into the dangers of São Paulo, an ironic tourism pamphlet.

Ninety-one people die violently in Brazil every seven hours. Ninety-one Americans have died in the entire Iraqi war thus far. It is safer to be an American soldier on the front lines of war than a Brazilian. . . . That dance troupe you want to see, that music hall you read about, the cathedral you'd like to visit, they are all too dangerous. If you are inside the cathedral, you are fine, but going in or out you could easily be assaulted. See those children there, looking innocent, they are part of a gang, they will take not only your purse, but your shoes and socks and pants and anything else they can. . . . Soares was robbed again just last week by two normal-looking girls on their way to a party. It is why Soares will come and pick me up wherever I happen to be. He knows I will never rob him. . . . São Paulo is no place to walk. Brasilia is dangerous too, because people know many people living there are middle class or higher. There is money to steal. American money is very popular to steal. Everyone will assume you are American. No one knows what a Canadian looks like. They will take the chance that they are robbing an American.

Notwithstanding the brutal description of the city, our fellow diners at the Italian restaurant all smile as if unaware they are targets for violent crime. I order calzone. A black man in a black leather jacket over a dress shirt plays a synthesizer keyboard and sings popular Portuguese songs. My mother claps louder than everyone else in the restaurant—her hands pudgy but tightly sewn from her operations, they make a distinct noise like slapping pizza dough on a countertop—and ten seconds before a song ends. The musician appreciates her enthusiasm and croons at me.

What's the song about? I ask.

Being in love. Like most songs, she replies wistfully. *This man loves his woman so much that he will walk across the desert to see her image in a mirage.*

What my mother thinks about love, besides that it exists ideally only in the movies, is unclear. Her love story was a tragic one because of my father's accident, that much would be obvious to the most inexperienced of lovers. But I'm beginning to sense my mother blames my father for something else, something that has led her not only to reject her responsibilities as a wife and mother, but to reject the loving part of herself. To redirect that love through filters and onto screens and the white pages of books, rather than live with it bubbling through her veins, boiling in her heart, rather than risk a night where the pressure of unfulfilled emotions explodes into violent tears and accusations and despair, her self's hot rains.

Did my mother expect her love to be perfect and pure and beautiful enough to cure my father? Like Bess in Lars von Trier's 1996 breakthrough film *Breaking the Waves*—a movie that left me a blubbering mess—did my mother believe if she made a deal with god he would reverse my father's paralysis? Or did she simply believe true love could overcome any obstacle—as so many do without imagining any obstacle might include the inability to work, chronic pain, inability to have sex, and the relentless crushing of dreams. In many respects, I'm beginning to understand that my mother still lives *in* love but always one step removed, like an expatriate who never relinquishes citizenship. My mother is the heroine of a love story gone so wrong she's scouring all annals and inventions of love to find out where her story went, when it will begin again.

Hearing me speak English, the crooner starts to play American songs—Beatles, Neil Diamond, Billy Joel. No one here thinks I'm anything but Brazilian when they set eyes upon me, until I speak. With my exotic mixed heritage, my abundant curly black hair and olive complexion, high Indian cheekbones, and my penchant for vintage clothing and party hats, I am not used to this, and find it liberating to blend in. The names here are magical: Fabrizia, Jona, Graziela, Nubia. The few words and phrases I have learned in Portuguese are solid—Soares says my pronunciation and accent are perfect Brazilian (I have always been a good mimic)—but they are few and far between: *bom dia* (good morning); *boa noite* (goodnight); *perdão* (excuse me/sorry); and my two essentials *socorro!* (help!) and *Onde fica banheiro?* (Where is the washroom?). I wish I knew how to say more! Language is the irrefutable indication to all outsiders that even if my mother introduces herself as such, we must not have had much contact if I know only a handful of Portuguese words.

Red meat and cheese and grilled vegetables settling nicely in our bellies, we sit back and enjoy the hit parade and my mother tells me about a cousin living illegally in the U.S. *How horrible to hide all the time,* she laments. *This is no life. To me, he is illiterate.* As she continues her monologue on the horrors of hiding, and the despicable decline of basic values, particularly family values, in contemporary society, I register that for my mother "illiterate" is the supreme insult. Nothing to do with literacy per se, but with a lack of complexity, integrity, compassion. I also note that she possesses no sense of irony. *Time is all we have,* she insists, applauding loudly for Stevie Wonder's "You Are the Sunshine of My Life." *Even God cannot give us back our time.* On the way out, we thank our gracious singer and ring a large brass bell hanging over the doorway for good luck. Ding dong. Ding dong.

Next, a Brazilian musical: *Constellation* at Teatro Imprensa. The plot revolves around the plight of a number of characters competing to win a trip to New York by identifying American songs on the radio. All the songs are from the American 1950s: "Blue Moon," "Only You," "Unforgettable," "Bario," "I Can't Help Falling in Love With You." From the fourth row we have a great view of all the slapstick action and fifties-style twisting and bopping and tap dancing.

After about thirty minutes, my mother leans over and whispers: *I am heartbroken. This is not the Brazilian music and dancing I asked for.*

I am stunned to discover she actually has tears in her eyes. *It's very interesting,* I whisper back. I normally don't like musicals; in my vision of the world people don't break out into inspirational song at the drop of a hat. To get me excited, a musical usually requires a twisted plot involving sexual deviants, monsters, cannibalism, the likes of *The Rocky Horror Picture Show* or *Hedwig and the Angry Inch*—but this musical is a cultural lesson so I don't think I'm lying. *I like it,* I reassure her.

At intermission, as I admire the fact that unlike most Canadians Brazilians dress up for the theatre—I can't spot a single person, young or old, in jeans or a sweatshirt—I elaborate: *It's like a translation, because they are not sung like the original American songs. Which is part of the point, I think. They're still Brazilians fantasizing about American culture and places like New York, projecting their dreams on Buddy Holly or the Empire State Building.*

Convinced I am enjoying the spectacle, she flips out a small spiral notebook and, now laughing contentedly, jots down thoughts for a review. At the end of the play, the performers line up at the foot of the stage and sing a song in honour of VARIG, the Brazilian international airline, which the audience applauds enthusiastically, and my mother explains that VARIG, like Air Canada, is in danger of bankruptcy. Brazilians are very emotional about their airlines because they believe the airplane was invented by a Brazilian, not the Wright brothers. After the performance, the actors, still in costume, congregate in the lobby to meet and greet audience members and hear their thoughts on the play. My mother strides right up, shaking all their hands and complimenting them on a fine performance that, thanks to me apparently, will receive a very positive review from her pen.

Later, as we prepare for bed, I insert the only purchase I have made on my own since my arrival—foam plugs I bought from the local drugstore while Aleshandro hovered outside—into my ears. Muffled due to the foam, as if spoken under water, my mother offers another one of her out-of-the-blue confessions:

Outside, Priscila, I am able to smile and be pleasing and forget the horrible things people say and do to me. But inside, I know it's doing much harm, much harm. You shouldn't judge me.

Then she laughs. She laughs a lot. Like I do. Our personalities are more similar than I'd like to admit. I, too, have found putting up a good front, keeping one's head up and smiling and laughing no matter what the circumstances, impresses people and makes them want to be around you, even help you. As I child, this is how I survived, forever pleasing those in authority—teachers, coaches, friends' parents—by being the child who surpassed all the others in test scores, who accumulated the most assists on a basketball court, who would enthusiastically offer to wash the dishes after a home-cooked meal. While there were certainly times, especially as a teenager, when my heavy-metal T-shirts and skull rings and penchant for morose poetry gave my melancholy away, rarely did this undercurrent of anger and depression interfere with my ability to excel and please. My teachers praised me for my stellar grade point average. My coaches could count on me to sink those crucial foul shots near game's end and to organize everything from extra workouts to team jacket orders. My friends' parents welcomed me as a positive influence as if math and science and geography scores rubbed off like chalk. *Look at what she's been able to accomplish, and under such circumstances!* "Such circumstances" being, of course, a sick father and a non-existent mother; and, later on, a fifteen-year-old living successfully on her own, going to school full-time and working full-time at a drugstore, paying her bills and gunning for university scholarships. Yet, deep down, deep down, the damage could not be eradicated, like toxic waste under soil. Like my mother, I would need to find an outlet for my dissatisfaction with the world; and, for both of us, this outlet is writing.

As my mother falls asleep, instantly, as soon as her head hits the couch pillow (and the snoring ensues), I recite possibly mistranslated poetry: *Ask whichever star/who watches over the deserted hours/why she is so distant/why my voice never succeeds to reach her there.* Who am I to this woman? Who is she is to me? Does she recognize our similarities? Our differing points of view and experiences? Am I her observer? Her audience? A figment of her imagination? While she sinks into her blue, a dimension which does her no further harm, I am like the lover Johana at the edge of the ocean dock, hoping Jacques will avert his gaze from the imaginary mermaids long enough to recognize her as the treasure she is, shouting: *I'm here! I'm real! I exist!*

My Mother and Me at the Italian Restaurant

3

mommie dearest

Greg Savitt: If you're acting, you're wasting your time. If you're not, you're wasting mine.

*

Christina Crawford: If she doesn't like you, she can make you disappear.

TODAY things take an inevitable bad turn.

After breakfast at the hotel, my mother phones Soares to take us to the Centro Cultural Banco do Brasil, or the Bank of Brazil Cultural Center, for an art show I marked in one of the tourist catalogues I found at the airport.

The building is stately and elegant, a bank established in 1901 that now houses exhibitions, and the friendly staff are all dressed like airline attendants in matching navy blue blazers and slacks and yellow scarves. Lights and shadows float across the entire architecture: the stairways, the towering green elevator doors (previously the safe doors with steel and brass handles and locks), the white walls and marble floors. The artist's work, *Claraluz* by Regina Silveira, a well-known female Brazilian artist, a series of moving lights, is projected like a white silhouette cut-out cubist collage from the ground floor up. Her other work, *Luna*, comprises two airy white balls that resemble planets, roll very, very slowly toward and away from each other as minimalist trance electronic music plays in the background. I can't help but feel sympathy with these two bodies as I observe the spheres approach and then repel each other. Contact is elusive and difficult and ambiguous and random.

After exploring the show and the historic architecture, my mother and I settle into the institute's gourmet restaurant, our chairs overlooking the section of light collage projected onto the stairwell. I was expecting a significant confrontation between us at some point, but I didn't expect it to unfold quite this way.

Like the actress Joan Crawford, the subject of the shocking tell-all accusatory memoir by her adopted daughter, Christine, that was turned into the infamous film *Mommie Dearest* (which single-handedly derailed Faye Dunaway's acting career), my mother suffered a series of miscarriages. Five to Joan Crawford's seven, I believe—my mother wanted a brood of children—nevertheless, she was successful at bringing two full pregnancies to term, whereas Joan resorted to adoption to fulfill her dreams of motherhood. I know my mother was proud of those pregnancies, and I have a vague memory of her telling me once that she wanted a daughter so badly, if she didn't have one, she'd have to make one up.

Did she do this after running away? I have an inkling that it is this imaginary daughter she has been escorting to the theatre, buying dresses for at the mall, reading placards to in art galleries, and sharing a tub of popcorn with at the movies. In only three short days, the intonations of her disappointment in the actual me are palpable. I don't dress the way she'd hoped (too much black, too modern). I don't speak the way she'd hoped (too analytical, too North American). I don't approve of her the way she'd hoped (too reserved, too skeptical). If she returned to the airport and waved her hands at another twenty-eight-year-old woman with dark hair curled into a bun, would she be just as happy or happier hailing her a cab and driving about São Paulo together?

As my mother clears her throat, I can tell she has prepared some lines for me today, a rehearsed speech. I wonder who wrote these words, and when.

I have not left Brazil for twenty years. I did not leave the city of Brasilia for seventeen years because I was so traumatized.

I do not expect this. I'm discovering I'm a terrible predictor of human behaviour when it comes to my mother. And that I could never write her dialogue. In that respect, she is an original. Her logic is utterly her own, and I have yet to figure out its fundamental principles. She abandoned us, forsaking a quadriplegic man to raise two kids on a flimsy pension and disability benefits, but *she's* traumatized?

What do you mean traumatized? Were you hospitalized?

I ask this because before I arrived in Brazil my mother sent some baffling legal documents from the Republica Federativa do Brasil and the Supreme Court of Ontario by mail to Toronto, what she called in her emails "a gift of truth." I could not make heads or tails of them. The ones from Brazil claimed my mother was placed "under serious specialized medical treatment" and then went on to state that she was awarded Brazilian custody of my brother and me. Some of the cultural implications in the document are also quite distressing: "It is clear from the proceedings that Petitioner [my mother], a person of high cultural level and fine sensibility was married to Defendant, a man of different origin and costumes [sic]." The documents she sent from the Supreme Court of Ontario clearly outline that my father obtained sole custody of his children "pursuant to an order of the Honourable Judge Doyle December 12, 1984." My mother accuses my father and "some Canadian authorities" of "a silent conspiracy . . . to keep my children away from any contact with me!" She concludes: "Both Amerjit and Priscila are both slaves in a so-called 'free' country. . . . God will certainly do Justice one day to my defenseless, poor children!"

In Canada, for the custody case, Jit and I were evaluated by psychiatrists and other doctors in the legal proceedings that ended with my father winning—seemingly by default, as my mother had "disappeared"—custody. I don't remember much about that time, only cold wooden benches and rides with my father strapped into the OC Transpo disability van. It's perhaps strange to be proud of a psychiatric report, but I must admit I am. The doctor writes of me: "Child exhibits extensive trauma. Child exhibits excellent coping mechanisms." I've taken this as a mantra of my entire life. Traumatized, sure, whatever, no argument there. But I can cope on my own. No need for doctors or counsellors or meds. Except wine.

We order lunch. *I don't remember. I don't remember.* A brush-off. But you started this, I think, and keep pushing. Day three: I want something more than discotheque shopping malls and Brazilian fruit and art exhibitions.

You just said you were traumatized when you arrived here. Did you seek help?

As if we are playing a game of chess, my mother pushes the salt and pepper shakers over to my side of the table. *There were bites on my hands and I underwent many body examinations to show the beatings.*

The implication shocks me. Utterly shocks me. But I contain myself, sitting perfectly still, waiting. Her monologue is just getting started. Her bright lips twitch. Is it my imagination or does she seem to be seeking out her light?

Social workers used to come to the house, don't you remember? Because your father made you tell the schoolteachers that I chased you with knives. In the end, the social workers knew it was your father who was the violent one, not me. But what humiliation. Don't you remember?

Now it's my turn. I lean back into my chair like a defence lawyer. *I don't remember. I don't remember much about you.*

I know this will hurt her. And I want to hurt her for what
she's saying about my father—I want to defend him, a man who
was also blessed with excellent coping mechanisms, I think, just
not perfect ones. Unfortunately, regardless of his heroism, he
wasn't a superhero, he was a man. The statement is both true and
false. I don't remember much about my mother—my childhood
memories of her are like damaged videotapes, lots of squiggly
silver static over somewhat familiar images, inaudible speech,
piercing noises, and stretches of blackness—but I do remember
some things, and I remember some very specific things that are
extremely pertinent to this discussion.

Childhood Montage

I remember I was often afraid of her. That I was never able to pre-
dict her violent rages against me, my brother, and, most alarm-
ingly, my sick father. I remember she once pinned my skinny
brother on his back and proceeded to shove a dirty sock into his
mouth and down his throat until he choked because he had forgotten to place the socks in his hamper. (Why are crazy mothers such sticklers for cleanliness—is it the lack of order in their
own minds they are bemoaning? My favourite line in *Mommie
Dearest* is, without a doubt, one uttered when Joan rages over a
perceived blemish on her immaculate house: *I'm not mad at you,
I'm mad at the dirt.*) She once held him underneath a burning
shower because he complained the bath she had drawn was too
cold. My own *Mommie Dearest* wire-hanger moment—the most
famous scene in the movie, when drunk and manic Joan terror-
izes the young Christine in the middle of the night, vandalizing
her room as punishment for hanging her clothes on wire rather

than wooden hangers (how a child would have the wherewithal to choose perplexes me), cited by critics as Faye Dunaway's over-the-top acting Waterloo—was when my mother threw me down the stairs along with her Remington typewriter because I hadn't asked permission to touch it. (Obviously, this did nothing to dissuade me from becoming a writer. In fact, I sometimes like to think that typewriter, tumbling down the stairs after me, imprinted itself on my bones.) Personally, I would like to defend Faye Dunaway for portraying Crawford in what was likely her actual narcissistic psychotic personality, something kept from the public and revealed only fully to her terrified children.

But my worst memory, which repeats on a quick loop in my mind's eye as my mother speaks to me over lunch, is my brother and I crouching in the thin doorway of the upper hallway, my father's bed just in sight through the slit, as my mother screams at him and keeps slapping his face, then horrifically, incomprehensibly, grabs his urine bag from the side of the bed and shoves the tubing down his throat. I burst in and launch myself like a crazed monkey onto her back while my brother kicks her repeatedly in the shins. I yank at her pearl necklace and it comes apart in my hands, the beads scurrying across my father's torso and adjustable bed, all over the brown carpet bedroom floor. *See what you make the children do to me?* I remember her shouting. *They hate me! They hate me!*

She was right. By then, we hated her. Her mood swings. Her rages. The unhappiness she sprayed on every morning like a nauseating perfume. I spent many years hating her, even as I ransacked her abandoned wardrobes of clothes (which were so flashy and out of date I would turn them into Halloween costumes and, once, an outfit for a disco-themed gymnastics performance in phys. ed.), her makeup bags of Avon products (including two tubes of half-used red lipstick—I have always associated Avon with her), her papers (rejection slips, an odd collection of romantic cartoons featuring a naked couple with oversized heads acting out moments of domestic bliss under captions of "Love is ... picking up his laundry when he's too busy" and "Love is ... telling her she's as lovely as the day you were married," and a personalized pad of paper "From the desk of Theresa Uppal" I've tucked away in my office but have never had the heart or the guts to use), and the photo albums. Even then my hatred outweighed curiosity. In fact, I think rummaging through her things was a coping mechanism (an excellent coping mechanism?), a concrete physical and mental outlet for the hatred. When the hatred was overtaken by ambivalence, I'm not sure. Perhaps I contented myself that it was an indication my own trauma was over? That I had reached stubborn if difficult adulthood?

Those pearls, like shiny white bullets, fly through my mind. And I feel the hot pangs of loss and grief and anger, and yes, hatred, once again, on behalf of my father, who had suffered so much already in his treacherous body, and whose humiliation at being forced by his wife to drink his own piss should trump any humiliation at being questioned by well-meaning public social workers.

I remember the social workers too. Either skinny young people with buggy eyes and bursting energy, clipboards in hand and the newest child welfare criteria on their lips, or overweight older women with receding hairlines and hoarse voices, who frequently forgot the times of appointments or our names. But I don't remember telling any of them my mother chased us with knives. I do remember unwrapping my lunch—a crumpled bag of Oreo cookies—and the astonished expression on the social worker's face when I calmly explained that no, there was nothing else besides the cookies because my mother said she was tired of us coming home with only half our lunch finished and so we could pack our own. I have zero memories of my mother cooking—I can't name a signature dish or family recipe she might have lovingly prepared for us after school or on special occasions, though I'm sure she must have cooked on a daily basis. When she left, I remember cooking for my brother and me from a "Junior Cookbook" I was quite fond of, and heating up frozen dishes for my father, but I've never had a talent for cooking, and I avoid it now as much as possible. I resent all those chicken dinners and pastas and pork chops I laboured over in our kitchen, which were greeted with little enthusiasm or gratitude. My mother hasn't made a motion toward the kitchen cupboards of our flat. Perhaps cooking, like sleeping, is also a waste of time.

When I came to Detroit or Chicago, I can't remember. . . . You wouldn't even speak to me.

The more baffling enigma: my mother's memory. She can remember the colour of every purse she's owned for the last decade, but she can't remember the city where she attempted a kidnapping.

I was a child. We were scared.

I had many lawyers—very expensive—working on bringing you both here. The case was in all the newspapers and television. Brazilians signed petitions. So you could join your mother and leave that house. (I've since tried to verify these phantom petitions and media clippings, but my research has not turned up any evidence for her claims.)

My father raised me, I remind her. I don't want her comparing herself favourably to the man who actually devoted all his scant resources to our survival. My father and I have our problems— my father is one of the strongest and therefore one of the most difficult men I've ever met—but they are ours and I'm offended by her insinuations and her assumptions about his facility as a parent, especially when she wasn't there as a witness. Many people, including me, believe if you can't have two loving parents, you can succeed with one good one, and although my father was not properly equipped to provide a stable environment for his children, he did instill in us valuable work habits, fundamental charitable values, the ability to cope with crisis, and an unquenchable desire to live and succeed. *I do not wish to hear anything bad about him.*

He knows what he did and one day he will answer for it.

She is pointing and waving her index finger at me, laying down the law. Things are getting out of control. While I don't believe my father was physically violent toward her—I have no memory of this, only of defending my father against my mother, and if he did lash out, she would have had the ability to overpower him—I don't need to convince her of this. Is she mentally ill? Delusional? Enraged she couldn't extradite us to Brazil? I sense my mother, patiently waiting for so long for her opportunity to speak, her time in the spotlight with her daughter as her active audience, has been stewing in the past, gradually cracking under the pressure. The storms in her brain are seeking a place to land. I must now be on tornado watch.

I need to calm her. Other customers overhearing bits and pieces of our conversation are now openly gawking at us arguing in a foreign language. *If you do not want me to judge you, you cannot judge him either. I will not judge either of you.*

This, of course, is a lie. I do judge them. No one with an analytical mind can help it, even if I'm coming to realize that my mother's life may be as sad and tragic as my father's. High hopes, sickness, debility, arrested time. Their life trajectories are, in fact, parallel. Like lit fuses of dynamite.

All I can tell you is my own experience, I continue. *And my experience is that after Detroit—it was Detroit, not Chicago—you never contacted us again.*

Right at the table my mother starts crying, wiping her eyes by pinching her napkin between her fingers and pressing it against her lids. Is she trying to protect her makeup? I think so. Her loud voice cracks with the tears.

I did not mean to upset you, I whisper, embarrassed I'm part
of a scene, in English no less, unfolding in a public place. This,
too, is probably a lie. Not that I enjoy watching her cry. I don't
like watching anyone cry. Period. I'm not embarrassed by it, it's
that tears are usually an indication of a loss of control, and loss of
control, for me, is always unnerving, even if I'm able to comfort
the sufferer. And for some reason it's even more upsetting when
a fat woman cries—as if no bulk is enough to counter the pain.
But I'm also irritated at her refusal to face the truth of the past
or the present. Why has she still not asked me anything about
my own life? Where I've travelled. What my PhD is about. If I've
been diagnosed with an illness. If I've ever been in love.

I am not a hurtful person. I have lived a hard life.

My father does not live an easy life either, I remind her again.

I know. I have lived a far better life than your father. And then
she smiles. A wide, smug, demeanor-stabilizing smile. Regardless of her tears, with that camera close-up smile, my childhood
hate for her, like a cold front to her rising temperatures, is helping the tornado take shape. I want to slam back, *I don't think so.
He knows his children. You do not.* But I don't. Not yet. Instead,
I say as calmly as possible, *Maybe. I don't know. Maybe not.*

I am not talking about material things.

*We did not have many material things growing up. We did not
have money. We did not live well,* I reply.

She shrugs as if those things don't matter anyway, are not
worth worrying about, although I suspect she has enjoyed financial comfort and some luxuries here with her work in civil service and academia and likely a family inheritance to boot. I am
silent as she finishes off her plate of ravioli and two extra pieces of
bread, and then, while I decline dessert, spoons mounds of carrot
cake into her red mouth, the temple of her ongoing monologue.

*I do not wish to live. Living is too difficult. Every day I wake up
and say, Oh God, I guess I am alive . . .*

This is blatantly contradicted by how strictly she follows her cancer doctors' instructions regarding diet and medication, but I am beginning to understand my mother is a mess of contradictions. How am I to know what she really thinks or feels? Or is every thought, belief, and memory dependent on what she wants her audience to believe at that moment? Almost everything she says contradicts something she said before. A conflict of extremes. Incapable of subtlety or introspection—a bundle of violent emotions tied together haphazardly with a flashy bow. A Pandora's box.

It is only because of my parents and my religion that I do not kill myself. People have said to me, "Theresa, God must want you to live." And so I live. I do not enjoy living. When my father was dying of cancer, I would have gladly given my life for his. Brazilians are nosy, they want to know everything about everyone. They think I'm a radical for not talking about my personal life. I will answer a question if it is asked, but then I'll forever label the person as unintelligent and I will never speak to them again. People ask me, "Does Priscila have children?" And I say I do not know. This is personal. I do not ask. I have a very close friend at the university. Very, very close. People would ask me, is she married? I would say, I do not know. I have never asked.

So, there's the answer, she's *proud* she knows nothing about her daughter. I can understand her avoidance of discussing her personal life with strangers—I'm guilty as charged, especially with lazy interviewers keen on reading literature as thinly veiled autobiography—but to not care whether your friends, or your offspring, are married or have children is an extreme case of willful ignorance. What do they talk about, just movies, novels, office politics? Well, I'm not going to play this role, I decide— avid listener without a speech of my own. I have a personal life and it should matter more to my mother than what I think about movies. *In North America, we think if you are not willing to share*

*personal information with a very close friend, then you're not really
a very close friend. And it's considered self-centred to never ask
someone questions about themselves, to talk only about yourself.*

My mother scrunches her face in disgust. *People who know
personal things about other people are common. I do not want to
be common. I want to be extraordinary.*

Now that she has polished off her dessert, my mother takes a
moment to survey the space. Several diners quickly shift their
gazes away. I suddenly realize I am afraid. Not just upset or anxious, uncomfortable or angry, but actually afraid. My mother is
hiding too much from her family, her friends, her co-workers, and
from me. Is she a psychotic? A sociopath? Perhaps, but I quickly
dismiss these terms as too easily flung about when someone's
worldview or behaviour is radically different from one's own.
Is my mother an actress? A performer? Does she think of herself as a person of flesh and blood or simply as "Theresa Catharina de Góes Campos" or that woman who left her husband and
two children for Brazil? The failed poet? The journalist? Movie
reviewer? The woman who refuses to answer questions about
the past, who refuses to know basic things about people because
that would be *ordinary*? I can hear her pleading with me, like
Joan Crawford with her own daughter in *Mommie Dearest: Why
can't you just act like one of the strangers on the street? Treat me
like you would a stranger on the street?* and me, like Christina,
shouting back, *Because I am not one of your fans.*

Dread is taking root in my bones. I should not have come
here. This woman has no interest in any story other than the one
she's constructed. A lesson I'm very unhappy to have learned. *At
least,* I tell myself, *I owe her nothing. Not even my own story. This
is my freedom. And my weapon. I can give her only what I want to
give. Nothing more. She doesn't ask, because deep down she believes
I will not be willing to give. I am not a gift who needs a recipient.*

I am a person with the free will to lay my love where I wish. Just like her.

My mother insists on paying all the bills (admissions, tickets, meals, clothing, cab fares), so even after the tense exchange she wipes her eyes, reapplies her lipstick, and signs the credit card slip. The trip is costing her, I know. Though I'm paying only for my airfare and a few souvenirs, it's costing me too. I can assure you that I as write these lines, years after the fact, I am still paying—the mind and heart send their own collection officers on their own schedules.

While we walk back to the square where Soares will meet us, my mother attempts a ceasefire.

All this is settled. We won't talk about it anymore. I should not have brought it up.

It is unrealistic to think it wouldn't come up, don't you think? I ask.

Oh. The day is gorgeous. Bright sunny thirty degrees plus. Not a cloud in the blue sky. Only we are burdened with severe weather warnings.

Nothing is settled. The dust has only begun to rise. Objects, people, memories, will all be swept up in the path. And this is Brazil. You can set your sights on the vast blue horizon, but there are miles and miles and miles of dusty sandy beaches shifting under our feet.

At the Pinacoteca do Estado, we stroll the sculpture gardens. This gives us both a chance to relax and take in the fresher air. When we do wander the gallery, surprise surprise, we reveal very dissimilar artistic tastes. My mother likes the Romantic period best, as well as portraits and realistic landscapes. Whereas I have little time for realism in painting, though I admire it in fiction and film; it strikes my eyes almost always as dull, unsuggestive, technique without artistry. I am an abstraction and expressionism fan. The world is not as it appears. It's a series of lines, shapes, haphazard gestures, bursts of colour, oblique symbols, dizzying ambiguities. My mother, impressionism. For me, impressionism is too calm, too placating, too pretty.

Graciously, she translates titles. She disapproves of artworks lacking titles. *Sem Titleo.* Apparently, she instructs visual artists to ask creative writers to title their art. I think the same of poems, that most poems deserve titles—it's writerly laziness to leave poems naked; however, I've always thought visual artists should be freer to name a stage or a period for a show, and not necessarily each individual artwork. Here I am taken by a contemporary piece by Pazé called *Cinzas*, or *Ashes*, a huge sculpture secured within a wall-size Perspex container, a landscape of straws of different shades of white and grey, resembling the cross-section of a rock or mineral. You don't notice the piece is made out of straws until you get very close to the container. This kind of optical illusion, made from common domestic objects, has always appealed to me. Clever. Playful. Uncanny.

I am also intrigued by Antonio Henrique Amaral, 1935, BR-1 SP, oil over screen, a work composed of bananas and banana peels (bananas being the natural symbol of Brazil) made to look like a woman with tremendously long hair. While clever, the piece is unsettling too, as it implies the woman's beauty is rotting away like a banana peel. As I am making notes on other Brazilian artists of interest, my mother whispers:

I am afraid of life. Afraid all the time. To live is frightful. I am not tough. I am fragile. I could not fight.

Jit and I are tough, I say flatly to avoid being suspected of bragging or posturing. And she nods. I know she is trying to explain why she had no courage, no strength to hold the house together for her children or even to keep in contact with them. Between Brazil and Canada, Canada would win. And I'm glad it did. For when

I look around this country, as beautiful and vibrant as some of its people are, as sublimely glorious as some of the mountains and beaches, I am aware of how many opportunities I would have lost if we'd immigrated here. We would not have been better off with my mother—able-bodied and employed and from a family of money and social standing though she is. Nor do I think it would necessarily have been better if my father and mother had managed to stay together. In any case, you can't change the past. It's difficult for me to see how my life would have been different; as an artist I'm surprised I have so little imagination in this respect. Or perhaps those childhood my-life-would-have-been-so-much-better-if fantasies are simply over. People who carry them around as adults like bandages for unseen hurts annoy me; no, offend me; disgust me. Here is life: deal with it. My brother and I dealt with it: we learned how to buy groceries and toiletries, how to pay bills and balance a chequebook, how to prepare a commode or empty a urine bag, how to walk on my father's arm to lessen the pain of tremors, how to score goals and baskets, how to earn highest-achievement plaques, how to graciously accept free clothes and toys and orthodontist work from strangers, how to garner invitations to our friends' houses for holiday dinners and vacations, how to forget some of our troubles with books and music and movies, how to use our imaginations to find our way back, how to laugh, how to raise ourselves, how to live life regardless. Here is my mother: this sometimes pleasant, sometimes frightening, damaged woman who gave birth to me. Then I think of my sad, stubborn, tragic father. It's impossible for me to believe our lives could have avoided suffering. But it's also impossible for me to believe we wouldn't figure out how to get through it.

I do not like competitions of any kind. If someone wants to share with me, I say yes. But if they do not want to share, if they want this chair, I will take the chair I don't want.

A single black bowler hat floats in and out of view as we stand in front of a white screen watching a film of a Norwegian cliff-side landscape. It's whimsical, lovely, the freedom of the bodiless hat in space, rising and falling like a magic carpet, without owner and without destination. Beside it is a sculpture composed of black sand and a sawed-off LP record by artist Mark Manders titled *Reduced Night Scene with Broken Moment (reduced to 82%)*. Something about this title makes me instantaneously melancholy and regretful.

What do you mean? I ask her. Competition has always been a welcome word in my universe. My brother and I could turn anything—eating cookies, riding bikes, carting medical pads from one room to another—into a competition, with rules and penalties, prizes and punishments. We still can. For us, competition permitted our inner desires to surface, allowed us to showcase our talents and devise new skills, pushed the other to do more, do it faster, do it better. And winning was expected of us. A typical South-Asian father in that respect—I believe "excellence" is a South-Asian's favourite word—second-best was never good enough. My father established a reward system for our academics, whereby we were given a small amount of money for each A+—not an uncommon practice, but the difference was if we didn't earn an A+ we were obliged to pay *him*. For us report card day meant a small windfall; we could buy new sneakers or computer games or go bowling. And in sports we were expected to be leaders, on the scoreboard and off the court, rink, or field, with Cs or As on our jerseys and MVP trophies. Yet I can't recall a single occasion when my father ever said he was proud of me. To express pride would indicate doubt of outcome. And an Uppal must succeed. Just not in the arts. I could participate, grudgingly, but when I excelled alarm bells sounded. My father pulled me out of a city-wide drama class after the instructor phoned to tell him I was the most talented student he had ever acquired.

And if I won a poetry or short story contest, my father would stay up all night studying each word as if they spelled a code of mental destruction. When I informed him I was unwaverable in my decision to pursue English literature and creative writing at university, he was inconsolable. In fact, when I was offered my professorship, he sighed with relief, wrongly concluding: "Now you can finally stop writing those books!" I imagine he was wary of me following in any way in my mother's footsteps, connecting her penchant for the arts with her declining mental state, the way my brother and I for a long time connected tropical landscapes with my father's paralysis. Nevertheless, regardless of the arena, my father understood the attraction of competition and winning fairly. Hadn't he been the first South-Asian in charge of all those Caribbean island projects? When I think of our test scores, our sports tournaments, I realize that without competitions we honestly might have been left behind.

I want you to understand my psychology.

Good. That's exactly what I want too, whatever that means. This is not a typical mother-daughter gallery chat, but a case study. I want to know what makes her tick, what keeps her living when she claims she'd rather die, what thoughts fill her day, what thoughts fill her night, what she has done with the past— where she has hidden those skeletons, if she's dressed them up in parasols or Arctic snowsuits, if she ever takes out memories like antique cutlery and sets a special table for them.

I do not like to fight for things. If someone wants to fight me, I hide.

She doesn't believe she's cruel; although she won't use the word, she's labelled herself a coward. It's the psychology of someone who, as a child, never had to fight for what she wanted. Faced with the possibility of competition, she bolts to avoid conflict, confrontation, failure. Whereas her children fought for everything they have. Failure was something we dreaded, unacceptable as anything lower than an A+, but something we had to acknowledge was a force of nature, like fire, we needed to heed. My mother fled to a world without flames. In that world, my brother and I are chairs my father was willing to go to war for. She simply sits in other chairs.

Soares has never eaten at the expensive revolving tower restaurant he has recommended for dinner, but he knows this is where tourists go to revel in the panorama of São Paulo, so he is confident I should eat there. To Soares, I am an aristocrat who deserves the very best of every sight and taste and experience Brazil has to offer, which is touching, especially considering that on his wages he would not be able to access most of what he tells me I *must* see and do. *You will dine like a queen,* he boasts. Apparently queens revolve while they eat.

The view is stunning, the bright lights of the mega-city like neon night flowers opening up to the moon. I am content to sink into the cushioned chair, sip a banana daiquiri pierced with a pineapple umbrella, and stare off into the mind-numbing waves of electricity and concrete while the floor moves slowly on its elliptical orbit underneath us. The last few days have been trying, although I have been loath to admit it and I have not cried or slept particularly badly now that I have a separate bedroom. But here, to puncture the illusion that I am taking everything in stride, my stomach gives out.

My mother is not impressed. Ordering delayed, she huffs when I return from the washroom where I have been dousing my forehead with cold water, my temperature having risen in a flash. I'm trying not to hold my breath or cringe as stomach cramps unfold in two-to-three-second waves while my mother regales me with stories about my childhood.

I want you to remember. You had a very good childhood. You used to put my lipstick tubes in the vase and clog it up and make your father very mad when you were toilet training. Your brother liked puzzles and was skilled at them. When you were silent I would know you were working on one of his puzzles. It would take you longer, but you would not get up and leave the puzzle until you had mastered it, even if it took you all afternoon.

Before our pumpkin soup appetizers arrive, I'm back in the toilet, holding my stomach and wiping sweat from my lips. *You had a very good childhood. You had a very good childhood,* I repeat to myself, trying not to puke. My mother has moved a good thirty degrees. The multicoloured lights of the tireless city assault my eyes as we spin.

Your brother loved his pacifier. We could go to restaurants because he would suck on it contentedly for hours. If the staff looked nervous, we would tell them not to worry, he would be very quiet, and he always was. When you were born, this was a different story. You wanted to touch everything. Do everything. My father would ask, "Is Priscila coming? Then I will not come." My parents were so embarrassed about your behaviour. At museums I would force you to keep your hands behind your back, otherwise you would try to touch everything. At one museum, you were given your own personal security guard.

Boar ravioli. Glass of red wine. Back to the toilet. Fruit cocktail dessert. Back to the toilet.

You had a very good childhood. You had a very good childhood.

On the way home, I attempt to place her stories among my jumbled memories. As my mother, she must insist I experienced a happy childhood, any unhappiness attributed solely to my father and her absence from my life. Nevertheless, she might be right. Children don't know anything different from what they have. I was a curious, energetic, bright child: I'm sure I threw myself enthusiastically into puzzles and games and sandboxes. I still do. My mother obviously took me out a lot, and when my hands were not forced behind my back, they were probably reaching out, often landing in hers. I'm told I was inconsolable my first year of kindergarten, that I cried and cried until the witch they called our teacher locked me inside the clothes closet until I stopped. I must have loved her something awful. But now?

I institute deep breathing. I can't afford to succumb to sickness here, where I can't speak the language, with someone I can't trust. I *must* not be at the mercy of my mother. Never again. If she was once maternal, all those bones have ossified from lack of use. She doesn't look at me like I'm her daughter—more like I'm her client or some unsympathetic defence attorney forced upon her by the state. And not for the last time I berate myself for not learning more Portuguese, not finding the extra time to play the tapes I bought with good intentions but poor follow-through.

Back at the flat, my mother asks if I liked dinner. I tell her it was delicious but that I suffer from stomach pains and need to take my medication now and be still and quiet in my room.

You must be a very sick person, she says, opening the bedroom door as I slip underneath the sheets. *Either that or you don't like Brazil much. It's propaganda that made you get all these vaccines before coming here. They are making you sick now.*

Although I miss Chris and know he's anxious for a full update on what has transpired thus far, when he phones I have no energy left to speak. My mother eavesdrops and peeks in at me whispering goodbye, her eyes wide, mouth silent but twitching. I am a disappointing image, like a black-and-white sketch of a missing person. Not the daughter she imagined. Like Christina Crawford, I too will end up typing out the transcripts of our mutual suffering, our battles over our memories, our lives. Who will sympathize with us? Are we both monsters? Feminists? Are we in competition? Is this a showdown between Canada and Brazil? Did I come to prove that I didn't need her? That though she didn't play fairly, I won? Who will get the enviable last word?

My mother is terrified, I now understand, that I am going to leave. That at any given moment, if I don't like what I've learned, I might simply and willfully disappear. The room continues to spin. I hold my stomach like a big, achy secret. I did not realize how scared she is. Even of me.

Mother at the Breakfast Table in São Paulo

4

ladyhawke

Mouse: How can I learn any moral lesson if you keep confusing me like this?

E VERYONE in the breakfast room is now worried about my stomach. Have coconut water. Have apple juice. Have guava soda. Brazil produces the best coconuts, the best apples, the best guavas.

The best water in the world, Soares insists, as I crawl into the back seat and buckle up for another smog-filled ride across the city. *Canada is nothing. Nothing. Like most people's heads.*

I do not mind too much when Soares insults my nationality. He has the warmest smile and laugh, a sonorous comforting voice, and a laid-back but professional attitude. He makes me feel safe and is a good buffer between my mother and me as he involves himself in planning our itinerary. Plus, I've noticed these national comparisons where Brazil comes out on top of any dichotomy are as commonplace as traffic lights or snapping one's fingers. "Brazil is the Best" chants in my head, an endless soccer match.

To top it all off, Soares is on time, to the minute, whereas apparently everyone else in Brazil is chronically late. My mother despises this, her only complaint about Brazilian character aside from the love of Carnival. *They do not plan. They like life to be chaotic. They do not care about ten minutes from now. Only now. Right now.* This distresses my mother, who, like me, is an obsessive planner and leaves herself dozens of "things to remember" notes: what to pick up, what to purchase, map routes, phone numbers, titles of books. Chris jokes that I'm never happier than when I'm making a list. I wonder if my mother has a special "things to remember" list about her children. *My mother is never on time,* she mutters. *She would even be late to pick up my father. Once they missed a train because she said, 'No train ever leaves on time.' When it did, she pointed out the two busloads of people the train station had to accommodate because they all showed up late thinking the same thing.* This mentality makes my mother and me both nervous. Think of the continual rewriting of the day's schedules. Think of all the missed connections.

We will do whatever you want on this trip, she says loudly so Soares can bear witness, *since it is once in a lifetime.*

Once in a lifetime. Yes, I agree, but it is interesting to hear her admit this whether or not she secretly hopes we will find a way to forge a relationship after these twelve days are over. My mother is a hopeless romantic (was a truer term ever coined?). She wears the Thai silk scarf I sent her from my friend Milton's vintage clothing store every single day. I've also been learning this by her responses to art. *Ladyhawke* is another movie in her 100 Club. It is the story of an ill-fated couple in love: the beautiful Isabeau (played by Michelle Pfeiffer), who, because of a corrupt bishop's jealousy, is cursed to be a hawk by day and a woman by night, and her lover, the stoic and regal Captain Navarre (played by Rutger Hauer—my mother must have a thing for Rutger Hauer—I mean she saw this film over a hundred times in 1985!), a wolf by night and a man by day. With the help of a lowly but good-natured pickpocket, Mouse (played by a wide-eyed Matthew Broderick), they must find a way to break the curse so they can finally embrace in the flesh once again.

My mother, it seems, has allowed herself to invent in her dreams at night, directing actors, composing dialogue, orchestrating music. Whereas I have tried my best to erase her from my dreams, censoring and editing her out, but have often found myself pondering her character during the day. Now we have been given the opportunity to meet and speak as real flesh-and-blood people. Will we decide on mercy and forgive, or will we arm ourselves with those lost years shell by shell for an epic family battle? The jury is still out. Perhaps we are both a little like Mouse, who laments having to face the awful truth of the curse: *I should have known better. Every happy moment in my life has come from lying.*

The Clock Museum, or Museu do Relógio Professor Dimas de Melo Pimenta: I tell my mother this is the next attraction I'd like to visit since we both value timekeeping. And I love clocks: grandfather clocks, glockenspiels, novelty clocks in the shape of TransAms or Betty Boop or KISS façades. But when we phone for hours of operation, no one answers. We chuckle at the irony and charge off to the Museum of Precious Stones instead.

Brazil is famous for its precious stones and Pedras Brasileiras is located on the fifth floor of a bank building, with no signage to indicate the museum is housed inside. I am told this is to discourage robbery. My mother and I are waved inside because of her journalist ID. She enjoys flashing it, like a secret service badge. Journalists in Brazil are offered free admission to all sorts of cultural activities, and are treated with deference and respect. *Since the dictatorship ended,* my mother adds, *we are not to be silenced.*

We walk into a colourful showroom of thousands of jewels (rubies, emeralds, diamonds) and geologic stones (agate geodes, amethyst chapels, tambled stones) encased in rings, necklaces, bracelets, brooches, hairpins, and objects with stones incorporated into their designs (clocks, jewellery boxes, wine openers, key rings, pyramids, dolphins, cats, hundreds of bonsai trees). Our young guide, a clean-cut, dark-haired Brazilian named Tom, speaks English and practically sings an aria as he shows off the glittering gems in a private tour, the pièce de résistance the largest natural quartz stone in the world, smoky quartz or *quartzo enfumaçado* from the north of Brazil weighing sixty-seven kilograms. More than me, I joke, as I examine the shiny tar-like sheen on its rectangular body shaft. He explains that the showroom is a business as well as a gallery, and most of their customers are airline employees, who know you can buy cheap stones in Brazil and hide them easily in suitcases or wear them through customs. Complying with this tradition, I buy several gifts from their lower-end selection: a desk clock, circular jewellery boxes, and corkscrews. My mother says we will tell Chris when he calls that we are so precious the manager tried to keep us for display. Her joke is charming and I am genuinely touched. My mother continues to surprise me. I make a note to add this to my own list of "things to remember."

Museums bring out our mutual good qualities—curiosity, appreciation for skill and beauty, an eagerness to learn—so we head out to another, the Museum of Inventions, also known as Inventolândia. This museum is located in the union building for inventors (makes sense), and here too we are given free admission and a private tour of more than four hundred Brazilian inventions. Many have to do with cooking and housework (and poking holes in coconuts), as well as machinery and toilet improvements.

As my mother takes notes in her small spiral notebook—we are also alike in our ability to turn any excursion into work—she lectures me about Brazilian infrastructure. *People can see and get excited about a new school, a new road, but what goes on under-*

neath the roads, they don't care about. *In Brazil, if there is a hole in the road, instead of fixing the hole in the road, they build another road.* But she loves that Brazilians "invented the airplane," and explains the genesis of this assertion here. According to Brazilians, if not the history books, the airplane was invented by an eccentric dandy named Alberto Santos-Dumont living on a trust fund in Paris, the first to have his own personal flying machine, a motorized dirigible, which he used daily to fly himself to dinner, shopping, and social occasions on the Seine. On November 12, 1906, he flew a kite-like contraption with boxy wings called the *14-Bis* 722 feet and was hailed all over Europe as the inventor of air travel. Only after this announcement did the Wright brothers contest the honour, claiming they had invented the airplane three years earlier at Kitty Hawk, North Carolina. Many historians still contend that according to the criteria established at the time, the Wright brothers' flight would not have qualified. Brazilians are especially sore around Wright brothers flight anniversaries. *Brasilia is shaped like an airplane. When we fly there, you will be able to see the outline of the city is an airplane. Airplanes are part of our family. My father was a pilot, and your Uncle Wilhelm and his children are all pilots. Very good jobs. Uncle Wilhelm is head of the Air Force and has met the pope. The most stressful job in the world is not an airplane pilot, as people believe. Studies show it is a university teacher or a public bus driver.* We spend two hours among the cramped shelves, inquiring incessantly about the light bulb changers and pet massagers, punch-proof tires, portable bidets, foldable pianos, wall paintings that convert into tables, combs for the bald, exercise equipment that washes lingerie, hats with cameras that take 360-degree photographs, and more.

Almost everything I order at lunch, my mother can no longer eat: cheese and sausage and pop. She orders soup and bread rolls and admits she is embarrassed by her weight—she could stand to lose thirty or forty pounds. *I'm glad you're skinny. Everyone in the family is skinny except for me. They like to tease me. In Brazil, if you're fat, you get liposuction. Not like in North America where fat is the norm. Brazilians sometimes eat as much as North Americans but we don't tolerate fat, we don't tell each other to feel good about our bodies. If you want to feel good about your body your body needs to look good. But I let them make fun of me. I've had too many surgeries for real problems, why would I put myself under the knife for cosmetic reasons?*

Although I don't yet know what to believe about the rest of the de Góes Campos clan, my mother has not painted a pretty picture. It is apparent my mother does not think highly of her immediate family, and this distaste is rubbing off on me rather easily since we've both lived lives where we've developed stronger bonds with friends and colleagues than with relatives.

They are jealous, she insists. *Jealous because I don't care about them. I care about my friends. My mother does not like me as much as she likes my brother and sister. Because I don't have a man. It's easier to fight with one person than with two people and my mother likes to fight.* (I notice she never says "your grandmother" or "your uncle and aunt.") *I embarrass her. She thinks a woman should have a man.*

I interject: *But she was with you when you left.* Which is true. It's the only memory I have of my grandmother. A tiny grey-haired woman who pitter-pattered around the house almost invisibly until bags were packed in a car headed for the airport under the illusion of picking up Christmas presents chosen out of the Sears Christmas Wishbook (a guitar for me, and a hockey foosball game for Jit). This bony woman was helping my mother force Jit into the car when I started screaming my heart out. *Yes,* my mother says, *I never said it would make sense. Nothing in Brazil or about Brazilians makes sense. I am just telling you that my mother does not like me very much. She makes plans to be away on my birthday when she knows I will come to Brasilia no matter what. She went away when I was in the ICU for my cancer. I am* visibly shocked by this. *Não, Não, I don't say a word. I try not to provoke her into a fight. I just smile and remind myself that when Pontius Pilate decided Christ had not done anything wrong and left it up to the people to decide who to set free, Christ or Barabbas the murderer, they picked Barabbas. I should not think myself better than Christ.*

Like the hawk and the wolf at sunset and sunrise, my mother and I almost connect at short intervals, excruciatingly close to understanding, sympathy, perhaps even clear-eyed sight. I try to hold on to these moments, these potential transformations, but they pass too quickly. Here she is again, my overweight mother in her loud formless clothes and bright red lipstick, following me incessantly with nonstop chatter from room to room, eyes glued on me as if I'm going to disappear into the ether. While I am learning a lot of interesting information about my estranged family, the relentlessness of the delivery takes a serious toll.

My brother has lived with the same woman for nineteen years. Common-law. His two daughters were taken away from him by his first wife. This makes me very, very angry. He has nothing to do with these girls, and they are not well. One has tried to kill herself, several times. My brother is a coward. He won't talk to his ex-wife, so his children have had no father. He's afraid of changing light bulbs. He also loses his teeth when he's anxious and so he has no natural teeth left . . .

It is difficult to identify the details my mother finds most significant about her family. Is my uncle's lack of teeth as important an insight into his character as the fact that he does not respond to his daughter's suicide attempts? How can she be angry at him for being a coward when she says she'll flee at the whiff of any fight? Like trying to collect water in a butterfly net, I can feel the coldness, the wetness, the rush of the motion, but can't trap my subject for further examination. And my True and False jars keep shifting, contents rolling imperceptibly from one to the next and back again like in a carnival shell game.

The only place my mother usually does not follow me is into the bathroom, and so I find myself retreating there, trying to catch my breath and indulge in a little peace and quiet by washing my underwear in the sink. Who are all these people she's telling me about, starting fights and losing teeth and flying airplanes? My *family*? I don't recognize the word beyond its six letters.

No, not that mall, Soares argues when my mother suggests the plaza she normally frequents to write her articles. *This is mini-shopping. You must take Priscila to the shopping palace.* So we end up strolling through a designer labyrinth, where you can spend R$3,000 for a handbag or a pair of shoes (approximately $1,200 Canadian). Strangely, considering the wealth the customers must possess, prices are signed in a curious manner: 199R x 15, or 49R x 20. I suppose the idea is that you instinctively surrender yourself to the object in question due to your attraction to the low numbers, even though you can (hopefully) do basic math and figure out the actual astronomical price.

I'm also amused by the opportunity to experience a culture where preparations for Easter are as extravagant as those for Christmas. In the middle of the mall is a display the size of a small town: fifty to sixty stuffed rabbits, human-sized, alongside other stuffed critters eating giant chocolate eggs and cookies. One glamorously attired rabbit is posed holding court with rabbit paparazzi while others in overalls and peasant dresses collect goodies from the fields. At Lojas Americanas, a popular department store my uncle with the missing teeth will later refer to as "paradise for housewives," thousands of chocolate egg baskets wrapped in bright pink and yellow and blue aluminum foil hang just in reach above our heads like palm tree coconuts. The sweet smell is overpowering. Customers are pulling these baskets down by the cartload as if wresting wishes out of stars.

I tell my mother that I remember, yes, I do remember (finally, one of the *good things you remember about your mother*) she used to hide chocolate eggs and rabbits in our dresser drawers and all over the house for Easter morning. *I am so pleased you remember,* she replies. I am pleased too. A happy memory of childhood. The kind other children must have. We both feel, momentarily, normal. Like we were once something called a family. Before the accident: our version of the family curse that separated us and made loving difficult, perhaps even impossible. I am reminded of a scene in *Ladyhawke*—a movie I must confess I find charming as well; I saw it for the first time when I was eleven years old and learned through Captain Navarre that hawks and wolves are wondrous because they both mate for life—when the shimmering Isabeau reappears to Mouse in the dead of night and he poses his most pressing question:

Mouse: Are you flesh or are you spirit?
Ladyhawke (Isabeau): I am sorrow.

My mother has suffered. Profoundly. I must remember this. She carries her sorrow around with her, in the silk scarf I sent her and in her crippled fingers, in her tacky clothing and bulky frame, and in the exhale of her eternal monologues. For her, there is no end in sight to her curse. Every night and day is torture. She knows she has children, but she knows she has no permission to love them. She gave up her mate. Instead of fixing the hole in the road, she built another road.

The father is nothing. It is only the mother who is important, Soares offers as he draws my attention to revolutionary monuments on the ride back. He likes my mother very much and wants me to stay longer, or else to come back very soon to visit her again. My mother translates all this to me. *You are very loved. Your mother wants the best for you.* I do not contradict him. My own Mouse, I smile at him and say *obrigada.* The man thinks I am a princess— don't princesses exist to be adored? Don't they exist for eternal love and happy endings?

Romantic gibberish, or is there some truth of love in my mother's heart? I haven't figured out how to talk with her yet. I am all ears, taking notes, jotting down observations, making judgments, but right now, I can't be sure I'm fully listening. I don't know what to focus on: pitch, tone, rhythm, notes, chords? My mother is a symphony without a score. And the soundtrack to this road movie, whether I press mute or not.

I love when you say my name, Soares coos as I thank him for the ride. *You say it with a perfect Brazilian accent, yet very soft, very soft.*

My mother writes the next day's pickup time on a free post-card—her purse stuffed with dozens from restaurants and cultural centres: advertisements for restaurants or perfumes, cellphone companies or swimsuit shops.

Soares hesitates before accepting the card. *Priscila is in command. I answer to her now.*

I would like to see the Treasures from Shanghai exhibit, 11 a.m.

It does not open until noon.

Noon then, Soares. Obrigada. Bon noite, Soares.

He closes his taxi door and we wave, laughing because it is impossible not to laugh when Soares is around. I suspect he is the one really in charge.

Museum of Precious Stones

5

god is brazilian

(dues é brasileiro)

*God: A human being is not a refrigerator which you can
return if it doesn't work properly.*

TODAY we are the only ones at breakfast, and over stacks
of pineapple, my mother tells me about some of the
rural areas she has visited in Brazil, partings in the green
where there are few people and no cars. Unlike São Paulo, where
it can take up to twelve hours to get to the airport and where the
government has been forced to implement a system whereby cars
with specific licence plate numbers drive on specific days and
some households circumvent this restriction by buying multiple
cars, my mother visited one town with only two registered auto-
mobiles: a jeep and a truck. One summer day, on the only road
in the town, they collided in a very serious accident, totalling
both vehicles. We laugh, but it doesn't surprise me. People are
born to crash into each other.

My mother also warns me not to talk about my religious beliefs,
or lack thereof, with the rest of the family. I was baptized, given

first Communion, and confirmed in the Catholic Church, as was my brother, and although my first novel is set in a nunnery, and I remember after my mother left that as an eight-year-old child I seriously considered becoming a nun—I was desperate to help children worse off than myself—I have since developed very little patience, even a repulsion, toward all religions, but, like any lapsed Catholic, especially Catholicism. (Although I confess—pun intended—that I possess a fetishistic fascination for a priest's long black cassock. Thank you, Alfred Hitchcock.) My mother and the rest of the family (except for her brother, who, my mother mutters, is also an atheist and refuses to go to church) are ardent Catholics, my mother and grandmother attending their respective churches daily, while the rest congregate at my grandmother's church on Sundays. Brasilia boasts some of the most beautiful churches in Brazil and I will experience church service there, she informs me. Ironically, I am not averse to the proposition—church architecture is fascinating (what people will build for gods or royalty has always amazed me)—but I am not given a choice in the matter. *I have a friend who has stopped believing in God since reading a book about how all living things were composed from a mass of jelly,* my mother offers, slathering the mango variety onto her toast, *but who created the jelly? I ask her. God, of course.*

Adamant in her beliefs, I'm sure my mother agrees with this line from *God Is Brazilian: God is like the wheel, the steamboat, and the airplane. He was invented by man, but that doesn't mean he doesn't exist.* She is convinced God knows the truth of everything and will reward her someday for her suffering. I don't ask her to define her suffering or why she thinks her suffering deserves reward, as I'm sure questioning her on this matter will only elicit bafflement at best, defensiveness at worst. Isn't it the reward system that draws people into religion in the first place? Do this, and you will get that. Maybe not now, maybe not in this life, but at some point, we promise, just believe . . .

As is mentioned in Carlos Diegues's brilliant film of a god desperate to take a vacation from the headaches of humankind, Brazilian miracles have been oddly overlooked by the Catholic Church, regardless of Brazilian religious fanaticism. Only very recently, in 2007, has Brazil succeeded in obtaining official recognition for a saint: Friar Galvão, who wrote Latin prayers on tiny balls of paper that, when swallowed, apparently cured a variety of ailments including infertility; he also healed a toddler considered incurable by doctors. I'm positive my mother would like to put her own name forward as a candidate.

In the movie, Taoca, a blundering but lovable young ne'er-do-well (played by the jubilant Wagner Moura) who owes money to loan sharks, accompanies God (played by the magnificent Antônio Fagundes) on his search for a saint to watch over the earth while he goes back to doing what he used to do before the earth and humankind were created: floating blissfully in the ether without a care. Taoca is skeptical, believing God created humans in the first place because he must have been desperately lonely. Although God insists, *I never needed company,* Taoca pities His fatherless, motherless, companion-less existence: *Poor fellow. Always so alone!*

Lonely or not, like God in the film my mother has become accustomed to living by herself, on her own terms, answerable to no one. She too is fed up with the stupidity and ignorance of humankind—her martyrdom, like that of most mothers, unappreciated by her ungrateful children—and while she might preach forgiveness, her real desire is for escape. Regardless of her relentless voice-over to our day-to-day activities, she is unpenetratingly alone. She speaks her version of the truth; however, perhaps like God, she doesn't really believe anyone is listening.

We're too busy being selfish and demanding and accusatory. I'm beginning to suspect she talks to keep herself company.

God Is Brazilian is one of her favourite films, and it's a masterpiece that touches even an atheist's heart like mine. There is a wonderful scene between God and his chosen saint, an honest and compassionate and hard-working man named Quinca with a severe stutter, which God cures for the duration of his attempt to convince him to step into God's shoes for an indefinite period of time and continue his good works. No matter what God does, including shortening day and night and inducing instantaneous seasons, then resorting to torturing the poor sop by dunking him repeatedly in the river and calling him a jerk, God's chosen one refuses to acknowledge his existence: *You're not going to convince me! . . . I'm an atheist!* By showing God in all his solitary vulnerability, along with brief moments where he displays the depth of his magic and mercy, Diegues does a masterful job of convincing his audience how much humans need and disappoint God with their actions, even if they must work against him or vehemently deny him in order to live more humanely. It is better to cease to believe in God than to cease to do God's work.

I am reminded of something very important: I didn't come here because I believe in my mother; I came here because I believe in myself.

Talking. Talking. The emptiness of words. I tell her Chris's sister died five years ago. She talks about the quality of Brazilian papaya. I tell her my brother was saved from drowning by a trucker. She talks about her favourite internet café. Talking. Talking. Her talking is a form of torture. If I endure, can I too claim martyrdom?

She continues insulting people by calling them "illiterate." I know I am lucky that both sides of my family have received post-secondary educations, but, as Quinca the unsanctioned saint points out, *No one needs a college diploma to care for others,* and it

sometimes seems like all my mother's education, instead of making her more humane, has enabled her to disassociate from real
people. Her millions of words joining other millions of words in
the sky like unreachable stars. The entity called my mother floating about alone in the ether.

Outside the window I see Hasidic Jewish couples and families, with their black suits and hats, headscarves and curly locks.
Does Brazil have a large Jewish population? I have no idea. In
my tourist brochure I added a question mark to the heading
"Museum of Japanese Immigration." I've already noted that at
least two or three of Brazil's major modernist abstract artists are
of Japanese origin, but I still know very little about why or how the
Japanese got here. (Since the trip, I've learned there are approxi-
mately one hundred thousand Jewish people living in Brazil, the
majority in São Paolo, where many Jewish families settled during
or after World War I. Jewish immigration was officially restricted
during the dictatorship of Getúlio Vargas under his Estado Novo,
or New State, in the 1930s, but individuals still managed to
immigrate through case-by-case negotiations. I've also learned
that there are more people of Japanese descent in Brazil than in
any other foreign country—around 1.5 million—starting with
165 families arriving by boat on June 18, 1908, to work in Brazil's
coffee plantations, thereby escaping poverty and unemployment
in Japan. Now there are so many Japanese-Brazilian citizens that
Liberdade, a district in São Paulo, looks more like Tokyo than a
South-American neighbourhood, and many claim that some 40
percent of Japanese-Brazilian descendants are now mixed race.)

The *Treasures from Shanghai: 5,000 Years of Chinese Art and
Culture* exhibit—on loan from the Shanghai Museum, and portraying the evolution of Chinese technology, art, and culture
through objects from the Neolithic period (circa 3000 BC) to the
Qing Dynasty (AD 1644–1911)—is jam-packed and we are not
permitted to carry anything inside with us, not a purse, not a

pen. My mother complains that she is a journalist and an exception for a pen should be made for her but the security guards shake their heads in the negative. Before we store our purses, she insists on applying her red lipstick one last time, forcing the coat-check girl to wait for her to complete the ritual, regardless of the hundreds of visitors in line behind us. Considering how anti-intellectual most of the world has become, how blissfully ignorant of world history, it's incredible to see the insatiable appetite we still possess for old objects. It's as if people no longer wish to understand the past, but still ache to touch it or own it. I suspect I'm the opposite. I'd rather understand the past than touch it, if this trip is any indication.

My mother translates the placards for me but I let her know that it's fine if she wants to look at other display cases; she needn't follow me about like a personal guide. *I only want to see what you want to see*, she replies. *I don't care for myself. Unless, of course, I am bothering you?* Not at all, I say. I feel guilty because I'm here to get to know her, not to see Chinese cultural artifacts, no matter how rare and valuable. I should be grateful, thankful, and I am. Sort of. But I am also resentful, suffocated, overloaded. Mistrusting. As if my mother has rewritten all the placards of the past to suit her version of her history—doctored photographs, fraudulent documents, reassigned dates—and placed them safely behind glass. As an archive, my mother is unreliable, compromised, her methods of selection and preservation seriously suspect.

Today she activates her "angel" reel: *I have never had a date since leaving your father* (neither has he—surprised?). *I am nice to everyone and I go to church regularly* (I'm not even sure you're nice to me). *I educate through journalism* (you give good reviews to bad art). *I live an angel life that everyone says is superior to others* (who is everyone?). I want to scream: How could such an angel leave her children and admit to being too fragile to contact them? But I know these stories aren't meant to counter this sentiment exactly; deep down she is terribly guilty and repentant. It's all so fucking Catholic, I just want to cry. And I can hear God chastising me, as Antônio Fagundes does his human companions in the film, lamenting human nature: *Why do you people only see the value of something after losing it?*

We will have lunch "where the rich people go," my mother tells me, at the MAM restaurant. It's not the first time that I wonder where my mother's money comes from: how much she earns from writing (I'm sure the pay in Brazil for freelance journalism is modest, as it is in Canada); translating (a job at the Senate might have been lucrative, but not general translating work, and she's retired from the Senate); teaching (she might have made a decent salary through university and college courses at one point, but she no longer teaches); inheritance (from her deceased father and through her mother's living allowances—her mother bought each of the children condominiums in the same building); and where her total income would slot her into the nation's economic class divisions (lower, mid, or upper-middle class). I wonder how much savings she has accumulated, if she's had to delve into those funds to pay for her cancer surgeries or her prescriptions.

Even with a generously funded medical system, my father's accident and subsequent illnesses (it's difficult to ward off infections when you can't feel them entering your system) were a constant financial drain. And as conservative governments in Canada and Ontario in the 80s and 90s slashed social and medical services budgets, my father's financial burdens increased (items such as the metal hoist for lowering him into a weekly bath were, under the new system, non-essential, and so we had to rent them at prohibitively high prices). Furthermore, my father didn't qualify for single-parent benefits because, at the time, the restrictive terminology indicated "single mother" benefits exclusively. Meaning that my father, paralyzed from the chest down, qualified for absolutely no parenting assistance, regardless of his condition.

Did my mother ever consider my father's financial burdens? Did she ever wonder if her theatre tickets and buffet breakfasts and hotel rooms were at the expense of school clothes or goalie pads or computers? Did she realize how much of our daily existence depended on social services and local charity? And how ridiculous it seems to me that while she was buying a hundred separate tickets to see this or that "marvellous" film, my father was making phone call after phone call and writing letter upon letter begging for fee waivers, free sports equipment, and discounts on medical supplies? But since I can't ask my mother about her financial situation or tell her about ours at the risk of it being misconstrued as emotional blackmail, I scan the menu for new Brazilian delicacies.

Cashew juice. I learn that cashews come from the end of a fruit—I honestly had no idea. I taste it sparingly, as it is not uncommon for people to discover they are allergic—American poet Elizabeth Bishop became so ill from it she missed her boat and remained in Brazil where she ended up meeting the love of her life, Lota de Macedo Soares, and settling down in the town of Samambaia for fifteen years.

Then, out of the blue, my mother asks me if Chris is religious.
I think we mean the word religious in different ways.
Oh yes, and when I—
I'm not finished, I say.
You see, you told me it was okay to ask questions, something I don't like to do and know you are—
If you ask a question, you should let that person answer it.
Oh. Her lips are trembling. I'm shocked as I realize she is going to cry, here, once again in a fancy art restaurant, because I need more than a few words and two seconds to answer her complicated question. *This is why I do not like to ask questions.*

There is no need to ask questions. Her shoulders are shaking now.
*I live a happy life inside my head and in my heart. There is no need
to ask questions and upset people.*

God hates questions. Questions imply doubt. Questions
imply freedom. God is the ultimate dictator. No wonder my
mother identifies with God and treats me like a misguided sinner. But I want to push the matter because it's becoming more and
more important to me that she's forced to acknowledge who I am,
whether or not she wants to, and whether or not she likes me. (I
realize that I don't care if she likes me or not. Or if I like her. Maybe
this is where I diverge from children of happy families. I don't care
about like or love any longer. I didn't have it when I desperately
needed it, so why would I seek it now from such a contaminated
source? I just want us to see each other once for who we are. Even
if it makes us unhappy.) *That's another obsession with you people,
being happy all the time,* God cries with exasperation in *God Is
Brazilian.* I know she's "happy" inside her head, acting the lead
role in a formulaic romance film where the martyr mother will be
showered with rewards and love in the end. I can sense that she's
frustrated that I have yet to drop to my knees and shower her feet
with tears and kisses. That I have yet to ask *her* for forgiveness.
Not the other way around, as I'd first thought. I'm not an innocent
bystander of a senseless accident. I'm to blame. I'm to blame for
some massive injury my mother has incurred. While I don't yet
understand this train of thinking, I must follow the tracks. I don't
want to crush her happiness, per se, but I do desire to shatter a
few of her illusions. The ones to do with me. I can't stand the person she has constructed inside her mind: a figment of her movie
imagination, a stock character actress right out of central casting.
I may also have a version of my mother living out her day-to-day
tragedy in the film set of my own mind, but at least I'm making
an effort to alter my projections along with her production notes.
She is making no like concessions with me. I am an audience.

And she only wants me around if I'm a doting audience. Like at a movie premier.

I will be quiet then, and let you answer the question. But when I'm about to, she stares longingly out the window.

I have upset you, I offer.

Your perception and experience are important, Priscila, she replies, without meeting my gaze. *I guess I need to learn how to communicate with you. I can still learn.*

This small admittance gives me hope. Communication is a skill; it requires updating and upgrading, focus and commitment.

You know, in Brazil, people all talk at the same time . . .

I too need to learn how to communicate with her. Learning has been my lifelong occupation. My mother's too. If we can't make an effort to adjust our methods, what kind of students are we? We both might be hyper-literate, but words are never uncomplicated. We are like warring countries that through colonization mixed long ago and no matter how separate our identity claims we are linked by history, blood, shame. And here is a confession I am loath to admit: I am ashamed she is my mother. She is ashamed I am her daughter. It's understandable to want to play along in an idealistic fantasy of pretend, at least to break the ice. At least not to take up more weapons between us.

As we re-emerge outside, I skip, perhaps like the little girl I once was, over to an amusing swing set sculpture, the seats upside-down busts of men's heads. *I love my name,* she coos as I plop myself onto the middle bust, kicking out my legs. *Theresa Catharina de Góes Campos. My name has benefited my life, my career. That's the truth.* She presents me her business card, the way children share a loved toy. Once again I note the startling title—Head of Ethics, Union of Journalists. But now a profounder irony intrudes: my mother's academic title—Professor of Comunicação. Communications is her field of specialty.

Like a disappointed child at the end of recess, I slump off the swing set and wander aimlessly about the grounds until I find a more suitable sculpture for our predicament. An austere minimalist geometric sculpture in white marble, two identical rectangular shapes each with one rounded side, one upright the other upside down (upside-down things speak to me here), like two figures, touching but essentially opposite. I locate the title: *Encontro e Desencontro*. Meeting and Unmeeting. By Arcângelo Ianelli, 2002. A recent acquisition. Potentially constructed on the day I discovered my mother by accident on the internet. Perhaps the day I left my first phone message or the day she responded by email to tell me how happy she was to know I like swimming. Meeting and Unmeeting. *Encontro e Desencontro*. A curse or a simple reality of mothers and daughters the world over? I can't *unmeet* her now.

In the "Making Of" segment on the *God Is Brazilian* DVD, writer and director Carlos Diegues discusses his love of road movies and how he utilizes the journey structure as the foundation of all of his films, even if specific characters are not literally rumbling down a road. When we choose a genre or a format, he argues, we're sectioning life, remodelling it into a structure we can follow and understand. I don't know what genre my mother and I are participating in. We too are definitely on the road, but whether this is comedy or tragedy, farce or satire, inspirational vehicle or warning exposé, I'm not yet sure. (This might be related to whether we are meeting or unmeeting.) I don't even know who's the good guy and who's the villain. I could easily be cast as my mother's worst nightmare. Could I also be her salvation? While I know it would please her to no end if I just wrapped my arms around her and begged, *Mommy, let's start over, let's cry until everything is healed between us and Jit and my father, and then let's hold hands and go shopping and to church*, I just … can't. Such a gesture would negate who I am. In life, unlike in art, I am a realist. My mother, an escapist. Can these two visions of life

ever meet (does meeting equal escapism, unmeeting realism)?
Even on the road in a once-in-a-lifetime miracle reunion? It's
cost us both enough to live through tragedy. What would it cost
us to pull together for a happy ending?

*I don't sleep for long, but I sleep without interruption when I
do. And I can fall asleep anywhere if I will it. At the doctor's office,
or on a bus, waiting for my mother to dress, anywhere. For this,
God has made me tireless.*

People think I am tireless too. This is an illusion. I need a great
deal of sleep: eight to nine hours per night. I don't sleep soundly
though. I suffer from vivid nightmares (violent chase scenes with
guns and knives, rapes, animal attacks, natural disasters) and I
wake dozens of times per night. Nonetheless, I'm blessed with
intense focus when I'm awake. And I love to work, love the chro-
nology of work, and having a lot to show at the end of the day, like
a pile of presents. If I don't have much to show, that's when frustration and depression descends in the form of self-doubt and
self-chastisement; but if I'm working well, just humming along
(Chris tells me when I'm typing without self-consciousness I
am literally smiling and usually humming a tune), I'm giddy as
I count pages (reading or writing), count miles I've run, count
items I can check off my to-do list.

Reunion with Mother: checkmark.

Ten Things I Can
Check Off My Trip to Brazil List So Far

1. Meet Runaway Mother for the first time in twenty years.
2. Buy Brazilian poetry books and attempt crude translations.
3. Go to a movie with Mother.
4. See a Brazilian musical.
5. Swim on a São Paulo rooftop.

6. Spark first fight with Mother.
7. Visit Brazilian art museums and exhibitions.
8. Encounter an elaborate display of giant rabbits in human costumes amid a field of chocolate eggs.
9. Discuss divergent religious views with Mother.
10. Try cashew juice.

Not bad for just a handful of days. I squeeze my mother's arm. *I am having a wonderful time,* I tell her, in part to convince myself and in part to thank her for all the bustling about she's been doing on my behalf. It's my version of an apology and she seems placated.

To Paulista shopping centre, she announces like a black-and-white film diva to Soares, who is reliably waiting for us, contentedly eating hot dogs grilled at the back of an old woman's car trunk. Soares explains she has served her famous hot dogs to presidents and movie stars.

But that is second-class shopping, Soares argues.

Maybe we can afford it then, I banter back.

Mr. Soares no understand why you no live here, the hot-dog lady admonishes, waving a bony finger at my nose. *If you like country, you stay. He try make you like country.*

That's sweet, I reply, and smile at Soares as he caresses his full stomach.

My mother tilts her face toward me and whispers: *Don't eat the hot dogs.*

As we drive along Paulista Avenue, a street Soares states is "paved with money," he points out that all the intersecting streets are named after countries, including a rue Canada. *Brazil is the second biggest country in the world, not Canada. Your mother has a big heart, bigger than Brazil,* he says.

My mother explains it is very common for Brazilians to claim
Brazil is the second biggest country because in Canada we have
too much land that people don't actually live on but in Brazil
people live everywhere.

It's not that we can't live there, we don't want to, I counter, and
Soares finds this incredibly amusing, chuckling to himself about
it for the rest of the ride.

*In Brazil, if you find a hole in the road, and throw a seed in it,
by morning you'll have glorious fruit. That is Brazil.*

I look at my mother, who beams from Soares's declaration. I
thought if there was a hole in the road, Brazilians built another
road. I suppose this is another option. Good. I sincerely hope he
is right.

At the shopping centre (another plaza where she's already seen
every movie currently playing) my mother buys me several items
of clothing: a playful leopard-print sheer blouse, a sci-fi-inspired
turquoise off-the-shoulder evening dress, and elegant black dress
pants with a sheer black sash. (I will end up wearing all three for
years to come.) My mother likes colourful, artistic prints, designs
of flowers or circles or wavy lines. She does not wear black and
does not like to see anyone in black, in honour of her father who
hated the colour. But she buys me the black pants nonetheless,
because, she concedes, I am Canadian and Canadians mistak-
enly think black is a colour. I am constantly offering to pay, but
she won't hear of it. *This is all I get to do for you,* she sighs, and
since she is somewhat right about this, I accept the gifts. I cannot
hide the fact that I do love clothes and Brazil is one of the centres
of world fashion. Here clothes are central to the personality of
the country. It's one of my only complaints about Canada; with
the exception of the French in Montreal, Canadians dress without imagination, thinking only of shelter from the elements and
comfort, like postal workers.

I also tell her how I will miss Soares once we are in Brasilia. I have grown so fond of him, I would like him to come with us. One of the other themes consistent in Diegues's road movies is the exploration of how strangers become attached to each other through the act of travel. Soares is part of our search for understanding, even if our lives are irrefutably distant in enumerable ways.

He is a good family man, she agrees. *You cannot pay for what Soares is. His kindness. And he is very fond of you too. He thinks you are beautiful.*

As we shop, I admit I am nervous about committing all the family names to memory, and ask my mother if she would mind creating a list for me of everyone I will meet in Brasilia. All the family members have been christened with Catholic names and names from the royal family, exclusively. My mother's name, Theresa, is typically Catholic, a saint name, but derives from the Greek and means "harvester." My own name also derives from Biblical origin: Priscila, or Prisca, was one of the founding members of the Christian Church. I have also been led to believe that the Samaritan woman who gives Jesus water at the well is sometimes referred to as Priscila. The name means "ancient, venerable." My brother's name, Amerjit, is Sikh meaning "forever victorious," and my father's, Avtar, "holy incarnation." Uppal means "stone." I am an ancient stone—difficult to move. Difficult, I imagine, to harvest.

You do not need to know anyone's name. Everyone is there to see you. But I will write you a list, like you've asked. Do you think I could buy a gift for Amerjit too? The most common question people ask me is if your father knows you are here. I say no, I don't think so.

Yes, he knows, I tell her. *And he's been good about it.* Which is true, although I could hear the disappointment and fear in his voice when I told him I'd found her and wanted to visit her, in

Brazil no less. To my father this reconnection is an indictment
of his parenting. I can't pretend to have no complaints on that
score, or I should say I can't pretend that I didn't used to have
complaints on that score—there are good reasons I left home at
fifteen—but I find it embarrassing when grown adults complain
about how their parents raised them, unless they were seriously
abused. In fact, I gave a talk recently where, to encourage the
English-as-a-second-language students to participate, they were
instructed to write their questions anonymously on pieces of
paper that would be drawn out of a box by the host. One audience
member asked: *How do you know when you've become an adult?*
Without batting an eye, I responded: *When you stop blaming
your parents.* I didn't prepare my answer—it was the first thing
that came to mind. Of course, this event took place several years
after my trip to Brazil, and perhaps in 2003 I was still blaming my
mother for some things, even if I didn't want to. I might still have
been blaming my father for some things too, but I didn't come
to Brazil to hurt my father. I thought about keeping the trip
a secret from him, but eventually decided dishonesty would be
even more cruel. My father raised me to be truthful, to confront
hard facts and ugly conditions. He didn't ask me why I wanted to
go, he just nodded the way he does when he receives bad medical
reports—disappointing, but expected.

*I wouldn't send the gift to the house—he still lives with our
father. But I can give it to him directly next time he visits me in
Toronto.*

My mother's eyes widen with hope. *Do you really think he'd
accept a gift from me?*

I hear God again—as an atheist it's contradictory how much I
enjoy representations of God in film (as well as priests and nuns
and monks)—telling the young orphan girl, Madá: *Everything a
human can imagine can exist, Madá. It's only a matter of training.*

I think he will, I offer, which obviously comforts her as she nods her head in agreement, a woman who can't fathom calling her son anything but Amerjit, even though I've told her several times that he legally changed his name to Jit. And I believe this to be true, even though when I took my brother out to inform him I was going on this trip he wished me luck but expressed no interest in hearing about the outcome and much more interest in whether or not the sausage on his pizza would be mild or hot and spicy. My brother has never refused a gift in his life—"free sample" is one of his favourite phrases, and we've both learned to accept kindnesses and aid from the strangest of places. Besides, it's hard for children to refuse gifts from their parents. A matter of training.

He likes sports, I tell her. The entire Erinbrook Crescent bungalow décor is an odd mix of deteriorated 1960s furniture, medical equipment, piles of files, and hockey and baseball trophies and posters; a testament to the twining of my father's and brother's lives. It is a combination that has scared off many a potential serious girlfriend for my brother, as within seconds of entering the premises and shaking my father's trembling hand these naive ladies soon realize that my brother's love comes with an extra-heavy burden.

Soccer! In Brazil we are the very best at soccer! We have soccer shirts, soccer hats, soccer shoes, soccer flags, soccer towels, soccer telephones, soccer placemats, soccer chairs. . . . Does he like soccer?

I'm not sure, I say with reservation, hoping I can guide her to the right gift, one that doesn't forcefully announce my brother is related to her or to Brazil. Her face drops for a moment, so I quickly add, *I'm not sure he has a favourite soccer team, but something soccer-related would be great.*

We settle on a silver desk clock in the shape of a soccer ball. (Innocuous enough to my mind that he need never think of

my mother if he decides to keep it.) As Soares drives us and our
many other packages tucked in the trunk back to the hotel, my
mother clutches the tiny ticking box to her heart.

Soares

6

stella dallas

Helen Morrison: I didn't know anyone could be so unself-ish.

AFTER only a few hours of stomach-cramping sleep, I wake to this mantra: *Everything must go well for the next few days. We cannot get into an argument. Everything must go well for the next few days. We cannot get into an argument.* I am so distraught by how little progress we seem to be making, I put my disposable contacts in twice. The bathroom mirror and sink go blurry—pricks of pain sewing flesh around my head, eyes gushing tears until I manage to flush them out.

Although there is nothing I like to do less when I am travelling than park in front of a television, I ask if we can watch a few minutes of CNN to keep up with some world news. My mother tells me she has three televisions in her apartment that are on all day long. She likes to watch several shows at the same time, especially soccer matches, whereas I don't even have basic cable. Top headlines: the Union of European Nations is becoming an even stronger economic force, and the escalating casualties in the war in Iraq. Brazilians are very critical of the Iraqi situation. Ads for

the Communist Party in Brazil feature posters of President Bush
sporting a Hitler mustache.

Today, as Soares escorts us about, my mother instructs me
never to engage in any sort of conversation with people on the
street. Men and women of all ages, children too, sell random
goods at traffic lights: candy, cellphone chargers, plastic blow-up
toys of Scooby-Doo and bunny rabbits, lottery tickets, bottled
water. Hands thrust bills and coins out car windows. My mother
never buys anything off the street. She keeps her hands and body
in the safety of the car. Me, I wish we could buy some of the fresh
fruit, but know better than to ask. Unless we are in a museum or
shopping mall, or people are wearing official badges and name
tags, my mother fears strangers. Soares's car is her protection
from the brutal urban reality of the hunger, poverty, and violence
of São Paulo. It is mine too.

The Museu de Arte de São Paulo is celebrating fifty years of
art donors by mounting an exhibition to highlight key philan-
thropists in the gallery's history. As I daydream about having
millions of dollars to spend on contemporary art, my mother
lists her accomplishments as a journalist (she is a "very famous
journalist," an educator "of the highest order," with "well-
respected friends"). I keep advising myself to just nod and say,
oh yes, that's great, and keep walking, but I'm horrified by the
tirade of conceit, and I can't help skepticism from creeping into
my daydream, wondering how much of what she says is true.
I searched the internet for information about her professional
activities before I arrived, and it is evident she is a publishing
journalist, has penned numerous articles, and contributed to
books; however, without knowledge of the Brazilian publishing
and academic scene, it's difficult to gauge her status in her field.
Does she think I am just as successful, completing a PhD in literature, having already landed a tenure-stream professorship at
the third-largest Canadian university, two published books of

poetry plus a novel that was even written up in a São Paulo news-paper before my arrival (my mother upset that the brief men-tion of her included in the article without consulting with me was inaccurate)? How is she to gauge my own accomplishments without proper context, without knowledge of the Canadian publishing scene and North American academic standards, and without having watched any of them unfold?

My mother's soliloquies reek of so much hyperbole that it would be naive of me to take her word for truth. I need to consider that my mother might be a compulsive liar. Delusional people fre-quently are. Deep down, I'm torn: I'm selfishly attracted to the idea of my mother as a top-tier journalist (for its implications of artistic heredity), yet I'd also welcome the karmic suitability of stripping her down to the realm of charlatan. Something I never would have predicted at the outset of this trip, it's become incredibly important to me to understand the scope of my mother's delu-sions and the uses of them in her life. Which means I'm trapped by her mouth: I need her to keep talking to reveal her uttermost dimensions even while it takes Herculean strength to keep my fingers out of my ears.

Then it occurs to me: maybe she knows I'm writing about her. Why didn't I think of this before? My notebook is as ubiquitous as my little black purse (I've even started to take notes while she is talking because she doesn't register my actions, and it's per-fectly acceptable for reviewers to be fiddling with pen and paper at exhibitions). Back in the safety of the São Paolo suite, bed-room door closed, I transfer the notes as quickly as possible to my laptop before falling asleep. But maybe she knows it's not all journal writing and lists of Brazilian artists, but a full char-acter sketch and psychological case study, detailed scenes and dialogue for an inevitable memoir, and she wants to ensure she is represented as an extraordinary woman who was victimized and is now victorious. The Wrongly Accused.

But I see her more as a Stella Dallas—a complicated figure, both tragic and despicable, a woman worthy of sympathy and contempt. If you've never seen the film, rent it. You won't be disappointed. You won't believe when the movie was made. At the time of the film's release in 1937, the role of Stella Dallas was certainly one of the most ambiguous female roles available for an actress at the time, and Barbara Stanwyck plays her with flair and unapologetic determination and desire. The young Stella Martin, born into a family of mill hands, fills her romantic head with love lyrics from India and high-society newspaper articles. The result is an infatuation with a rich man whose father killed himself, Stephen Dallas. One day they meet and he takes her to the movies, where Stella longingly admits she wants to be *like the people in the movies. You know, doing everything well-bred and refined.* When Stephen marries her, Stella thinks she's been granted her grandest wish, but all is accoutrement—unfortunately, Stella's still a lower-class mill hand's daughter with garish tastes and little elegance, a woman more interested in fancy parties and endless martinis and fur coats than in her newborn daughter. Eventually, Stephen gives up on changing her shallow ways and moves out of the house and to another city, renewing a love affair with an old childhood sweetheart who is now a widow. The two want to adopt Stephen and Stella's daughter, Laurel, but Stella vehemently refuses. By today's North American standards of motherhood, and our inherent distaste for anything that reeks of class-consciousness, perhaps someone like my mother would side with Stella and claim Stella was a feminist, a woman refusing to accept the standard female roles offered to her. However, I think that Stella's tragedy is related to an inability to love unselfishly. It's only when she realizes that her daughter's future might be seriously hampered and even harmed by her infamous reputation and foolish behaviour that she's spurred to take painful action. Stella disowns Laurel for her own good. Stella's ultimate triumph occurs at the end of the movie as she stands defiantly behind a gate in the rain, accosted by a police officer, watching her daughter marry her own rich prince, Richard Grosvenor III, in the living room of her ex-husband's home. Stella walks away from the festive scene, fierce satisfaction visible in her eyes; her mission complete, all her previous mistakes as a mother erased by one unselfish decision.

Over the years, there have been many people, especially women with children of their own, who have intermittently accepted me into their lives as a surrogate daughter, who have said of my mother what two women on the train say about Stella Dallas: *Some women don't deserve to have children.* And it would be easy, as my mother hurries about the gallery waving her arms in the air, smiling desperately, announcing, *I want to be doing marvellous things all the time. Marvellous things like movies, plays, exhibitions, and when they take my journalist card I feel marvellous,* to chastise and ridicule her (or write her off as mentally ill) as women chastised and ridiculed Stella Dallas for wanting so much for herself at the expense of her child. But who doesn't want to feel marvellous? I do. Stella does. Some people are just not capable of seeing how their desires affect those around them.

And although some women have welcomed me into their lives—as a teenager, usually because one of their sons or daughters was a close friend, then later on as a responsible and promising young artist and academic—offering "motherly" advice and affection, meals and sometimes even board, I have always known, deep down, the designation of "honorary" daughter was a deliberate, albeit well-meaning, illusion. Most of these women were happy to include me in their roster of dinners and Sunday afternoons and family movie nights because I was grateful and rarely any trouble whatsoever, and because it also made them feel good about themselves, like charity work, to create some sense of familial comfort for my tumultuous life. But if push came to shove, if my grades dropped and I became a drug addict, or if I hooked up with some meathead boyfriend, or if I got sick and needed help paying my bills, I knew without a doubt that the telephone would stop ringing, the invitations to dinner would stop arriving, not to mention that no matter how much free work I performed for some of these surrogate parents I would never receive an allowance or inheritance.

There was one woman whose name is so painful to my lips that I cannot utter it, even here. After moving out of my father's home at fifteen, I rented a room from her and so lived with her and her ten-year-old daughter, a child with tons of affection and energy who leapt into my arms whenever I walked through the door. "We've fallen in love with you," this woman declared, and then one day she and her fiancé, a reserved well-to-do medical doctor with a passion for jazz, took me out for brunch and proposed that when I went off to university I could return for vacations and visits like other students back home to their families. It was strange that while I was contemplating the ramifications of this arrangement—how much hurt this would cause my father, how wonderful to gain a spritely little sister—I was still paying rent, but a lease is a lease, right? And then everything changed. First, a friend of her fiancé's—a twenty-something musician— asked me out. A week later, I arrived home smelling of beer after a long-weekend camping trip with friends. All at once, she claimed I was a bad influence on her daughter, she was worried I'd come home one day and tell her I was pregnant, and so she thought it best if I found somewhere else to live. Adopted child to abandoned child. Just like that. I loved her more than I could remember ever loving my own mother. I never heard from her again. And only once did her daughter seek me out—without her mother's knowledge, I'm sure—when I was working the counter at the drugstore; she literally ran into my arms and wrapped her legs about my waist as she used to do, planting kisses all over my cheeks. When she bolted out the exit—perhaps her mother was shopping in the mall or waiting in the car—her brown wavy hair bouncing through the air, I felt a longing so painful I thought I had been shot in the chest.

There is a big difference between a real child and a pretend child. A pretend child can never be a burden. Never be complicated. Never disappoint. I've learned to accept each and every gift from a surrogate mother as just that, a gift, a kindness you can never count on again. And I have valued every delicious meal and night out, every expression of interest in my schooling or my books, every birthday gift, every warm hug I have ever received. Eventually, of course, all these women become consumed with the lives of their real sons and daughters. But I do wonder if some ever think about me, if at Christmas Eve or Easter dinner while passing the mashed potatoes or cranberry sauce they ever ask, *Do you remember Priscila? When Priscila used to join us? What a story! She didn't have anywhere else to go. She became an author, you know. We always knew she would land on her feet.* Now when anyone says "You are like a daughter to me," I can't help but die a little inside.

I lived with my biological mother until the age of eight. Since that time, I have now lived with her a grand total of five days. Five days! One hundred and twenty hours! Maybe seventy awake. Do I have a right to judge her after only this? Consider her guilty or wrongly accused—and of what charge exactly? Does anyone "deserve" to have children? I have known women who are natural caregivers and nurturers born to raise children, and those who have not a single affectionate bone in their bodies—biology gave each equal opportunity. What did this woman think motherhood would entail? I have no idea. Except that she must have hoped it would be "marvellous." For some lucky mothers, I'm sure it is. Did her children disappoint her? Does she think she disappointed them? Or does she put the onus for everything on a freak accident that ruptured her perfect marriage to the man of her dreams who once read her Indian love lyrics?

If it were up to me, I'd write nothing, she tells me. *I'd just be going out and enjoying what other people create. I go to these places early so I can talk to people. It's the people I am most interested in.*

While I know this statement from a woman who has not asked her estranged daughter more than two or three questions about her own life in five days of conversations seems baffling, disingenuous, even irritating, I am acutely aware that she adamantly believes what she says. And the truth is, I've met this type of person before—one who claims to care deeply about the underprivileged, the oppressed, but who shows little genuine interest in anyone but themselves and never goes out of the way to help a suffering human being. My mother cares more passionately about the landscape painting in front of us than she does about me. Or about the landscape. And she thinks that means she cares about people. That's the truth. Plain and simple. I just want to find out why.

I love myself. I really love myself. I do only what I want, she announces as we cross into another room. *When I came from Canada things were very difficult for me. I had to start over professionally.*

And we had to start over emotionally, I want to say. *We are now a family defined by so many pains we don't know which to choose for our coat of arms.*

I had an amazing childhood, she gushes, stretching her arms as wide as the room. *I was happy all the time.*

I add my own voice-over: *We were sad all the time. Angry all the time. Happy only when we could forget. When we were reading books, or playing sports, or watching movies . . .*

My father only allowed me to read the New Testament until I was an adult, she continues. *I was his favourite. My father begged my mother to visit me in Canada. I did not want her to see how I was living. It was embarrassing.*

Maybe strike up some music here: *But you didn't care how your children were living.*

I live, I die, makes no difference to me. But I do not want to be in the hospital or in a wheelchair. This I could not stand at all.

Because you've seen it. And yet, where is your empathy for those of us who have lived with it longer than you and for the man who has had to endure his wheelchair for the sake of his children for this long and more . . .

Your father hates Jesus on the cross, likes Jesus resurrected much better. Victorious, not a victim.

Zoom in above my father's mechanical bed. *My father has only crosses in the house. . . .*

Voice-over rebuttals kept to myself, my stomach cramps again, this form of silence toxic, corroding from the inside. I'm starting to panic and I think it has less to do with meeting my mother, as maddening as she is, than with the fact that I've put far too many important things into the hands of someone I do not trust. It is hard to live with someone twenty-four hours a day you do not trust, especially someone you are dependent on to negotiate a foreign country for you. And yet, my mother believes she is being generous with her time, her emotions, her monologues, and her overbearing love: a philanthropist of the heart. The problem is I'm not a charity. I wish women who speak of love would understand that.

I would like to rest a bit at the hotel. This pleases her. Because my stomach is still bothering me, she informs me she will leave me there tonight while she works on her articles at the internet café in the shopping mall. I can sleep.

Annoyingly, I am hurt. A break from the relentlessness of my mother's orbit would be nice, but I don't want to be stuck in the

hotel from afternoon until morning. Besides, she has proudly
proclaimed several times that she has taken a hiatus from working during my visit because she wants us to spend as much time
together and see as much of Brazil as possible. Has she grown
bored? I'm offended—I thought I was good company, desirable
company; most people think so, why not my mother?—then dis-
card this train of thought as it matches too closely my mother's
own. And if she's really so worried about my stomach, wouldn't
she want to watch over me, offer me hot compresses and ginger
ale? I know she hasn't acted like a mother for some time, but this
would be more in line with what real mothers and daughters do.
Wouldn't she want the opportunity for such a screen test?

I offer to accompany her later to the shopping mall, after a
short nap. She can work and I can buy some souvenirs. *Oh no*,
she replies, tapping the car seat definitively. *You will stay at the
hotel. I will go out and work. You will stay in bed.*

Once back at the hotel, the fight begins.

My mother paces the small living room like a caged animal.
*You are never happy. You are always upset. I do not understand
why you are acting like this all the time when I have done nothing
but please you and be wonderful to you.*

Excuse me? My forehead is moist with anger. I'm trying not to
lose it now.

*I have done everything for you and you are not happy. This is
very hurtful. Very hurtful.*

I'm hurting you? How?

*Your stomach is bothering you. You want to come back to the
hotel. You have something every day that bothers you. You are far
too sensitive.*

I can't believe my ears. I look about the living room, with its
orange-brown décor, fold-out couch, my underwear drying on
the backs of two chairs, then back to my mother's face, her eyes

electric and whirling like projector reels, and I can't stand it any longer. If she's going to accuse me, I'm going to countersue. *I'm far too sensitive?*

Yes.

I'm far too sensitive?

Yes.

YOU are so full of yourself, I spit, advancing toward her. *You spend the whole day talking about yourself, never once stopping to ask me anything or to let me speak. You talk, talk, talk, all day, and you never listen.*

I ask you all kinds of things today and you are still in a bad mood.

You don't ask all kinds of things, and when you do you give me no time to answer, you ignore my answer, or you talk over it. And to say I am always in a bad mood—I have told you often how grateful I've been to you on this trip, how wonderful the museums and exhibits are. But if you expect me to just listen to you all day long about yourself and act like everything on this trip is a marvellous dream, mother and daughter side by side as if we've never been separated in our lives, you are completely unrealistic.

Frizzy hair wild, my mother stops her pacing and juts out her chest as if she's conscious of taking up as much space as possible. *Then, Priscila,* she says, smiling condescendingly, *if I felt this way about someone, I would leave.*

Like a tranquilizer dart, the thought takes hold with a vengeance. The room starts spinning, my mother's smile widening in slow motion, my legs buckling underneath me. I lean against the couch. I can't believe that I have been so trusting that I have not printed out a schedule of return flights to Toronto in case something like this happened. My thoughts are muddy but logical: I will phone Chris, order a cab to a Holiday Inn, get the hell out of here on the first available flight, rescheduling fees be damned. But, as with any breakup, I want to be clear on who is leaving

whom. *I come here after twenty years to see my mother who abandoned us and you are telling me to leave?*

My mother's smile does not waver—when did she learn to
use smiles as weapons? *If your purpose here is to be mean to me,
then yes. I did not abandon you. I left your father. There is no need
to bring up the past. It does nothing. I live only in the present, Priscila. I do not care for the past.* My mother, utterly calm as she
says this, slaps her hands dismissively. There is no ambiguity in
her decisions, in her philosophies, or in her ways of handling
unpleasant situations. If I am not prepared to submit to her reality, I am not welcome. She won't even accord me the leap of faith
or poetic licence she grants without a second thought to a filmmaker's universe, or a poet's lines, or splotches of paint thrown
upon a canvas.

I grip the arm of the couch, force my words forward: *I believe
in the present, but also in the past and the future. You can't control
time.*

And in a moment the slow motion ceases, her calm speeds
into anger like a thunderclap, her hands waving about manically.
Her face is white. She powders it, but it is whiter than it should
be for someone of her natural complexion. It looks like it's cracking, like bad cement. *You have no right to judge me. You will not
believe me no matter what I say, so what's the point? You want to
throw garbage at me. I live a fine life. Mother and father do not
live for the child. Mother and father do not exist. I live for myself.
I have my freedom. People like me. If you don't, that's fine. You
don't have to come here and spend any time with me at all. I will
not let you be mean to me.*

I am being mean to you because I have a stomach problem?

Instead of answering, she shrugs. I don't have to understand
her logic, I just have to accept it.

*I am being mean because I sometimes don't agree with all of
your many, many opinions, or think that everything unpleasant*

in life is worth escaping from? Why do you think I came here?

She scurries into the adjoining kitchen and from behind the protection of the counter stares back at me as if she is pondering a new appliance. *I don't know. I have a fine life here. I escape to the movies, I enjoy myself.*

I really can't stand it. *You think you live a better life than my father?*

Vigorous nods. *I know I do. I know I do.*

I don't think so. He knows his son and his daughter. You don't.

My mother is her own storm cloud. She looms, energy bubbling. Nothing can contain what is about to explode. I know this. Now she knows too. The room cringes, awaiting the blow. *Don't you threaten me. You have come here to accuse me.*

This is ridiculous. I am the one who found you and approached you and made the trip to a foreign country, a foreign city. I don't know the language, and I don't know you at all. You're a perfect stranger to me.

My mother steps back. This last statement surprises her. And hurts her. And silences her.

I don't know you. You can't expect me to pretend twenty-four hours a day that I do. I'm sorry if I can get overwhelmed or frustrated or upset in small doses. If you weren't prepared for that then you are completely unrealistic. Do you have any idea how difficult a decision this trip was for me?

My mother tosses up her hands—I am not playing by her rules. *I do not want people who do not like me around. You are going to educate me? I don't have to ask you anything. This is a democratic country and no one can demand anyone else listen to them.*

After all these years, you don't want to listen to anything I have to say? You don't want to know what I've been doing or thinking or feeling all these years? Is it possible my mother has concentrated so fully on what her own narrative line will be, her own extreme close-ups and grand speeches, that she never once expected an answer, a dialogue, some editing? Is it possible my mother has never imagined me with a mouth?

No. I don't. Not if you're going to hurt me. Spit garbage in my face. Put me down on the carpet and stamp on me! I talk all the time. If you do not like who I am—

She has worked herself into a frenzy now and, good literary critic that I am, I jump into my role as adversary. *You know almost nothing about my life, your own daughter's life, and you're not even curious to find out? Isn't this why you would want me to come?*

And then my mother surprises me. Beyond anything else she will say on this trip, this is the statement that makes me want to wrap my hands around her neck and throttle her until all her words are swallowed up in suffocation, and accept my jail time. *No. I know you very well. In the last six days I know enough to write a book about you!*

Luggage packed. Cab on its way. Plane on the tarmac. So long, crazy lady, time to speed out of here. Forget all about you. Let Stella Dallas's words to Helen Morrison foretell my own future: *In a little while, she'll forget all about me . . . she'll love you just like you were her real mother.* This woman is a bloodsucker. She drained our piggy banks when she left, our piggy banks! She feeds on other people's lives, their vital and creative energies, to escape her own. She thinks she's a critic, but what has art taught her about living? Obviously books and movies and theatre haven't prepared her for dealing with the real world. Art has only prepared her for delusional victory—a victim of circumstance wrongly barred from her family who will be vindicated in time. As audience, we don't get to see Stella Dallas's lonely nights lamenting her bad decisions, wallowing in the pain of knowing she is unfit to be a good mother and that her daughter has been spared further humiliation and harm with her freedom to live life without her. The movie ends before this life sentence of mis-

ery, with Stella's one unselfish act culminating in a happy marriage for her daughter. Few are capable of such unselfishness. My
mother is not among them.

What the hell am I doing here? I've never had any urge to visit
Brazil. I've dreamt of Paris, London, Berlin, Stockholm, Mel-
bourne, St. Petersburg, Vienna, Oslo. Never São Paulo. Brasilia.
Rio. For years, I could not have cared less where my mother
was, if she were alive, if she had a passing thought about me—
it wouldn't take a genius to figure out she likely fled back to her
homeland, I just didn't want to know for sure, and she didn't
want to find me either. Total willful blindness. On both sides.
And now I'm trying to convince her that she should listen to
what I have to say—*what do I have to say indeed*? Why didn't I
compose even a single speech for this very moment in all these
years? Why did I think it would be better to act like an observer,
a note-taker, a researcher, detached writer, when I'm an active
participant whose life will be affected by this course of events,
who might very well be harmed, permanently harmed, by the
human windmill in front of me? I wanted to give her the chance
to simply be, be who she is, as she is, without fear. I wanted to
be as neutral and unobtrusive as possible. I wanted to believe I
was taking the higher road. How stupid. How Canadian. Even
peacekeepers carry guns. I didn't pack a single weapon, and now
have to cobble together defences as the need arises. *I don't appreciate your sarcasm.*

*I don't understand sarcasm, or irony, or hints of any kind. There
are many things in life you have to deal with that you don't appreciate. My friends told me you came here for vengeance.*

Nice friends. *Vengeance? That's ridiculous.* I knew this wasn't
going to be an easy trip, but I am not a quitter by nature. I will bang
and bang and bang on a wall until it falls down. (It is only after
this trip that I learn the other option is to just walk around.) In my
mind, I hold my luggage back from the belt, unpack my clothes,

put down the receiver. I will not make a dramatic exit, which will only please my mother's theatrical sense of her victimhood. *This is why you need to listen to me. You don't have accurate information. Just once in this entire trip, I want you to listen to me.*

When my mother rains, she pours. *I don't have to do anything you ask. I am not your student. See, the child is telling the mother what to do, pointing her finger at me?*

Who is she talking to? Who is this "see" directed at? Is there a jury behind the curtains, in the breakfast nook, crouched with binoculars in the washroom? *I am an adult.*

I am fifty-seven years old.

We're comparing ages now? Granted, I suppose my mother never imagined herself, nearly a senior citizen, confronting her estranged daughter off the plane from Canada in an apartment suite in São Paulo. It's clear she imagined only gourmet dinners and shopping escapades, gallery hopping and loving hugs. Perhaps in her version of *Stella Dallas* the daughter notices her martyr mother outside in the rain and lifts her bridal veil to offer one last look of gratitude for all she has sacrificed. But not in mine. And it occurs to me now that I've always imagined us fighting—not about anything specific, but I sensed we would naturally butt heads—then me running off into a closet, crouching into a ball, breathing in the stale smell of clothes and papers and old shoes, my brother knocking lightly on the sliding doors to offer me a slice of cheese or an apple, a ritual I performed regularly as a child to escape the heaviness of our home, and which I haven't indulged in since I left that house. In the closet, I felt safe, contained, as if I'd grown a boxy shell. Frequently, I'd even fall asleep, neck curled underneath hanging shirts and dresses, legs crammed tight to my chest. When my brother couldn't stand it anymore, he'd go the opposite route, battle fear with fearlessness, recklessness—he'd construct a ramp out of bricks and wooden boards and invite all the neighbourhood kids to watch him flip his motocross through the air, building the ramp higher and higher until he would finally spill, or speed down our swimming pool slide on that same motocross, which would invariably end with him crashing headfirst bike-upon-body into the water, me the little nurse with alcohol swabs and Band-Aids swearing on my life not to tell our father. I take a quick glance at the entrance closet, barely large enough for a broom and an ironing board, and imagine retreating to its delineated space, but know it won't do. I might be someone's child, but I'm still an adult. I didn't come here to hide. I'll need to be more like my brother now—risk everything even if I crack my skull on the concrete.

If you cannot listen to someone, you cannot have a relationship with them. Communication must go two ways. I am asking you to listen to me so we can build a real relationship. What we have now is based only in imagination. I know this isn't easy, but it's necessary if we're going to meet on equal terms.

I will not play your game, she counters. *You don't believe God, why would you believe me?*

My face is as hot as my mother's is cold. *I am not playing a game. This is reality.*

She wipes her hands together, harshly. *I don't want your reality. I don't want your threats and accusations. You could have found me any time. I am all over the internet. I am everywhere. My work is everywhere.*

I did not come here to threaten you. Or accuse you. Or seek vengeance. Your friends are wrong to tell you this. I came here as a gift, an opportunity. This is what I've been trying to tell you. I came here to get to know who you are and for you to get to know who I am. Do you want to know who I am?

She doesn't respond, only settles into the chair with an unwavering eye, ignoring my little white flag waving in the wind. The truth of the situation hits me like a bullet fired after the declaration of a truce: I am the true perfect stranger. She trusts me even less than I trust her.

I step into my temporary bedroom and shut the doors. Not a retreat, but an intermission. Let the prima donna gather herself for the second act. Within seconds I hear the buzz of the television.

When I am able to convince myself that maybe this ugly fight is actually our first genuine breakthrough and it is imperative that I recommit to the original program—like I said, I'm not a quitter by nature and so my ability to reassess and retry is vast—I open the doors and ask my mother if she has decided on our evening itinerary.

I have always hated the Apocalypse book of the Bible, but when its title was changed to Revelations, I thought this was wonderful. There will be no more tears. I don't want to cry anymore or to remember any tears, Priscila. I really wanted my marriage to work.

Surprisingly, considering the well of emotions my mother ought to have stirred in me by now, I have yet to cry on this trip. I sincerely hope my reaction is not an unconscious desire to disobey my mother, but her words trigger my first sensations of tears: eyes watering, nose plugging up, throat pulsing. I did not intend to defeat her, only bruise her a little for the sake of a fairer fight. Of course she wanted her marriage to work. I'm sure when she said her "I do's" her future was bright and happy. Her tall, handsome husband was climbing the government ladder at a relentless pace; her starter home included gorgeous hydrangea bushes and a swimming pool; her sex life produced two precocious offspring and might have been extremely satisfying (I will never have the guts to ask); she was raising children and writing poetry and articles for magazines. I am sorry her dreams were crushed and damaged her so extensively in the process.

My parents' experience is probably the reason I'm so skeptical about marriage. *I'd rather wake up every day and choose to be with you than promise to be with you no matter what we do to each other,* I've said often to Chris, who also has no interest in the religious or civic institutions of marriage. And yet, I know such an attitude actually absolves my mother from fleeing a marriage she couldn't stomach any longer. Leaving a marriage doesn't need to mean abandoning one's children though. Many marriages end in divorce. Does my mother resent my relationship with Chris? My finding love and a supportive partner in life at the age of twenty-one? Is that why she doesn't want to hear about how we met, how we like to spend our time, how we celebrate our birthdays or book launches?

I'm coming to the conclusion that trauma exists in manifold disguises. My father's trauma was physical, touchable, requiring immediate medical intervention. One part of his body no longer able to communicate with the other parts. Permanent paralysis. To look upon my father, wincing as he grabs hold of the hoist to lower himself into his wheelchair, his daily experience of pain, discomfort, and disorientation is evident to all. Inarguable.

However, there are other forms of trauma, less easily detectable, but just as insidious. As someone who has studied trauma theory and written about trauma in my academic and creative works, I use the word carefully and purposefully here. For some a severed dream is as permanently altering and debilitating as a severed limb. I believe my mother is one of these people. A form of mental illness, perhaps, but activated by circumstance and not easily understood or treated. There are no prosthetics available for severed dreams, no surgeries, no equipment, and only the most unsatisfying of medications (those that stop one from dreaming or feeling the burden of the lost dreams). In the face of unreachable dreams, many of us learn to adapt, cope, invent new dreams, especially if we've had a hand in pushing ourselves away from those dreams in the first place or over time. But when those dreams are taken from you, snatched violently away without any permission on your part, the rupture left in their place can offer little chance for recovery. In the case of my father, his immune system was attacked. In the case of my mother, her imagination. She's been living in a state of crisis ever since. Phantom dreams as achingly futile as phantom limbs.

I need to be the strong one, I tell myself, all the evidence points to that. She is a victim not of you but of herself. A victim of her imagination. She needs the distractions of art to function on a daily basis, the way your father needs his medications and his homecare workers. If you want access to her mind or heart, you need to be patient and gentle. Lost in the blast long ago. Even she doesn't have the keys. So I swallow the tears, freshen my makeup, and join my mother in the lobby.

The fight did open up something in my mother: an old wound. Over dinner, she unwinds the outer bandage to offer me a peek.

I was going to die. Just die if I stayed. I tried to get in touch with you and your brother. Your father would not let me. No one can get angry at me for that.

It is hard enough for her to admit this much. I think about one of the claims from her legal documents: "The palsy turned Defendant into a violent and intractable person who was unable to accept the reality of being disabled and under a State Pension." The palsy turned the Plaintiff into a violent and intractable person unable to accept the reality as well. Who could, so easily? I've often speculated that if dealt the same cards I would not have fared as well as my father—I imagine I'd be consumed by bitterness and anger, depression, alcoholism, potentially suicide. My father was brilliant and possessed boundless energy; I'm sure he thought his brain could will him out of his situation if he tried hard enough. The doctors and nurses, I'm told, admired my father as he pushed himself every day at the parallel bars, carrying his body weight with one arm, his legs attached to metal braces, hoping against hope for a synapses reunion. He was never rewarded for his efforts. At the end of each session he was just as disabled as he was before. Outside the hospital a new life was waiting for him, an incomprehensible life with a new vocabulary and few options, a life he didn't sign up for. No fault of his. One with a disappointed wife, who also could not accept the new reality. And two clueless children.

I proceed lightly, gently, but am determined for her to understand my own point of view. *I think you were sick. My father was sick. You both made decisions that you felt were right. I don't think they were right, but I understand why you made them. All decisions have consequences. I was affected by those decisions. You can't expect me to pretend I don't have mixed emotions. I do not want to bring up the pain of the past, but you can't pretend it doesn't exist for me. It does. I was eight years old. My entire life, who I am, is shaped by what happened. You're asking me to pretend I am not who I am and that I did not live the life I've led, and I can't do that. I am happy to be here with you, I am having a nice time. I want to get to know you more, but I won't pretend the past never happened. There were consequences to you leaving. I had to take care of my father and my brother: shopping, cleaning, cooking, medical procedures. I had a Visa card with my name on it at ten years old. I was so old and worn out by the time I was fifteen that I left home and have been self-supporting ever since. It was easier for me to work full-time and go to school full-time and earn A-pluses across the board than it was for me to keep that household functioning.*

My mother has stopped eating her leafy salad and is listening to me. Actually listening to me. It's the longest and most honest speech I have been permitted so far on this trip. She takes a

breath and stops. She's thinking. Actually thinking about what
I've said. She takes another deep breath.

*I can't face these things, Priscila. I know you want to talk about
them. If I have to face them I am afraid I will die. I am afraid I will
break and the breaking won't end.*

My mother is more insightful of her psychology than I have
given her credit for. She's not oblivious; she's desperate. The
woman has been in survival mode for over twenty years. She's
utterly exhausted, and that exhaustion shows itself in her frizzy
hair, her bloated face, her clashing clothes and shuffling body, but
now she knows no other way of life. She must play out this fugitive role until the end. Of course she's scared of me. She implies I
have the ability to murder her. With my presence. A few words.
No knives or gas leaks or gunshots: just memories.

You don't have to, I assure her. *Just understand that I can't
cover up my mixed emotions every second of the day.*

My mother points to her chest, the hard lump of her cancer
tube. *I lost your father and both of you. You lost only me. You need
to think of that.*

I will. I've never considered it in such a light.

And she's never considered that I had to assume responsibilities in taking care of my father and our household—a task that
she, as a grown adult, found too burdensome to handle. *I remember so little about you because we didn't talk about you. Except
when we were angry. We tried to forget.* I know now she thought
she was providing us a better option than a weak, disappointed,
hysterical mother. Like Stella Dallas, she thought she was offering
us escape from her. *From* her.

My mother's parents liked my father but were against her
marrying him because of the differences of culture. They did not
want her to marry any Canadian when she accompanied them
to Ottawa, when her father accepted his post as military attaché.

It is the only time I disobeyed my father's wishes, she says sadly. *I married for love.*

I remember some happy things, I offer. Over the last few days, I've been ransacking my brain for morsels of tenderness to keep in my pockets for such a moment. *Easter eggs and my giant multicoloured teddy bear—which I still have—your red Avon lipstick tubes, your hairbands and bobby pins, you pulling me to the mall in a red wagon, the ice cream man and my kangaroo flavour—grape with vanilla inside—you'd buy me a whole box for the week, and vanilla cones and ice cream sandwiches for Jit.*

Do you remember I took us for swimming lessons?

And suddenly I do. I do remember. The chlorinated pool. The yellow arm floatation devices, and that Jit was a far better and braver swimmer than I was, repeatedly diving to retrieve dropped objects, though I loved actually being in the water more than he did. How we splashed about and swam circles around my mother, calling out for her attention and approval. We must have loved her once. We must have. Even Jit.

Our outdoor parent. The one who took us to bus stops and dentist appointments, to softball games and choir. The one who cleaned the pool and tended the garden: zucchini, tomatoes, green peppers, and four strawberry bushes. The one who bought us birthday presents and Popsicles and ground corn for the petting zoo. The one who taught us to sing and skip and slide and swim. But, to her disappointment and my own, I don't remember her driving the brown Mustang or making paper snowflakes with us and decorating the entire house with them.

We allow our memories to fade into the music of the traditional Brazilian band playing in the café, which my mother finds "soothing." I too am comforted by the mix of the piano with the soft Brazilian drumming and chanting voices. They are all religious songs, my mother tells me, that people sing outside of church, folk songs, and a couple of songs by recently deceased soprano Bidú Sayão. Couples begin to dance, holding each other close, some even kissing as they move to the music.

The last time I danced was with your father.

When I first fed my mother's website through the automatic translation feature, my mother's name appeared as Theresa Catharina de Góes Fields. Fields? She must have married a white guy, I thought. Whoa. In all the intervening years, it's astonishing that I'd never imagined her remarried. Did she start another family? Do I have half-siblings? My mind raced through the possibilities. But I soon figured out Fields was simply the English translation of her maiden name, Campos.

You've never dated anyone here? I risk.

My mother's eyes remain fixed on the band: *I am still a married woman, Priscila.*

She is stating a fact: irrefutable. I feel sad now watching the public displays of affection on the dance floor, knowing both my parents have had no romantic life other than in their imaginations for the last twenty years, probably more. For someone as romantically inclined as my mother, as idealistic about love, this absence must cut her deeply. She must project herself into her movies as much to experience the lost joys of candlelit dinners and shared desserts and drawn bubble baths and strolls through public parks as to follow a plot or admire a filmmaker's craft. The failure of her love to save her marriage from ruin must have been more devastating to her than leaving her children. The realization that love, no matter how pure, how total, cannot overcome all. Happily ever afters reserved for fairy tales and movies.

We share our table with a mother-daughter couple originally from Russia who emigrated to California. The daughter, a stunning blond with severe blue eyes and high cheekbones, has recently separated from her husband, a Brazilian she met in Argentina; the mother is helping her set up her new apartment, though it is clear she wishes her daughter would return to live with her in the United States. Among the folk music and chatting up strangers she will never meet again, my mother shines in her element. The Russians open up easily to her, are enamoured of her grand hand gestures and her operatic voice, and they tell us all about the Russian delicacies the mother imported from California specialty shops. These are the first people, outside of my mother and Soares, whom I have been able to speak to at some length since my arrival. A mother and daughter helping each other through a tough family matter. I hope some of their caring will rub off on us, bring us a little luck. From what I can ascertain, my mother isn't holding a grudge and I admire this trait in her. The issue isn't really talking about the past—she wants to know she's been forgiven for the past. Or at least that I won't hold it against her.

Later, as we head off to bed, for the first time since my arrival my mother does not kiss me goodnight. Perhaps this is what equal terms means. No victims. No victors. Just each of us alone in the dark.

Encontro e Desencontro

7

freaky friday

Fortune Cookie:
A journey soon begins,
its prize reflected in another's eyes.
When what you see is what you lack,
then selfless love will change you back.

CHURCHES crammed with believers and repentants. Upper-class shopping malls with fish-eaters. The streets ghost towns.

Normally on Good Friday my mother would be fasting, but because of the cancer she has been given permission to eat. Just no meat. Without any qualms about talking to people while they're trying to perform their jobs, my mother brags to the breakfast pianist about my accomplishments as a writer.

You are very proud of her, he replies after finishing a light-hearted tune on the keyboard.

Yes, she is so young and successful in such a competitive field. A month ago, she posted an article about the famous Canadian writer who will be visiting Brazil, if only two cities: "But Priscila Uppal intends to come back to our country. . . . I must admit that the poetess and *romancista* is my daughter." Yes, she is proud.

Nobody inquires as to whether she's played a role in any of my accomplishments. It's probably no coincidence that we are both teachers, writers, and art enthusiasts, though I can't pinpoint any specific memories of my mother, aside from regular crafts and colouring books, that would have contributed to the formation of my artistic side. My mother's nursing duties kept her unhappily away from her typewriter, but I don't think her resentment made me value the act of writing. Could it be simple genetics? Is there an art appreciation gene in our code? I loved my books as they could always be counted on to transport me out of the house into a world of adventuring talking dogs and ugly ducklings who transformed into beautiful swans, or tortured princesses and goblins living under bridges, or funny blue monsters who didn't recognize they were monsters until the end of the book. I could block out my hysterical mother with books. And my father's sickness. But I'm not convinced my passion for reading as a child is the key. Although psychologists are not necessarily in agreement with me, I think the most important years in determining who you will become are your teenage years. Which is one of the reasons Freaky Friday movies—a comedic genre based on temporary body switching starting with the original 1976 *Freaky Friday* starring Barbara Harris and Jodie Foster and spawning several remakes as well as adaptations of the genre such as *Body Switch, 18 Again,* and even *Shrek the Third*—have been so popular, so consistently, for decades. A middle-aged person forced to remember what it's like—physically, emotionally, intellectually—to be on the precarious cusp of adulthood. A young person forced to appreciate the tough decisions and burdensome responsibilities of adults. We squirm as the adult trapped in the teenager's body once again experiences raging hormones and crippling insecurities, and we laugh as the child in the adult fakes his or her way through important business meetings or pretentious dinner parties. In the Freaky Friday genre, once body order is restored, satisfaction lies in the knowledge that parent and child have gained an understanding of each other's worlds. Father and son, mother and daughter, now love out of compassion rather than merely blood.

My mother missed my entire teenage years, from my first AA-cup bra to my first traumatizing menstrual period, my first nauseating hangover (vodka mixed with grape Kool-Aid—I wish I was kidding), my first embarrassing sexual experiences (is a hand down my pants supposed to feel this icky and pointless?), my drama productions (I played Barbra Streisand's role in *Nuts* and was relentlessly recruited for air-band competitions because of my long flowing hair), poem and story publications in the high-school papers (usually about frightened siblings, the dynamics of teenage friendships, and suicide), my academic and sports awards (I won top ranking in classes as varied as accounting, English literature, biology, and phys. ed.; MVP on the basketball team, and other sports ribbons and trophies including for bowling—again, I wish I was kidding); she missed absolutely everything. I am an unknown quantity buttering toast, sharing watermelon slices. If only we could switch bodies for a day, even a couple of hours, I think. I'd like to know what's going on in that layered head, what she really thinks about the state of her existence and the young woman who shares her DNA and her hotel room.

He says you are very beautiful and that you look like me. What else could a mother want? As if sensing hesitation on my part, my mother adds: *You do look like me. You also look like your father.* Then, *I did not marry your father to stay in Canada. Canada is no better a country than Brazil. There is no democracy in Canada.*

Revelations as one decides which jam jar to open. The thought had never, ever, crossed my mind. I figured if she fled Canada so easily, she would never have married to stay in it. Plus, she's not expressed or inferred or hinted at a single characteristic or feature from Canada she's missed. Including me. Not "I used to love poutine" or "Canada has the right idea about universal health care" or "Does that Group of Seven still paint trees?" or "I miss skating with you on the Rideau Canal." From the lack of references, one would imagine she'd never lived in or travelled about Canada, when she actually spent the better part of her twenties and thirties there. Maybe Canada, to my mother, is an imaginary place, a land far, far away, where she stores all the bad and sad feelings. Canada is a villain who turned her life unfairly on its head. Who dished out a brand of justice she can't accept.

I pile endless pineapple on my plate. Brazil has the best pine-apple. My Brazil enthusiasts are right about this. We both eat tons of it; and as we do, I decide to prepare a mental list of all the things I love about Canada (a list I can replay in my mind whenever my mother decides to dismiss its value to me).

Ten Things I Love About Canada

1. I love that I don't need to know how to drive and can walk outside almost any hour of the day, relatively unafraid.
2. I love that if I'm sick I can go to my doctor's office or emergency and not worry that I'll have to take out a loan to pay for tests or procedures.
3. I love *Hockey Night in Canada* (Don Cherry's tacky suits and Ron MacLean's groanworthy puns).
4. I love Canadian lakes and rivers and the Rocky Mountains and Algonquin Park. Most of all I love the longest skating rink in the world, and love love love that it's in my hometown.
5. I love the Canadian Pacific railroad and the rolling food and drink carts.
6. I love Canadian books: *The Handmaid's Tale, Basic Black with Pearls, Beautiful Losers, The Apprenticeship of Duddy*

Kravitz, Fugitive Pieces, poetry by Gwendolyn MacEwen and Irving Layton and A.M. Klein and Anne Carson, George F. Walker and Judith Thompson plays.

7. I love our political system, which allows for more than two parties and for coalition governments. (Like my father, I love Pierre Elliott Trudeau.)

8. I love that the city I live in is home to millions of people from around the globe. And I love that this means I can find, at a moment's notice, a restaurant to satisfy any culinary urge.

9. I love French Canada, especially their artists: writers Anne Hébert, Marie-Claire Blais and Hubert Aquin, painters Jean-Paul Riopelle and Paul-Émile Borduas; poutine and tourtiere and molasses candies; how they dress and speak and smoke; even their snobbery against the English.

10. I love my Canadian passport. (Which should *not* need a visa to visit Brazil.)

Satisfied, I wipe my mouth clean of yellow juice.

Many of the museums and exhibitions and stores are closed today, except the Museu de Arte Brasileira, specializing in works by local as well as internationally renowned Brazilian artists. As Soares drives us there, my mother, offering an unintended ironic commentary on the holy day, takes the opportunity to tell me Brazilians care very little for fathers: *Only the mother is important. It is said that a child can have many fathers but only one mother. The mother can take the child and find a whole new family. When judges ask children who they would like to live with, they always say the mother.*

I let her talk. I know this bias isn't that different in North America. Fathers come and go, mothers are steadfast. No one loves you like your mother. A mother's love is eternal. Et cetera. Et cetera. It's why people make a special face of disgust when

I'm forced to reveal my mother ran off when I was a child. The issue is that the look of disgust is usually directed as much at me as at this invisible mother. As with perfectly good furniture left out on the curb, passersby brace themselves for ugly smells or hidden stains or cracks as they open drawers and lift cushions; otherwise, why would anyone throw out a perfectly good chesterfield or vanity?

Then, changing her mind again at the drop of a hat, my mother gestures to a young couple playfully lifting their two children like swings between them, out for a stroll on this very sunny day. *Family,* she points. *Look at how beautiful, how happy a family. If you have a good happy family, I think everything in life is so much easier for you.*

Romantic Flashback

So, it's probably a minor miracle, I think, that I've ended up in a stable, loving relationship, but I'm thankful that I have. When you grow up with sadness in place of love, you sometimes think sadness itself is love, a landscape that makes you feel at home, or a favourite genre of film or art; sadness is your element, your aesthetic; instinctively, automatically, you move toward it.

Chris grew up a morose teenager in a small town north of Toronto, the only son of a disastrous second marriage that saw his firefighter father turfed out of the house for alcoholism when Chris was only three years old. His four siblings, older than him by a good decade, had their own problems, which likely began in earnest once their father died in a car accident leaving Chris's mother, a woman without maternal instincts, a young widow with four small children. After some false starts and punishing labour jobs, Chris returned to high school to finish his diploma when a teacher took an interest in him, dangling the possibility of university under his nose. We ended up meeting each other the week before university actually began; we'd both managed to earn large entrance scholarships to study literature and creative writing and the master of our college hosted a reception for scholarship recipients. As Chris likes to tell it, *I had long hair and silver skull rings and there were a lot of geeks in that room with pocket protectors, and then there was a beautiful woman with purple-black hair in a black leather Harley-Davidson jacket and a miniskirt with the word "die" written on it. I decided to walk up and talk to her, and it's the best decision I ever made in my life.* After three years of solid friendship, while we watched each other pair up and break up with other people, Chris finally confessed he was in love with me. We've never turned back.

Neither of us may ever have experienced a good happy family, but we have experienced good happy love, and I hold on to this love as tightly as my purse as my mother tries to convince me that everything in life, not just biology, begins and ends with mothers.

My mother quiets as we enter the museum atrium, a stunning display of several famous statues by Aleijadinho, Brazil's finest baroque artist, born in 1738 to a Portuguese architect and black slave woman. In his twenties he contracted leprosy, a condition that left him with crippled hands and legs. Some of the finest churches in Brazil were miraculously decorated by Aleijadinho. A Brazilian Michelangelo. Revered like a saint.

In stark contrast, we then enter an exhibition of contemporary artworks by J.R. Duran featuring huge two-storey-high glossy photographs of scantily clad women—not necessarily Easter-approved entertainment, but then again we are the only visitors here—and my mother slips four postcards into my palm. No need to whisper as even the security guards are nowhere to be found, my mother positions herself in front of a topless woman astride a blow-up alligator, kissing its snout.

It never occurred to me that you or Amerjit would have to do anything for your father when I left. I thought you would all go live with his family. Or they would give him money.

I don't interrupt her, because I don't know how to respond to her mistaken assumptions. While she was packing her luggage in our basement, her own mother helping her pick and choose what to keep and what to leave behind, or maybe on the plane, two empty seats beside her like unfulfilled wishes, she must have convinced herself of many illusions regarding our future lives.

Childhood Montage

My father's two brothers did help out, at first: the one immediately driving overnight to pick us up and take us back over the border to Syracuse until after Christmas; the other accepting us into his household and enrolling us in a West Bloomfield, Michigan, school, until my mother dropped in unannounced, terrifying everyone like an envelope leaking white powder. My brother and I had some good times with my cousins in Syracuse: two boys about our age who built model airplanes and motorized sports cars and the younger girl with so little to fear in her life the only punishment her parents could wield was the imaginary sceptre of The Boogeyman. In Michigan, our older cousins introduced us to Led Zeppelin and AC/DC, to horror movies like *Rosemary's Baby* and *Halloween*, to piano lessons and softball leagues. My brother was enrolled in a special after-school math and speed-reading class, whereas I was placed in swimming and cheerleading (something I didn't even know existed and found ridiculous, but my status-conscious aunt kept insisting would help me "belong"). I still remember the look of bewilderment in all their faces when Jit and I, kids completely uprooted from our surroundings and severed from the care of our parents only months before, presented them with our mid-term report cards: Jit had earned 100 percent in all subjects except two: English and woodworking, I think, and I had managed the most singular of feats, a *perfect* report card: 100 percent in every subject. My cousins touted those report cards around the neighbourhood like a parlour trick or freak show: *Have you ever seen such a thing in your life?* My uncle was a sweet and warm man who tried to make us comfortable, but it was clear my aunt was chewing at the bit to ship us back to Ottawa. After her wish came true, we received a yearly "Christmas Newsletter" bristling with vacation highlights to Hawaii and Thailand and job promotions, the kind that Chris and I parody by sending out a yearly "Bad Newsletter," which includes a list of "People Who Owe Us an Explanation" and "Places Never to Visit Again." A one-page letter with a Christmas card to display on our mantel. To my knowledge, never once did such a letter include a cheque.

After Michigan, we ended up in the countryside with the French-Canadian foster family, who were also well-meaning but baffled as to what to do, a grey-haired couple who baked us cakes and biscuits and taught us how to care for the rabbits and chickens in the barn and then how to deliver them to slaughter. After several months, my father joined us there, the town allowing us all to live together in the abandoned community centre—essentially a gymnasium, its colourful circles and court lines intact—a makeshift home with Styrofoam frames separating one room from another.

Later that year we returned to our home in Ottawa and my father was able to sponsor two relatives to Canada: a young half-brother by a different mother who was more interested in driving a cab and marrying as quickly as possible and moving out to the west coast with barely a look back, and an older sister we all just called Auntie (I've never known her actual name), a tiny frail woman, the spinster of the family because of facial deformities incurred by smallpox, who learned basic English by watching soap operas like *Days of Our Lives* and *The Young and the Restless*, and *Hockey Night in Canada* (she developed a strange obsession with Zdeno Chára), and who fled back to India at any meagre invitation for months and months at a time. Not that I blame these relatives for seeking escape from us—they were out of their element, drowning in medical procedures and the odd behaviours of precocious but weird children old before their time. Our family was a curiosity to social workers, teachers, nurses, homecare workers, neighbours; like the Crazy Kitchen at the Science and Technology Museum, the furniture adjusted in size to appear as normal as possible but the floor slanted so that it was a struggle to get from one end to the other without succumbing to dizziness. Our family would never "belong."

Because you said I don't ask you any questions, I have come up with a list of six essential questions for me to know. I would not have done this otherwise, but since you said it was okay for me to ask questions about you, I have made this list.

Close-up

A postcard: a blurred view of an amusement park swing ride across a purple background, a black silhouette of a girl on one of the chain swings in the foreground. On the reverse:

<u>Six</u> *basic questions for me*
(I have always loved you and Amerjit very much. I <u>love</u> you
both!!)
  1. *Did you ever love me? (when I was with you at home)*
  2. *How about Amerjit?*
  3. *Do you love me presently?*
  4. *Does Amerjit love me presently?*
  5. *Is this trip helping you to love me?*
  6. *Is this trip better or worse (ref: feelings) than you expected?*

For only the second time on this trip, tears gather at the corners of my eyes. The illusion that we were making any progress
completely shatters. I am shocked. Speechless. The childish pleading reminds me of the photocopies of homemade holiday cards
my mother sent me along with her "gift of truth" legal documents, cards I might have made with her hovering over me as in
my memories: one of a pink flower and a heart speared with an
arrow where I've written "I love you! Very much!" and another
with the most rudimentary rabbit for Easter that says "I like you!
also I love you! AND the bunny likes you too. And she is calling
you to say 'Hello I hope it'll be a good day.'" My mother even
wrote the dates on them: October 24, 1982, and April 4, 1982,
the year she abandoned us. I never thought the cards were sent
as a "gift of truth," but, like the other documents, the mounting
of a defence. The postcard questions assault me with their inap-
propriateness, the unleashing of an offensive.

How can this woman demand declarations of love from the
past and from the present? What kind of monster child would
deny loving their parents when they were defenceless children?
What kind of question is it whether Jit would love this woman
"presently" when he doesn't know her from a hole in the wall,
when he wouldn't even be able to recognize her voice?

Phase two: a second postcard, the exact same image on the front, dated SP 17/4/03: *Dear daughter Priscila: I travelled to Detroit and I came back to Brazil . . . without even a smile at me . . . to keep as a good memory!! And for 9 months you were inside my body! Your mother Theresa Catharina.*

Phase three, Phase four, Phase five: the remaining postcards attack, attack, attack, accusatory statements about how badly she has been treated and how her children ought to feel sorry for her and love her.

I am reeling from the shock-and-awe onslaught, the blows hitting all kinds of sensory targets in my brain and body, but am determined to remain outwardly calm and collected. One of my excellent coping mechanisms revs into high gear. I learned long ago that breaking down, folding into a mess of tears and dysfunction, only gives the cause of your hurt more power. I recognize the benefits of releasing some of the pain in private, but I refuse to allow pain to overwhelm me. I always tell myself I have better things to do. Even if it's meant that at various times in my life people have found my ability to control my emotions and function at a high level, regardless of pain, offensive. When your friends and colleagues are spending thousands of dollars on therapies and medications to help them work through their feelings about their relatively kind and supportive but imperfect parents, when you're able to keep a woman like my mother at a relatively safe emotional distance so as to minimize damage, you come off as arrogant or smug at best, at worst a cold monster. On a basic level, people don't want you to be able to cope. They want to pity you, feel sorry for you, have you turn your skin inside out for their view. I remember one of our friends, a psychiatrist in training, asking me once: *Do you feel things like other people?* I thought *he* was crazy. *Do you read my work?* I replied. I feel things just like other people (sometimes I think I feel them more authentically than other people), but I try to use those feelings to become a stronger person, to gain understanding of the world I live in. I love the Buddhist proverb *Pain is inevitable. Suffering is optional.* I wish I could show my mother how art exists, at its best, to help us heal our lives, not to mask them.

For now, I hide my disappointment and soften my anger by concentrating on the exhibit. When I decided to make this trip I told myself I would go to discover as much as I can about who my mother is, whether I like her or not, so that I am not left wondering for another twenty years. In this respect, the trip is fulfilling my goals. I am seeing who she is. *Whether I like her or not.* And it's true, I don't like her, I can't force myself to like her, but I must find a way to appreciate this "gift of truth" and plod on. Even if she's incapable of knowing me.

I turn away, silencing the postcards by shoving them into my purse.

So . . . ?

These women with their long, sour faces, mounting animals and wearing studded dog collars, seem a hundred times more tasteful than my mother. I imagine myself melting into the photographs, perhaps the one of a topless woman in a chain thong posing on a Harley-Davidson motorcycle. Or maybe I should attack one of Aleijadinho's treasured sculptures? I want the security guards to handcuff me and send me back to Canada. But I can't quit, because I want to meet the other members of the family. If I don't do it now, I know I never will. It would not be fair of me to judge them in relation to her.

Instead, I collect my voice: *These questions are all about you.*

Yes, my mother nods enthusiastically, as if, like an improving student, I've finally come around to her way of thinking. *That is what is important to me. Do you love me? This is an essential question. You told me I could ask anything I wanted about your life.*

My mother is shaking, I notice, but I don't care. I don't exist. To her my emotional life is only significant as it relates to her own feelings. If I were to bleed, I'd be bleeding for her. If I were to cry, I'd be crying about her. I repeat to myself the truth of my situation: *I have no need for a mother. I have no need for a mother.* I grew up just fine without one. I wouldn't know what to do with one. I am not her daughter in any real sense. What can I say? I won't be forced to admit love when I don't feel love. That would be the worst sort of emotional blackmail. Treason.

I don't remember doing anything bad to you or Amerjit.

Jit. His name is Jit, I sigh, a gut reaction—I've given up on altering her vocabulary, just as I've given up on altering her personality. I wish she would give up on altering mine. *It doesn't matter. You don't remember. To know would only upset you.*

Do you . . . do you love me?

In the Lindsay Lohan and Jamie Lee Curtis update of *Freaky Friday*, in one of the most touching scenes of the film, the daughter trapped in her mother's body the day before her mother is set to remarry delivers a toast to welcome her new stepfather, something she has been loath to do since she is still grieving the death of her biological father three years earlier. She announces the family unit is now ready to *make a little room.* It's a beautiful phrase, as if all love required of us was a slight crowding of chairs, a transfer of a bookshelf or bulky lamp to the basement, a holding of breath to endure a tight elevator squeeze. I wish. I wish it were so easy.

My instinct is to burn the postcards, but I know I will take them back to the room and place them carefully inside an envelope stashed in my carry-on luggage. The postcards are evidence. Evidence my mother is a maniac. That I've been justified in not seeking her out all these years. That some mothers really need to be kept away from their children. Storytelling is by nature hyperbolic. Plus, for some stupid reason, people want to believe we *should* have good relationships with our family members, that a mother is a mother and a father is a father and you're stuck with them, no matter what. I can already hear it: *She didn't really do that, did she? She wasn't really so bad?* But look, look here, I will reply. Look at these postcards. Who would hand this to one's child?

I don't know you.

Rage in my mother's eyes. Pure, unadulterated rage.

I can't love someone I don't know.

Isn't that the lesson of the body-switching genre: that true love and understanding can only come with empathy?

She tries to snatch the postcards. I zip my purse, shelter it against my hip. My mother always has something between her teeth or on her lips—a speck of pepper, a flicker of mint, a lint fluff—she doesn't register it until she checks in her lipstick mirror. I keep silent, as usual, as she walks briskly out the door, cookie crumbs on her chin, and wonder how can she walk through life so obliviously.

I consider putting stamps on the cards and sending them home. But I already know the Brazilian postal service is seriously unreliable. The prettiest postcards are frequently confiscated by clerks and pinned up in the post offices. Those aware of the situation hide postcards in envelopes so the postal workers cannot see them. And I don't want these cards stolen, or misplaced, or forgotten. They are my fortune cookie, my earthquake. They are the first real letters I've ever received from my mother. Therefore, for some stupid reason, I treasure them.

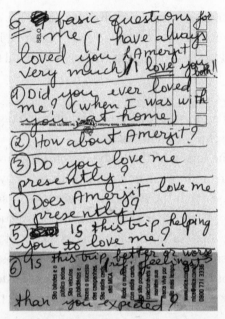

Postcard of Essential Questions

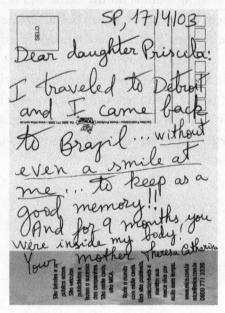

Postcard of Guilt

8

throw momma from the train

Larry: A guy kills my wife, but he can't even kill his own mother.

TWO MEN SWEATING in the middle of the blistering desert are informed by a third that someone is planning to build a city right where they're standing. They both start laughing and can't stop. They die laughing.

I have been warned that Brasilia, the capital of Brazil since April 21, 1960, when it was changed from Rio de Janeiro, built purposefully in the middle of the desert and now a UNESCO World Heritage site, is very dry and very, very hot; many transplanted Brazilians have trouble adjusting to the new climate. I can't wait—São Paulo to Brasilia please! Step on it! Not a moment too soon!

You do everything quickly, my mother points out as she meticulously covers every item in her suitcase with a plastic bag. *The only two things I do fast is read and write.* But I also remember her confessing that she has never known what to do with her hands, and that my father was always asking her to control her hands. Taking her sweet time packing gives her something useful to do with those hands.

As we drag our luggage down the lobby hallway, with my mother wearing the same orange outfit she wore to greet me at the airport—perhaps this is her "travelling ensemble," the way mine is my loose-fitting black jumpsuit—she rips a piece of paper, a message for another guest in the hotel left by accident on her bag. *Now the clerk will be made to pay for his carelessness,* she says smugly, as if she has executed an extremely ethical act. I am horrified, imagining the unknowing guest who won't receive the message my mother has destroyed.

Maybe she'd be somebody you'd like to kill, I hear, the voice of Danny DeVito arguing with Billy Crystal about swapping murders—Crystal's ex-wife for Danny's mother—in *Throw Momma from the Train.* I can't help it—I love this movie. Danny DeVito and Billy Crystal at their best. Now that I'm a published writer and a professor of English and creative writing, Billy Crystal's Larry, a writer with writer's block teaching the craft to a group of misfits and losers, is even funnier. And Owen. What a perfect name for a boy with a mother complex! *Owen loves his momma.*

Owen's momma is grotesque to the nth degree: physically, emotionally, spiritually. Played by ghoulish Anne Ramsey in her most famous film role, even her voice assaults; spit flies with every hoarse syllable. Relentlessly, she demands Owen perform disgusting tasks, such as removing her earwax, and is constantly belittling him and smacking him upside the head. Owen retreats into an imaginative world of matricide revenge fantasies. After seeing Alfred Hitchcock's *Strangers on a Train*, Owen has an epiphany and approaches Larry to murder his mother in return for him killing Larry's ex-wife. I've been thinking about Owen's momma a lot lately and the taboos associated with matricide in such myths as Orestes and in the horror films *Carrie* and *Psycho*. *Maybe she'd be somebody you'd like to kill.*

I used to wonder, often, if my mother was dead. My brother tells people she's dead—it's easier than explaining our family history to acquaintances, business associates, or first dates. I've even considered over the years whether or not I wish her dead. Or, if informed of her death, whether I would cry or feel more than indifference to her passing. I know as a child, when I was afraid of her rages, I cursed her and hoped she'd die. But children wish their parents dead all the time—not understanding death as permanent, desiring only temporary relief. Over the last week in São Paulo, there have been many moments when I would have welcomed a mute button, a trap door, a panic room, or a teleportation machine. I confess I might also have envisioned a coffin.

The humour in *Throw Momma from the Train* stems not only from the usually repressed desires to kill one's mother or an ex-lover, but also from the psychological reality that these beings are spiritually unkillable: not with pillows, poisons, knives, axes, or high-speed vehicles. The two bumbling would-be murderers botch suffocation, falling down stairs, death by trumpet (Owen's momma wakes to screech out one of the most bizarre lines in cinema: *What a dream I was having! Louis Armstrong was trying to kill me!*), and throwing the overweight beast off a train. The movie is a comedy, I would argue, not only because no one actually dies, but because both men manage to turn their pain and trauma into creativity; they publish books—Larry, his new best-selling novel called *Throw Mamma from the Train*, and Owen, a pop-up book simply titled *Momma, Owen, and Owen's Friend Larry*.

I'll admit that one of the things keeping me by my mother's side at this point is the fact that I'd like to write about her. I can hold my disappointment in check if there's a purpose to enduring the torture. I can withstand the knowledge that my mother has no interest in her daughter, in me, if I'm permitted a window into her psychology. I can even calm my nerves, wary of shared DNA, if I can pinpoint how my mother turned her real life into a fantasy. I'm willing to endure her for a book for all the other children of disastrous, neglectful, and narcissistic parents, who beat themselves up for not being able to alter their gazes, not being able to create the love that would salvage the past, turn it into the turbulent backstory of a triumphant comedy. For those out there who reunite with lost mothers and fathers, dreams of reconciliation packed tenderly in their carry-ons, who land to the horrific discovery that they were better off without these parents, better off with the deep and searing pain of lost love they learned to live with day after day instead of this irredeemable pain of hopeless reunion. The problem with most books and movies about family reunions is that they share the same arc: strained family relations that through forced contact and conflict result in newfound understanding, acceptance, and love. The same predictable, unrealistic arc. While I've loved art my entire life, art doesn't always prepare you for life. I suspect the vast majority of prodigal sons and daughters end up sorely mistaken and disappointed with their homecomings. My book will be for them: my people. No book, no daughter. The truth is ugly. For both of us. And I can't throw her off the airplane.

While we wait to board, my mother hands me a flimsy piece of notepad paper. *Your schedule in Brasilia,* she says flatly. I'm relieved my handwriting is distinct from hers. Her ones look like skinny triangles, and her Ps curve into loops at the stems.

SUNDAY:
10:40 a.m.: leave to church
11 a.m.: Mass at D. Bosco church
~~1:30pm~~ 1 p.m.: Hotel Blue Tree (restaurant)

~~17 hr~~ *5 p.m.: Coffee with cookies at the Hotel bar*
7:30 p.m.: Dinner at Patio Brasil Shopping

MONDAY:
noon: check-in at the Hotel Blue Tree
1 p.m.: Lunch at Restaurant Bargaço
7:30 p.m.: Hotel (or Cinemark Hall)

TUESDAY:
noon: check-out Hotel Blue Tree
1 p.m.: Lunch at Pier 21
7:30 p.m.: Dinner at Academia de Tenis

WEDNESDAY:
6:15 a.m.: leave to airport
7 a.m.: check-in at the airport
8:06 a.m.: VASP flight to Guarulhos

Then several postcards: names of the people I will be meeting with indicators of family or social ties as they relate, not to me, of course, but to my mother:

CARD ONE (amusement park photo):
Victoria: my sister/irmã
William: meu cunhado (my brother-in-law)
Elizabeth: minha sobrinha (my niece)
Walter: meu webmaster
Guilherme: sobrinho (nephew)
Fernando: irmão (brother)
Rosana: cunhada (sister-in-law)
Fernanda: sobrinha (niece)
Succoro: empregada e guerida amiga (employee and friend)
FAMILIA CAMPOS minha familia some members

*It is a big family, there are many more! Uncles, aunts, cousins,
　　great grandparents...*

CARD TWO (psychedelic Motorola cellphone ad):
Maria des Gracas: tia gracinha (great aunt)
Ana Margarete: her daughter
Julia: husband
Heloisa: my lawyer
Bete: Maria Elisabete
Raquel: her daughter

CARD THREE (Motorola ad):
Áurer César: Professor
Ione: his wife
Cláudia Verô: Nica his daughter
Ricardo: her husband
Nicola: their son
Artemis
Adrianna: Guilherme's sweetheart
Elaine e ELCI
Flavio and Camilla his sweetheart
(At Blue Tree Brunch)

We are flying VASP, another Brazilian airline, and my mother counsels me not to be alarmed by the runway, which is on a plateau a couple of storeys higher than street level—it looks like we're taking off from the roof of a building. From my window seat, I can clearly make out cars and bustling people and a hot dog stand. *That stand was completely smashed by an airplane wing once landing on this very runway,* my mother laughs. *That's how close we are to the city. Luckily, he saw the plane and ran down the street! No need to be nervous, Priscila, I've survived three plane crashes in my life.* Preparing for takeoff, the Brazilians unanimously genuflect. *Oh shit,* I think, sinking further underneath my seatbelt. *To die beside my mother would be the worst irony of all,* I pray. Am I praying? Yes, I am. Please don't tell anyone.

You know the quality of a pilot only second by takeoff, first by how he lands, my mother informs me. A criticism from a family of pilots. From a woman who has survived three plane crashes. *I am always last to leave the plane.*

It's a short flight, barely enough time to study the postcards and wolf down a snack. As we approach Brasilia at night, my mother reminds me to observe how the city lights form the outline of an airplane. Here are the wings. Here is the body of the plane. Here is the nose. The tail. The advantage of a modern, planned city: vision and order. My mother admires order. Safety. Stability. Predictability. As we land, the pilot boasts that Brasilia is home to the largest flagpole in the world. Why not? I come from a country that boasts the world's largest mallard duck, badminton racket, chuckwagon, and snowman. The world's largest flagpole is nothing to sneeze at.

Three women and two men await us at the arrivals ramp. Two of the women, standing side by side in front of the others, are petite, in tasteful pantsuits and light overcoats.

I am your grandmother, the light-skinned white-haired woman in her late-seventies with sparkling blue eyes tells me, grabbing my hand with her bony fingers.

I am your Aunt Victoria, the freckled woman with auburn hair, thin lips, and soft voice, chimes in.

I am your Uncle Wilhelm, and this is your cousin Elizabeth and her boyfriend Walter (both Ws pronounced like Vs), a round-faced, clean-cut, short man directs, pointing at a tall, shaking, dark-skinned girl and her nearly inert equally dark boyfriend. True to my mother's descriptions, the women are all skinny, and Walter and I, the two outsiders, the only ones in black.

I turn to my mother, who looks anxious but puffed up. I managed to do it, her face and posture convey. Look here: my prodigal daughter. Feast your eyes.

No one has ever come to meet me at the airport, she whispers behind me as I finish shaking hands with my new relatives. *This is not normal. You should feel special.*

I know this is not normal, the way Billy Crystal knows Owen's home life is not normal in the fabulous scene when he is introduced to the trollish mother as Owen's Cousin Patty. *You don't have a Cousin Patty,* she snorts. *You lied to me,* Owen exclaims, and whacks Larry on the head with a heavy frying pan. Who are you? I think, scanning all these faces for signs of friendliness or lack of sanity. Is my mother a product of you people? Or is she an original?

Because it's late, we eat at the airport on hard plastic chairs at metal tables. Everyone is smiling. Smiling and staring at me and then into their teacups. Nobody really knows what to say, except: *How was your flight? Did you like São Paulo? Did you see any movies?*

For this first hour, I try to match faces to my mother's stories, like a memory card game: *Victoria has the best marriage because she and Wilhelm have never had a single fight. My father died of cancer at eighty because my mother fought with him. His own mother died when he was five. Then his father married the other sister. Then she died. Then his father married the next sister. Then she died. This went on until he had married all five sisters, and all five died.* (What was sister number five thinking? It's a Gabriel García Márquez novel! Only those without ties to South America would believe in an artistic genre called "magic realism." In South America, this is realism.) *So, my grandfather hated the colour black, and all black clothing. Victoria's life revolves completely around her husband. The night of her marriage was the first night she'd ever slept away from our mother and father. She returned home several times, crying that she loved Wilhelm with all her heart but couldn't sleep. Mother was angry and sent her back. My brother Fernando has decided not to stay in Brasilia for Easter this year. He does what he pleases. Except he drives Mother around whenever she likes. He'll drive, but he won't speak. He doesn't speak to anyone. If you meet him, which I don't think you will, he won't speak to you. You should be offended. We all are.*

I am thinking my grandmother and aunt look so elegant, refined, controlled, so diametrically opposed in body type and temperament to my mother, when my grandmother leans across the silver table and says: *I never imagined meeting you with a table between us. I imagined I would be able to embrace you, hold you close.* She looks heartbroken, her blue eyes pleading with me to rewind the tape and film again. *Did you cut your hair?*

So my grandmother imagined this day. The admission makes me more comfortable. *No, it's just hot, so I've tied up the sides,* I explain, highlighting my two Princess Leia buns. If this family advocates slimness, it also seems to expect its young women to have long hair. Check. Check.

The last time I saw you, you were showing me how quickly, how beautifully, how eloquently you could write. My grandmother, unlike my mother, speaks precisely, calmly, intent on communication. She squeezes my hands. She has very long fingers, pianist fingers. *Do you want me to write something for my mother? you asked. And then you did. You were writing even then.* When she smiles, her white face and hair light up; she looks like a Swarovski crystal.

I rise to refill my cup, but two other people my mother knows stand in my way. I don't catch their names because I am already overwhelmed with information and greetings. The woman has red hair and a wide mouth and immediately swarms into my personal space, while her pigeon-like husband nods and keeps nodding like a bobblehead doll.

Your mother looked everywhere for you. Everywhere. We were all involved, signing petitions, writing letters—everyone hoping she would one day find you and bring you home. What a day! What a day! Look at you, so beautiful! She hired private detectives. The FBI was involved. No one could find you. Now here you are. Here you are!

Is insanity contagious? How is it this woman, who knows my mother, talks in absurd fantasies just like my mother. Instinctively, I recoil. Pour hot water from the carafe. Stir my tea and sit while my mother chats with the couple in Portuguese, the red-haired woman hugging her, the man three steps back, nodding, nodding, agreeing to god knows what.

After they leave, I'm informed that because tomorrow is the "big day," it would be best if we called it a night.

I don't want to go, my grandmother pouts, pulling my arm so I will bend to her level. *I have just found you. It breaks my heart to leave you. But I will see you tomorrow, and so will have pleasant dreams.*

I look forward to seeing you too, I reply, genuinely wishing I were spending the night with her or skinny Aunt Victoria, who has done little other than smile and ask me repeatedly in spotty English to visit her house, all while her husband snaps photos of us. Before I can think of a way to make this happen, the extended family has vanished and I am alone at the Brasilia airport with my mother.

What those people said, I start, *makes no sense. You didn't need to hire private detectives. We were only away from the house for a year. We lived in the same house. FBI? That's American, not Canadian,* I chuckle. *What were they talking about?*

Even though she wipes her mouth with a napkin, a pastry flake remains on her lower lip. She eyes me coldly. *They shouldn't have told you those things. They are worse than illiterates. They just wanted you to know I was looking for you. They pretend to know more about me and you than they should.*

We were in the same place you left us. I'm not sure why I'm pushing this point except that I want to identify where my mother believes the truth lies.

You don't want to hear my side. That's been obvious since you landed, my mother responds, rising and pushing our luggage cart. *And you're not going to get anything else out of me. You only want to use what you learn against me. I can see that. You are not a trusting person.*

The barometer of my psychological wellness, my stomach, cramps again. I don't know how to respond to my mother's insults, her resentments. When I told her that growing up many of my friends' families invited me to spend holidays, special occasions, and small vacations with them, she was annoyed. *But those people are not your family. You were entertainment for them,* she scoffed. *They were there for me during tough times,* I insisted. *Some even let me live with them when I left home, before I could find a suitable room to rent.* But she waved me off, never once asking where I've lived. And she wonders why I don't trust her.

I'm just trying to understand.

No, you're not, she snaps as I follow her to the taxi stand. *You don't understand, but you will. You will understand that I expect nothing from you. Nothing! And then you will be sorry.*

Close-up

Are you . . . are you threatening me? Should I even get in this cab?

No. My mother's face a traffic barrier.

That's a threatening face.

Extreme Close-up

Puffy red lips: *Brazilians don't threat. We just do.*

For the first time, I understand that maybe *I* am someone *she'd*
like to kill. Living is acceptable as long as I don't contradict her,
disagree with her, or force her to confront her memories or fantasies. People would have comforted her, praised her, built shrines
to her even, if her children had died tragically in an accident, if
they had died for want of a mother's love. I think she would have
welcomed my death as a relief because I've been dead to her anyway and death ends the other side of the conversation. My existence a hologram, a mirage, as ethereal as light and air, she's been
wrapping around her heart like a fine protective sheen, taking to
bed at night for support like a water bottle or a night light. Alive, I
too am a monster. A monster she needs to slay to retain her peace.
I don't live in a fantasy world—that's all I've been trying to say.

 *I did not go to Canada to bother you. You forget, you are in MY
place and you will do as I say. This is MY family, Priscila, remember that. Not yours. You made your choice for twenty years. You
love your Canadian culture.*

 I note that my mother has pushed me outside the family
circle. Physically, emotionally, spiritually. I am not permitted to
think of anyone I meet, including her, as family. Therefore, what
are my options: tour guides, research subjects, zoo creatures? *I
made these choices at eight?*

 *Eight, nine, ten. You're still making this choice. You don't want
to live in Brazil. You think Canada is wonderful. You people who
go and destroy other people are wonderful. You and the Americans. And you come here to destroy me too. And I have cancer. If
cancer will not kill me, you will not kill me.*

 Maybe she'd be somebody you'd like to kill. If my mother con-
vinces herself that my unwillingness to smother her with kisses

is a choice between Canada versus Brazil rather than a reflection on her, then it's political, not personal. Never mind that Canadians are not exactly known for going about and destroying other people—it's significant that she sees me as part of this Canadian offensive. Like my father, she uses sickness to avoid unpleasant conversations. Instead, she throws our luggage into a taxi trunk, squeezes into the front passenger side while I crawl into the back and weigh the pros and cons of throwing myself out of the moving vehicle as she speechifies nonstop in Portuguese to the driver until we arrive at her building. Her home. Where she doesn't live most of the time.

My mother's home: clutter, clutter, and more clutter, overlooking quadrant S Bloco J (S indicating the south end of the city, J her particular building complex). Photographs and movie posters, like for *Persuasion* (*Persuasão* in Portuguese), line her walls, and stacks of paper (newspaper, books, loose-leaf sheets) cover every shelf and corner of the two-bedroom condominium—at least I think it's two-bedroom; I can't tell because all the rooms are snowplowed with paper, with only a single bed in the room at the back. Also, Catholic trinkets: miniature crosses, Virgin Mary icons, saint cards, mixed among framed photographs of family members, including the grandmother and aunt I have just met, and a few photos I sent her which she has inserted into frames at least one size too large. The Campos clan celebrates a lot of family occasions together, but this could all be an illusion of film. I count six, not three, TVs.

Worse than a frying pan to the skull, two hangings assail me: one a photograph, one a painting.

The photograph: me in a floppy red hat and red blouse, right before my first book launch. Unpacking my first book, I flash a large, proud smile to the camera. I sent my mother this photograph, as well as a couple of others, before I arrived, so she would know what I look like and feel more at ease. I should be flattered she was pleased, but it unnerves me to discover she had the photo blown up to poster-size—a nearly life-size version of me nailed prominently among portraits of Jesus and the Virgin Mary. The only thing more disconcerting is the massive painting to the right.

The painting: the long-haired woman almost looks like me— large brown eyes, dark eyebrows, curly dark hair, high cheek- bones, long nose. However, a glance at the two smaller figures beside this prominent one dissuades this notion. The big-haired woman, who, I might add, is painted from the chest up naked, her nipples hidden by wispy clouds against a bright blue sky, is my mother, what my mother must have looked like when she was my age. Which is why the painting is painfully anachronis- tic. Beside this woman, who possesses the tight fresh skin and undaunted, blissful expression of a naive twenty-something, are two childish figures, one on each side, like criminals beside Jesus, I immediately think, even though there is nothing explicitly reli- gious or gothic about the picture. The children gaze peacefully ahead, blissful in the clouds with their mother-goddess. A min- iature yellow sun peeks out to the right. I know who these two children are, but I can't bear to confront their vacant faces, espe- cially as they don't look right somehow. What is it? I stare. I keep staring. I move closer to the atrocity.

My mother mistakes my gawking as admiration and beams: *I had the painting commissioned from my friend, a brilliant artist. You like it, no? Isn't it beautiful? It's my favourite painting. I was so clever to commission this, no?*

Clever isn't the word. In a state of numbness, I nod so I can get closer to the children, figure out what's wrong.

It was painted ten years ago. I brought the artist pictures of you and your brother, from when you were small, but asked her to age you to be older, so that we could be together in the painting! But still as mother and children. You see! She wanted to paint a portrait of me, and I said I refuse unless I am painted with my children. Clever, isn't it? May I have permission to tell her you like the painting?

Clever isn't the word. Again, I nod. It's not the poor artist's fault. What else could she possibly do, instructed to age children six or seven years above the original photographs? My face is drawn exactly the same as my mother's, in the same shade of brown (this is wrong because my mother's skin is white, not brown). My brother's slightly darker with a wider, redder mouth. We look like midgets, a freakish concoction of infant and mature features. The portrait a circus. A family circus. Without a father.

I teach a graduate course where we study twentieth-century artworks (literature, film, visual art) focused on three classical myths: Orpheus, Icarus, and Medea. During the Medea section, we examine a painting by American Bernard Safran, known for his *Time* magazine portraits, simply called "Medea," featuring a 1950s mother in pearls staring defiantly at the artist, her two male children holding on to her (or is she holding on to them?) hoping for something: protection, acknowledgement, mercy, love?—it's difficult to tell. Fierce debate always follows: what it expresses about motherhood, American culture, the controversial classical myth. I am tempted to bring in this painting of my mother and her two children, inform my students the title is "Medea," and record the ensuing discussion. In fact, I wonder if part of the reason I've been fascinated by the Medea myth is because my mother reminds me of Medea, sacrificing her two children to hurt her husband and flee the foreign culture that drained her of her magical powers.

Dizzy, sick to my stomach—I ache to break out of her painting, float away with the clouds that must exist beyond the frame. I'm angry she's trapped and distorted us for her own comfort and entertainment. I can't imagine what her friends must think of this travesty. And I now realize that despite having spent the last nine days in hotel surroundings, regardless of my mother's overbearing presence, I was saved from complete immersion in her psyche and world. Now here I am. Freud and Jung would have a field day. I need to look at this space from a psychological point of view, from a writer's distanced point of view, in order to stand it. I need to keep my horror and disgust to a minimum so I can analyze what's going on. Otherwise, I will take a knife to this painting and choke my mother with my bare hands. So, I look at it this way. This apartment is my mother's mind: messy, loud, passionate, illusioned, delusional, nostalgic, Catholic, sentimental, cluttered, aggressive, distressed, unapologetic, unlivable. I have a ticket for a tour of this mind, but at the end of the tour I will escape out the exit.

Removal of couch cushions; it suddenly dawns on me that this is where I will be sleeping: in the living room, on her pull-out couch, underneath the giant photograph of me and the epic painting of the mother goddess and her two bucktoothed children with bad haircuts (am I sporting a South American version of a mullet?) floating in the blue sky, staring at rivers of paper and Virgin Mary ceramics and a large screen television it took my mother five years of diligent saving to afford. I have been head-whacked into the world of black family comedy. I can hear my soon-to-exist nightmares start to giggle, then laugh, then bellow.

Family at Airport upon Arrival in Brasilia

9

alien resurrection

happy easter, felice pasqua

Ellen Ripley: Any questions?
Human hosting an alien: Who are you?
Ellen Ripley: I'm the monster's mother.

SUCCORO, my mother's shrivelled housekeeper, arrives early in the morning (I guess maids don't get holidays off in this country), while I am still lingering uncomfortably in my fold-out bed. The night was, surprisingly, chilly and, not surprisingly, I had a lot of trouble sleeping. My dreams involved volleyballs, frying pans, and book launches. I am looking forward to seeing my grandmother and aunt again though, as I believe they are genuinely happy to meet me and eager to know me better. *Succoro and I have never fought. Not once. She likes me very much,* my mother states proudly. I'm not sure if it's common to fight with your staff here or not.

Succoro serves me eggs and toast and, while I am eating, I present my mother with a York University tote bag full of gifts—mostly York mugs and pins and notebooks, since I didn't really know what to buy her but know she's proud I'm a professor. *I was waiting for Easter,* I explain. She hurries away into the kitchen to open the bag in front of her cleaning lady, yelling out thank-yous for each gift as she uncovers it, while I watch CNN. In Toronto, the SARS epidemic continues, shutting down hospital wings, placing patients and staff under quarantine, and destroying tourism, and the temperature is nine degrees Celsius. Here the temperature is thirty-five. Enough to make your head melt. When my mother reappears, she is wearing the York ring and a costume bracelet of silver and gold beads from a second-hand store in Toronto. I noticed she stopped wearing the scarf I sent two days ago. Maybe this is some sort of truce. But when I politely refuse a Tic Tac, she says to Succoro, *Jesus and Barabbas,* as if I have chosen to crucify a saint instead of refuse a candy.

We cram into my mother's algae-green Gol car—my first experience of my mother behind the wheel—to visit my grandmother. Although she kept boasting in São Paulo about what a wonderful driver she is, how careful and skillful, not five minutes strapped inside the car I know I've been had. She thinks she's careful because she's irritatingly fussy, but she misses very important signs. Even backing into a large parking space with her compact vehicle turns into a long-term project. While sightseeing parts of Brasilia, pointing out where she has worked, where the president and past presidents have stayed, lived, or dined, she jolts, stops, and starts. The reference point of presidents is not unusual here—identifying a place in terms of the president's relationship to it. In Canada, people would find it laughable if we spoke of prime ministers the same way. The city, erected in forty-one months, was built on red desert clay with a population of five hundred thousand in mind. Now five times that many people live in Brasilia. And the city is built on a flat plateau. The flatness of the city is frequently cited as a cause of madness.

When I came to Brasilia in 1965, I fell in love. The urban designer, Lúcio Costa, was a genius. I love our Super Quadras— this translates into "series of boxes." Isn't that wonderful, a whole city built like square boxes, every neighbourhood orderly like every other? We even have a lake. A completely fake lake! They built a dam to divert waters from the river over to a construction site in the middle of the desert. What ingenuity!

As my mother lurches about the city, I have to agree. The city's most stunning architecture, designed by Oscar Niemeyer, is ultra-modern, smooth, sleek, curved, and egg-like, framing the landscape within a science-fiction universe. When you encounter the immensity of the lake, the picturesque trees and flora on the sides of roads, it is very difficult to believe that not a single aspect of the world you have entered is natural to its environment. Everything transported and transplanted. Spliced. Cloned. Only when you double take at a glowing white cube in the middle of a field of grass does the uncanny aspect of the city jolt you: artists built this city according to their dreams. And now the dream is locked: no one is permitted to construct a building that will contrast or contradict the original abstract architectural vision, part of its status as a UNESCO World Heritage site, the first such city to be granted the honour after less than thirty years. There is something extremely comforting in this kind of consistency, order, and wholeness. Lúcio Costa even went so far as to dictate the uniform colour for bus drivers. But there is something frightening about it as well: as if the rage for order was deemed necessary to contain the irrational, brutal, unsatisfied passions of its citizenry.

I'm starting to wonder how much of my mother's psyche is elusive to me because of culture rather than nature. If I learned

```

one thing on a six-week cross-Canada trip I took starting in Victoria, British Columbia, and finishing on Prince Edward Island, it's that landscape and environment are responsible for everything: weather, diet, clothing, industry, economy, and especially personality. If you live among the Rocky Mountains, you can't help but climb them, spend your days looking up, seeking adventure. If you live where you can see for miles without a single obstruction, not a hill or tower or farm, you become a master of patience, of seasonal planning. If you live on an island where the soil is so red it literally stains your skin, no matter where you travel that sand never rubs off and you always feel homesick. São Paolo's commercial hustle and bustle and arts institutions suit my mother's hunger for constant entertainment, endless sensory input to fuel her fantasy life. Brasilia seems to feed her need for order and predictability. But she grew up in Rio de Janeiro, I can't forget this, a city with a reputation for complete disorder and dysfunction and a mess of contradictions; a city of brutal violence on the one hand and the largest dance party in the world on the other, with one of the tallest art deco sculptures of Christ on top of a massive hill, watching over its mansions and apartment complexes and millions living a precarious existence in the *favelas* day and night. The old capital city. My mother's family one of the first to move from one capital to another. One of the first to exchange one set of dreams for another. And proud to do so. When my mother first set foot in this futuristic city raised from dust in the desert, she would have been just a wide-eyed little girl, her own dreams like the new species of plants, just beginning to take root under the sun.

Two main highways vein into the city and out east, west, north, and south to the Super Quadras; each Super Quadra meant to be self-contained, with its own set of stores, restaurants, nightclub, church, park, and school. Lúcio Costa wanted to create a city of "happy families"—no wasting too much time in transit because
```

everything essential would be close by. My mother's apartment building was the first residential structure erected. While I love the modernist architecture of Niemeyer—elusive, stark, clinical, yet still dreamy; many buildings look like spaceships out of *2001* or the Alien series—the Super Quadras, with their grey boxes on top of grey boxes, like giant hives, leave me empty, fascist in construction to my eyes, even after only one day. Lúcio Costa also seems to have designed one adult erotic video store in each neighbourhood—I suppose to deal with any unhappy families.

We will be attending church in my grandmother's Super Quadra, not just because she is the matriarch and as such the unrivalled queen of the Campos family, but because her church is considered the most beautiful in Brasilia outside of the Niemeyer cathedral. The Church of Dom Bosco is named after the Italian saint John Bosco, who in 1883 dreamed the latitudinal and longitudinal coordinates of the new city of God. He documented the dream in his journal. Brasilia was built on those coordinates seventy years later, in the middle of a desert no less. Constructed out of hundreds of panels of bright blue stained glass, rows of which open and tilt diagonally when it is too hot and shut when it rains, light floods into the church, baking us all in a heavenly blue glow. *It's gorgeous, Grandmother,* I say as she escorts me around the inside perimeter on this very bright, blistering day.

It's funny, at once I call her "grandmother"; I have yet to call my mother "mother" even once in front of her while I've been here. I have simply avoided this admittance, though she calls me daughter constantly and refers to herself as my mother to whomever we encounter. Likely it's another thing my mother finds hurtful about my behaviour, although I'm not doing it to hurt her—I don't have the Canadian passive-aggressive gene, I'm not adverse to confrontation when necessary. I just don't *feel* like her daughter. Regardless of similarities in physical characteristics or predisposed likes and dislikes, our healthy appetites and vivid imaginations, our connection doesn't feel natural. I'm a different species. One perhaps invented in a lab, a clone of a daughter that didn't quite progress according to plan, developing mutations or defects like the clones made of Ellen Ripley in *Alien Resurrection. You're not human,* the characters keep reminding her. She knows it's true, but lives like a human nonetheless. Not that I feel like a granddaughter. I don't, but I don't really know what a granddaughter is since my father's mother died giving birth to him and his own father died before I was born. And though I've spent a lot of time with other people's mothers, I haven't spent much time with other people's grandmothers. Therefore, a grandmother is more of an imaginative construct to me and I'm willing to explore its dimensions with this thin, smiling woman with the deep wrinkles and sparkling blue eyes that match the church's stained glass windows. Besides, I'm desperate to be protected among the other members of the family. If it wasn't for meeting them now, I don't think I could survive this trip—I would likely cause irreparable damage if left exclusively to my mother's care for much longer. As I said, I'm not adverse to confrontation when necessary, and without more buffers or interference I fear I will become aggressive and bar teeth in my defence to achieve distance. My mother has even taken to shadowing me to the washroom now, standing outside stall doors while I pee, lecturing me on a variety of subjects from her opinions on Jesus to vegetarianism to cancer treatments to Brazilian beaches. I am grateful for the novelty of new faces and the mandatory silence of a church. Plus, my mother has mentioned that my grandmother despises the portrait painting hanging over her couch, so it's clear my grandmother possesses superior taste and judgment. I might be an alien creature, but I can sniff out who wants blood.

During mass, I sit on a short wooden pew in between my mother and my grandmother, both dressed in baby blue to match the church. My Aunt Victoria and her daughter Elizabeth, who I encounter for the second time as an extremely beautiful, painfully shy young woman, are seated behind us, both in white tops and blue denim pants. All the women here wear airy blouses, the men dress shorts and short-sleeved dress shirts—it's so hot! I wear a simple fire-truck-red one-piece cotton business dress. Nobody cares about exposed shoulders, even on a special mass day. Heat commands all.

Split Screen

I still can't quite believe that it's Easter and I'm attending mass with my mother's side of the family. I can't remember the last time I've been to mass, let alone a holiday mass. After grade eight graduation, I left my Catholic high school for a public one and don't think I've ever attended a mass since. My father never pushed the issue but has since expressed his sadness, on several occasions, that I no longer believe in God. Whereas I express astonishment that someone in his condition still does. Not that we ever made too much of a fuss on holidays. While I've always adored celebrations—any excuses for happiness—as we grew into teenagers my brother and I spent more holidays outside the home at the houses of friends, where we'd be separately treated to sliced ham and roast beef and mashed potatoes and stuffed turkeys and shortbread cookies and pumpkin pies, not our usually holiday fare of take-out pizza. No additional meals: lunches, brunches, day-after breakfasts, or visits to the houses of other family members; these were reserved for real families with real holiday itineraries. No gifts to unwrap. For us, a card from my father, picked out by a homecare worker, in a simple white envelope containing a modest cheque, which we were told we could spend however we liked but were strongly encouraged to save for our education.

Then we'd watch an action flick or comedy in the living room until my father would be transferred back to his bed by a homecare worker eager to end the day. And when I first left home, I remember several years of spending Christmas Eve alone, tipsy on red wine, watching the midnight airing of Alastair Sim's *A Christmas Carol*—a movie I still insist on watching each and every Christmas Eve, no matter where I happen to be. Even the old lady I moved in with after the woman who wanted to adopt me reneged on her offer—a gentle but lonely white woman in her eighties who would count the days per week I'd spend out late because she needed a boarder to help pass the hours, not because she needed the money—would find herself picked up by one of her four sons on Christmas Eve (*I wish I had girls*, she confessed. *Boys will pay your bills for you when you're old, but they don't visit like girls do.*) I offered to work Easter, Mother's Day, Father's Day, New Year's Day, and other holidays at the drugstore to earn time-and-a-half. The only day I didn't like to work was Canada Day—a national party with strangers out on Parliament Hill, dancing to rock concerts and cheering on acrobats tossing and eating fire, open bottles of beer and wine and glow-in-the-dark necklaces and headgear, red maple leafs everywhere; I guess I felt more Canadian than part of a family. Now my usual Easter routine is to either skip the holiday entirely—aside from a handful of chocolate eggs—because it generally falls smack in the middle of end-of-term marking and a trip out to visit Chris's family takes up too much time, or we end up across town eating delectable brisket and scalloped potatoes courtesy of one of my surrogate Jewish mothers.

The priest instructs us to join hands with our neighbours and between pews. The significance of the seating arrangement now hits me as I am forced to hold my mother's and my grandmother's hands, a genetic chain. I must have held my mother's hand as a child, I must have, I tell myself, though this is the first time in at least twenty years. Besides flesh cushioning bone, I feel nothing to my left. No warmth or goosebumps, no sudden flood of memory. I might as well be holding the hand of a stranger on a bus. But my right hand feels at ease, secure, connected. I know already that I am fond of my grandmother, even if I haven't yet figured out how to understand her role as accessory in my mother's disappearance. She is elegant and exudes grace and power. My mother resents this, has told me her father treated my grandmother like a queen, "carrying her everywhere," and that her brother and sister also treat her like a queen and do everything she desires. I gather my mother is baffled by the fact that my grandmother commands much more attention by silence than she does by speech. Her body, though thin, bony, and arthritic, is the stronger of the two, and I am drawn to it like a magnet.

After the service, without hesitation my grandmother takes my arm and directs me to the large wooden cross at the front of the church and the marble statue of the crowned Virgin with baby Jesus to the right of the altar. She, too, is enamoured of art and draws my eye to the fine craftsmanship. My mother is now second fiddle, and I do feel bad for her—I go back and forth on this tidal shore of emotions—it's not easy to know you are not as liked as you hoped, and my mother must feel this intensely within her immediate family circle. Definitely the black sheep, the stain, the unfortunate experiment that went terribly wrong.

The Hotel Blue Tree: a gorgeous red ribbon–shaped five-star hotel, designed in the modernist aesthetic of, of course, Oscar Niemeyer, with geometric lobby tables and chairs and glorious bright blue pools. My mother has invited a troupe of family and friends to meet me at their extravagant Easter brunch buffet. Tomorrow, we are going to stay overnight in the hotel as a special treat.

The smell of chocolate accosts me before we get near the restaurant entrance. Chocolate eggs, chocolate bunnies, chocolate

fountains, chocolate truffles, chocolate cookies, chocolate cen-
trepieces, chocolate trees—yes, chocolate trees the size of adults.
And the buffet boasts rampant hot and cold dishes: omelets,
hard-boiled eggs, sausages, frittatas, pancakes, waffles, cinnamon
buns, croissants, pasta salad, green salad, crab salad, chocolate
cake, cheesecake, pineapples, mangos, watermelon, pears.

And then the people assault begins: twenty-five well-wishers
to congratulate my mother on her daughter's arrival and to check
me out with fanfare like the final float of the Easter parade. I wish
I'd brought one of my hats. Keep calm and carry on. Keep waving. Keep on waving until the end.

Before I have a chance to put down my purse—*in the middle,*
my mother insists, *we must both sit where everyone can see us and
speak to us*—an old professor friend of my mother's—he must be
Áurer César from the card—juts in to inform me that in Brazil
they do not hide eggs or have Easter egg hunts on Easter morning. The chocolate eggs and bunnies are a new thing of the last
twenty years. Could have fooled me. A chocolate bunny at least
five feet tall guards our table.

*I met your mother when she was eighteen and attending the
university. You look exactly like she did then. Exactly.* His wrinkled
eyes sparkle.

I smile because I realize this is intended as a compliment,
that people are attempting to forge connections by saying I share
my mother's nose, dark-brown eyes, writing talent, but it only
reminds me that no one actually knows me here. In fact, I have
my grandmother's nose and eyes, shape not colour. I have my
mother's hair and hand gestures. I notice over the course of the
brunch that the people who I think are the most sincere in trying
to get to know me are those who have not resorted to this kind of
perfunctory comparative statement. I guess I should be thankful people are being kind and leave it at that. Keep on waving.
Though I really wish I had a hat. With a veil.

She was terribly, terribly timid, he continues. Hard to believe. He obviously likes her a lot. When I am about to venture off to the oasis of food, he stops me with a tweed arm. *People want to meet you, not watch you stand in a line. I will bring you food.* So I sit. He doesn't ask what I'd like to eat, but I don't care, I'm not fussy. This buffet isn't about food. Like the chocolate eggs littered on each seat, family and my mother's friends fill out around me. A melody of languages erupts into a translation experiment.

Uncle Wilhelm and Aunt Victoria both speak English. Cousin Elizabeth, although she has taken English lessons and can identify English words and phrases, is much more comfortable talking in French, which she learned when they were stationed in Paris; her father teases that *she learned no English in London, and maybe even forgot Portuguese.* I have no idea if my cousin Guilherme, Elizabeth's brother, can speak French or English, because he doesn't speak to me, only to his fiancée in Portuguese. Everyone is talking over one another, repeating questions in different languages, translating answers back and forth. I'm trying to keep calm and collected and decipher broken English and French as they decipher my foreign tongue. At least we have such delicious food to share—when I can't think of anything to say, or when it's apparent that the person in front of me has no idea what I am saying, I just smile and bite into a pineapple or warm chocolate croissant.

Once everyone has settled somewhat into their seats, plates piled with breakfast goodies, my mother passes around the original photograph of me before my first book launch. Uncle Wilhelm asks me about it, and while others are engaged in their own Portuguese conversations, I am suddenly aware that the group is half-listening to me at all times, like a puppy underneath the table whose little barks attract excessive attention.

What does this title mean, How to Draw Blood from a Stone? he asks, putting down his camera. His voice is boisterous; due to his job, he's a man accustomed to conversation with foreigners. He doesn't speak to me like I'm his niece, but more like I'm an invited dignitary.

Do you have this expression here? I ask my mother.

Yes, yes, she responds, nodding vigorously.

The exact same expression? I query again.

Yes, yes, except here we say tears from a stone.

Now I know these two phrases can't possibly mean the same thing. *It means you can't pay?*

Pay? Pay what? my mother asks.

I explain the implications of the English title to the table.

You see, Priscila has followed in my footsteps, my mother beams.

Only in writing, I say as cheerfully as I can, so it seems more like friendly banter than a correction. *We write very different things.*

Uncle Wilhelm nods, pours me watermelon juice.

We do write very different things. As far as I know, she's never published a book of poetry or a novel, only articles on the internet.

Tell me the plot of your novel, Uncle Wilhelm commands as I indulge in my first *brigadeiro*, a rich dessert made out of chocolate and sweet milk, like fudge. Not my last.

I oblige, outlining the murder mystery aspects of the story and the genesis of "my little nun" narrator.

How does it end?

I can't tell you that. You have to read the book! I counter, and we both laugh, Aunt Victoria tapping affectionately on her husband's hairy forearm.

It ends with the girl dying and then deciding that because there is no judgment there is no forgiveness, my mother intercedes.

Did she really just do that—not only give away what happened to the girl but offer a misguided moral interpretation to boot? Does my mother's rudeness and narcissism know no bounds? I guess this is what family holidays are like for some people, a constant struggle to keep one's cool among the outrageous behaviour and infuriating comments of one's relatives. I've always suspected I've been spared such nonsense by growing up in a fractured family, and now I've been proven right. *No,* I say, unnerved by having to defend my work in front of strangers, *that's not correct.* I hope my voice sounds explanatory, not condescending or angry.

My mother recoils like a snail into her bulky frame. *Then you tell him.*

I take a moment to collect my thoughts into an English explanation that I hope can be easily understood. I am about to speak when—

Art has many interpretations. Some people say the ending is sad, others that it is happy, and they have watched the same movie.

Maybe it has to do with reading in another language. I direct my words to Uncle Wilhelm and Aunt Victoria in an effort to ignore her outburst. *Because—*

Priscila and I have only communicated by email until now, my mother booms over top, turning this way and that so it is clear she is addressing all her guests, *because speaking in person someone can very easily become upset when the language is not exact . . .*

That's the last straw. No more sympathy for this woman who won't even let me speak about my own work to people who have asked me directly about it. Who has misread my novel and doesn't care. Now I regret sending her my books before I arrived. She has projected too many of her own emotions and judgments onto the pages, dismissing or ignoring the actual content. The last page of my first novel is very specific about forgiveness. Not another valid interpretation, this is outright misreading—and careless reading is upsetting, even dangerous. I'm embarrassed, hoping the guests won't think I am being unkind to my mother in arguing with her, that they will appreciate my frustration, but it's hard to tell. They are her friends and colleagues and relations, not mine. And we're supposed to be on "good behaviour" because no one really knows how to behave. This is a warm brunch, but not a comfortable one. I am the prodigal daughter after all, from Canada, who has plopped into their laps like a strange Easter gift. Unwrap with caution.

The ending of the book does not take such an easy view of forgiveness, I say. *One of the virtues of art is complexity.*

Art is not complicated. You might not understand your own book, but I do. My mother looks about her people, smugly sipping her juice and smiling that wide-faced steel-armour smile. She's been waiting for this day her whole life. Waiting patiently for me to unroll the stone.

I'm done waving. Now I really need a hat with a veil. A black hat with a black veil. I realize my mother doesn't want forgiveness. She wants to be resurrected.

After a second (or is it a third?) round of desserts, my grandmother once again pulls gently on my arm. An Easter present. For me. A mink stole, given to her on her birthday in 1975 when she was living in Ottawa, from Dworkin Furs on Rideau Street. *And now it is going back to Canada on my granddaughter!* she exclaims, wrapping the dark-brown and black fur around my shoulders.

I know people get angry about fur. I don't want you to get hurt. So I've made this wine velvet covering, my grandmother explains, extracting the fabric from a second bag.

Secured with snaps, the covering envelops the entire stole, the red unleashing a festive Christmas air. *Now I have two stoles,* I say, thanking her.

This only looks right on someone tall, which is why I barely wore it, and why I did not offer it to Elizabeth. It has been waiting for you.

Everyone is snapping pictures. My digital camera (not yet commonplace) is a great conversation piece with no language barrier; everyone wants to experiment with it and experience the novelty of viewing your photo seconds after taking it. So I oblige for a good twenty minutes, even though I'm boiling under the weight of the stole, ridiculous attire for the desert heat.

As Elizabeth and Guilherme play fashion photographer, grandmother tells the story of her silver anniversary party. They discovered, after the event, that no one had remembered to load film into the camera. Everyone in the family, except my mother's brother, my Uncle Fernando, who wore a suit for the only time in his life and refused to do it a second time, dressed up again several days later for new portraits.

It isn't the same. You can't reproduce it. There aren't enough flowers or other decorations. It isn't the same day, she reports sadly.

I'm sorry I didn't get to meet your husband, I reply. And I mean it.

Enormous and blue, her eyes take me in like a planet with gravitational pull, and as she squeezes my arm I have the urge to lift her up into the sky. *You have a picture. It is 1975, your birthday, and he is holding you.*

Yes, I reply, *yes, I have this picture.* I do have this picture. I remember it now. It never meant anything to me before. It's at my father's place in a box of other old pictures that never meant anything to me, but I'll retrieve this one. That's when I met him, she is telling me. It's all right. I was loved by him. I was a loved granddaughter. Perhaps I am sorely mistaken, but I feel as though my grandmother must have been convinced to try and help my mother take us away from Canada out of love, not out of spite or anger. She seems genuinely regretful to have missed out on our lives, all the photos that exist without her.

As everyone calculates their bills, I am asked, for the third time today, to visit Uncle Wilhelm and Aunt Victoria at their home. I relate this to my mother, but she refuses to alter her plan and says briskly that we cannot. Guilherme, who is apparently a

bit of a vain showboat, and his stereotypical blond fiancée soon-
to-be Air Force wife invite my husband and me to visit them in
Recife the next time we find ourselves in Brazil. *We have beautiful beaches there. Very warm. Lots of good shopping. We say there
is a shopping gene in the family. You must have it too.* I laugh. I
suppose I do. Now I know where it comes from. Now I also know
Guilherme can speak English. The benefits of an Air Force education: flight training, weapons training, and language training.
No wonder my mother is a triple-threat.

Next I am driven about the oddly named artificial Lake Paranoá
and then to the Oscar Niemeyer cathedral, in architectural terms
a hyperboloid structure, designed to mimic hands in prayer, the
white beams (fingers) interspersed with swirls of blue, yellow,
and white stained glass, with a below-street-level entranceway—
a tribute to persecuted Catholics forced to practise their religion
underground. *Because of the glass, only crazy people attend mass
during the day here,* I'm informed, *you could burn alive in the
noon heat.* In front stands a massive statue of the four gospel
writers, where old women sell dried flowers. *These are the only
flowers natural to Brasilia,* my grandmother tells me. *All that was
in Brasilia before was red dust. A dream wrapped in red dust.*
      At the base of the ramp entrance, we are halted. Because it is
Easter and a late-afternoon mass is in progress, tourists are not
permitted entry. Dozens of disappointed foreigners stand squint-
ing behind a rope barrier and two very stern security guards.
This, however, does not deter my grandmother.
      You will see the church, she whispers. *Follow me.*
      Because the elderly are revered in Brazil (if you can live this
long in such a dangerous country, you must have learned a thing
or two), no one interferes as my grandmother walks past the
rope barrier and into the church, very slowly but absently lifting

her head up and down and weaving from side to side, as if she doesn't quite know where she is.

Look at as much as you can. The angels above you are beautiful, and the confessionals, and the shroud, and then come back for me, she instructs, kneeling at one of the pews, pretending to pray. *You have about ten minutes.*

I do as she says, gazing upward into the swirling light at three angels in descending order of size, the smallest on top, attached by cables to the ceiling, as incense fills the room and a dark burly security guard trails me, monitoring my movements through his walkie-talkie. I proceed to the modern confessionals, minimalist wooden containers, confessor on one side, sinner on the other, talking through a hole in the shape of a cross. I have less time with the shroud, which looks like a corn sack but is rumoured to possess the imprint of Jesus—I can't find it and feel silly, like I'm looking for the face of Jesus in an artichoke or grilled-cheese sandwich. In my periphery, my grandmother rises and delicately weaves toward me. Believers kneel, then sit. Communion is about to begin and we have drawn attention, so I take my grandmother's hand and lead her slowly back up the grey ramp to the outside twilight like a real granddaughter would.

Thank you, I say, squeezing her fingers. *You are sneaky, Grandmother.*

Sometimes, she smirks, *this white hair is very powerful.*

To Pátio Brasil shopping plaza, top-floor food courts, which house everything from fish and beans to tacos and beef teriyaki to McDonald's and pizza. Here various friends of my mother's, who were not invited to the brunch, eagerly await us. Each coos about how much my mother loves me and how I should return to Brazil many, many times. Before landing in Brasilia, I decided not to blame the rest of the family or my mother's friends for

her behaviour. I do not refuse love. I did not survive my childhood and other difficult times by refusing love—I've needed to
detect it and accept it from the most unlikely places. Anyone
can love me. My mother, my next-door neighbour, my students,
God. But it's my choice whether or not to return it. Just because I
share blood with someone doesn't mean I share, or should share,
an emotional bond. Too much manipulation and exploitation
justifies itself under the heading "but we're family." As for my
mother's friends, since she doesn't share personal information
with them, I assume they are all colleagues and therefore might
have very different emotional lives and values than my mother.
I should not recoil from them because my mother is repulsive. I
should welcome the opportunity to discover what good qualities
they respond to in my mother.

Your mother was very kind to me after a horrible divorce, one
confessed as soon as she shook my hand. *I am a single mother
and your mother doesn't look down on me,* says another. *If I didn't
have my group of female friends, I would be so lonely; my husband and I separated a few years ago,* admits a third. These lonely
women seek solace in each other, especially in a machismo society where attractiveness and desirability depends on your ability to interest and keep a man. I can't quite tell if they actually
like *her* or what she seems to stand for: a strong career woman
who doesn't need a man, or children for that matter, to fill her
days and give her satisfaction in life. An admirable role, but my
mother doesn't quite fit the bill. Or at the very least, she's pecu-
liar casting.

A woman in her nineties dressed entirely in layers of black lace
and a pearl choker is my mother's favourite aunt, Aunt Maria des
Gracas, whom she calls Aunt Gracinha. I think my mother forgets
that she's said all family should be loved equally and unconditionally, but never mind. My mother is also Aunt Gracinha's favourite
niece. I'm amazed this ancient woman, who sits as quietly and

calmly as a black-cat figurine, lives alone with all her faculties intact. Apparently, my mother spends every Christmas with her. I am about to ask why she doesn't spend Christmas with the rest of the family, but stop myself. Evidently there are tensions that go further and deeper than Easter; no one wants to allude to any of them today. My grandmother, rather than complain that my mother has not yet ordered us food, rises from the table, orders her own—a plate of vegetable rice and a cup of coffee—and carries it back on a heavy tray. She hands the bill to my mother. I love her.

Did I *feel* that correctly? Is it love I'm feeling for my grandmother? Do I even know what that means? Or is it just that I've recognized the aura of someone who has no intention to hurt me—an instinct I've relied on for much of my life. Chris has so much family that family is a word and concept as ordinary as tea or car or book. For me, family is a landscape I am travelling through, staring out the window and taking notes, unsure of what I'll retain when it's all over; attempting to overcome my barrier as a tourist but fearful, no, terrified, of crossing over into unsafe territory and exiting the bus in case I'm robbed. I've never loved a female family member before; but I trust her, implicitly, with my heart. I am confident she will not crush it. Or hold it for ransom.

As I try this new love on for size, she explains some family history:

My father, your great-grandfather, Dr. Custodio Fernandes Góes, was a composer and a professor at the National Conservatory in Rio. Piano and violin and full orchestras. A street is named after him in Ipanema in Rio, where we are from originally—I wish you were going there, but I would worry so much, it is a very dangerous city, but then you could see the streets named after your family members, you could stand outside our old home. My mother was one of his piano students. She was seventeen and he thirty-nine when they married.

I guess she had a few things to teach him, I interject, risking a joke.

My grandmother laughs, her blue eyes twinkling even under the harsh neon lights of the shopping plaza. *She did. My father was a Romantic composer and adored my mother, who was very beautiful. His songs were frequently sung at graduations. When I graduated, I sang my father's songs. Sometimes the lyrics were written by your Great-Uncle Carlos, Custodio Carlos Góes, who wrote poetry and a very famous grammar book. A street is also named after him in Ipanema in Rio. And their cousin Arturo Nones da Silva was also a poet, and yes, he too has a street named after him in Rio. All were Romantics.*

Incredible news! I had no idea there were so many artists, and poets no less, in the family. It makes me hopeful that maybe the bulk of my DNA might be traced outside my lunatic mother. For some inexplicable reason—inexplicable because these dead artists are known only by name—I feel proud. This is a family tradition I don't mind embracing. I set a new impossible goal for myself: I must have a street named after me. I dream that Erinbrook Crescent will one day be renamed Priscila Uppal Crescent.

Can I get any copies of the scores or poetry?

My grandmother puts down her spoon. *Are you interested?*

Of course. I know I can't read the Portuguese, but I would still like to see them. I can read some music. I taught myself as a teenager because I desperately wanted piano lessons, but we couldn't . . .

My grandmother shakes her head in wonder. *No one else is interested in these things. Music doesn't run in the family anymore.*

Poetry should count, I venture.

Yes, of course, you are a poet. You have the music gene! My grandmother looks delighted as she calculates where she's kept the box of all those old papers. I do note, however, that she doesn't consider my mother part of this genetic inheritance. Has my mother expressed no interest in the works of her ancestors? Is this another sore spot between them? Is my mother so fearful of competitions of any kind, even with dead family members, that she has ignored this treasure house of artistic archives? It must not have been easy for her to have aspirations of artistic greatness and to find herself standing in the wings. Is she jealous of my success too? *Your grandfather died three years ago: February 2, 2000,* she adds. I am interested in that too.

One of my mother's friends, sour-looking and frumpy with dark arching eyebrows and jet-black hair in a fuzzy purple sweater and purple lipstick, tells a joke: *A divorced woman finds a bottle one day, rubs it, and a genie pops out. The genie is old and tired, so he offers her only a single wish, not three. That's all he has left.*

Okay, then I want Israel and Palestine to be at peace.

Impossible! the genie cries. I don't have that kind of power. You must pick something else. Something smaller.

Okay, then a man to love me forever.

Let me see that map, the genie replies.

I laugh hard, perhaps inappropriately. What a sense of humour this purple woman must possess to spit out a joke so clearly on target in terms of the evening's crowd. Good for you, lady, I think, as she devours a slice of chocolate cake.

One of the unique things about the Alien series is that each movie is filmed by a different director. In the hands of French director Jean-Pierre Jeunet, the metaphor of the alien assumes psychoanalytic proportions whereby women, in their capacity for motherhood, are monsters. Ellen Ripley, played in every Alien movie by the tough-as-nails Sigourney Weaver, has been cloned to produce a baby alien (she was impregnated as a host human at the end of *Alien 3*, two hundred years previous, and committed suicide so as not to propagate a viscous predator—now there's a truly unselfish mother). The military, using a computer called "Father," plans to use the aliens as weapons of war. This baby alien is a female, a mother, and queen, and Ripley warns them that her alien daughter will end up killing them all. Through the cloning process, Ripley has acquired some of the alien DNA. The other crew members consider her "not human." However, it is the only other main woman character in the film, Call, played by Winona Ryder, who is not human, an android. These two women are outcasts, freaks, monsters. The most powerful scene in the film occurs when Ripley discovers the lab housing the failed cloning experiments, all the different mutated versions of her-self—grotesque bodily dimensions, extra limbs, eyes and teeth peppered about—locked in glass cases. Stunned, she stares at the fleshy remains of her exploited DNA, a ghastly hall of mirrors, and torches the place to the ground. Johner, played by the brusque Ron Perlman, describes the act: *Fuckin' waste of ammo . . . must be a chick thing.*

At the end of my notes on *Alien Resurrection,* I've written: *MORAL: No creature wants two mothers.* I'm not sure I want one. There's a reason stepmothers embody evil in the fairy-tale genre and overbearing mothers are a recurring trope in horror films. The ability to create life harbours the opposite: the ability to kill it. Some women can't resist this urge, as strong as the urge to procreate, to control the product of one's flesh to its end. With-out her children, my mother lost control of a very important area of her life. No longer could she count on affection, attention, admiration, obedience, at a moment's notice. My mother did not plan this life. I must remember that. She didn't know what to do when she was plucked from her romance and dropped into a horror. The heroines of horror films must fight, fight until their very last breath to survive. My mother was not built for fighting, or running, or bloodshed. Every night she moans loudly, like an injured dog, before falling asleep. Is she crying, or praying? I cannot tell. But she seems, like these other lonely women, to miss expressing a maternal largesse. One of the most distress-

ing horror movie images ever has to be Ripley drowning in the
bosom of the Queen Mother alien, mother and daughter hugging and caressing each other. Hungrily. These women too look
at me hungrily, even once they have wiped their faces with nap-
kins. Will their appetite for love ever be satiated?

And I wish someone could explain to me why it is that in
science-fiction movies—think *Alien Resurrection*, think *Gattaca*,
think *Brazil*, think *X-Men*, think *Avatar*, where distant planets
are colonized, where robots are so advanced they can pass as
humans—these revolutionary civilizations can't seem to eradi-
cate simple paralysis, or at least give these military guys an electric wheelchair! I know I'm sensitive to the portrayal of disability
in art because of my father, but doesn't it point to a truly deficient
imagination if plot twists depend on the inability of humans to
design effective prosthetics or mobility aids when they've managed to build elaborate spaceships and project themselves into
new bodily forms?

Nobody asks me about my father. Nobody asks me if I have
children. Has my mother prepped them? I bet she has; either that,
or they're afraid I'll ask them similar questions. No one wants
to be put on the spot. There is blood underneath their eyes and
purses and plates of noodles and fried fish and cans of Coca-Cola.
Streams of blood and anger and lost years no one wants to recall.

Furthermore, maybe my mother fears I'll explain why I don't
have any children. If she asked—I'll bet an entire year's salary
she won't—I'm not sure I would tell her the truth. Better to let
her think that I'm too focused on my career, that I'm waiting
for Chris and me to purchase a house and build a nest egg,
that there's no need to rush in today's world, where a woman of
twenty-eight can accumulate a lifetime of experiences before
settling into domesticity, that I'll change my mind once the biological clock starts ticking a little faster. How to explain to my
mother what is nearly impossible to explain to most friends and

other family members: when I imagine holding a baby of mine, I am overwhelmed by nausea. Always have been. So much so that I took the pill for over a year before I even thought about losing my virginity. I'm just grateful I've managed to find a partner who has as little interest in reproducing as I do. Even if it makes me seem like a monster, let me confess that when I see newborn babies, especially newborns with scrunchy red faces or drooling lips or with spittle on their shirts, I feel disgust. I am a caring and generous person—I frequently put myself out for friends and strangers alike—but I don't have any sentimentality toward motherhood. Ultimately, never mind all the propaganda to the contrary, I think procreation in our society is a selfish act. Millions of unwanted children exist in the world. Why not put your intense motherly pangs to work to give these kids a fighting chance? But I know I'm in the minority here. I've watched dear friends undergo painful and expensive fertility treatments for the opportunity to carry a child. And I've witnessed the sincere satisfactions and intense joys many experience feeding, cuddling, and playing Lego and tea party and Transformers with their children, even unplanned and unexpected children. I frequently offer to throw the baby showers. *That way I don't have to talk to anyone about breast milk or poopy bums or stretched labias.* My friends think I'm funny, but they also know I throw a damn good party. Just don't involve me in baby discussions. Once I nearly passed out when a pregnant friend mentioned she was thinking of saving her placenta and eating it at a later date. I feel woozy now just writing it. *Besides,* I like to tell people, *I have way too many children already at the university. Their parents screw them up and then I help them sort out the mess. My talents lie with this age group—eighteen to twenty-five or -six—when they want to become adults but don't know how. When they want to leave their childhoods behind.* And I do think of them as my "kids." Just kids whose bums I've never wiped.

As we disperse, my mother gushes that the day has been "so emotional, so delightful," then has trouble remembering where she parked her car. It is painfully clear my mother has rarely been the focus of the family, able to set the agenda and command the centre of attention. When I explained our intense Brasilia schedule to Chris, he christened it my "media tour." He also said, *You're your mother's accessory.*

And I am on display. *Look how beautiful. Look how intelligent.* Always mentioning my books, my professorship. To think she has never once asked me how long it took to write my novel or what courses I teach. She desires a picture-perfect mother-daughter weekend without any of the work. Well, I suppose we're celebrating Jesus coming back from the dead. Like Ripley, who when characters exclaim *I thought you were dead,* counters *Yeah, I get that a lot*; she doesn't have much choice, being who she is, whatever combination of human and alien, so she keeps living. My mother and I don't have much choice either. At least I've made the decision not to reproduce. Not to risk birthing monsters. As the British poet Philip Larkin advises in "This Be the Verse," to avoid the cycle of parent-to-child neurosis: "Don't have any kids yourself."

Come to me, my little one, my mother coos, closing her eyes and turning herself about the parking garage like a child playing pin-the-tail-on-the-donkey. Opening her eyes, she steps forward. Astonishingly, her little green Gol car appears. As my head thumps against the roof all the way back to her condominium, I consider how I believe art and magic are meant to facilitate revelations, while my mother believes they are meant to perform miracles. And today, for the most part, her wish has been granted.

My Grandmother Therezinha at the Church of Dom Bosco

10

the myth of
fingerprints

*Warren: It's been long enough that I can't quite remember
that I shouldn't go.*

T HE HOTEL BLUE TREE, as already mentioned, is not
actually blue, but red to symbolize the workers' union.
Oscar Niemeyer, born in 1907 in Rio de Janeiro and
inexplicably still alive and kicking (Oscar will die only years
later in December 2012, days away from his 105th birthday), is
an unapologetic atheist and Marxist. I'm glad that there is such
a prominent, beloved Brazilian who has shunned Catholicism
(and built the famous cathedral!). The hotel neighbours Palácio
da Alvorada (Palace of Dawn), the official residence of the president, and also designed by Niemeyer. In fact, the city of Brasilia
is essentially Niemeyer's artistic DNA. Under the directive of
visionary president Juscelino Kubitschek (a Brazilian equivalent
to American president John F. Kennedy, Kubitschek campaigned
in 1956 on the slogan "50 years of progress in 5" and was hailed

"a poet of public buildings"; there is even a twenty-eight-metre-high statue of him and a memorial museum with a sepulchre for his sacred ashes), he also designed the Brasilia Palace Hotel, the Ministry of Justice, the Ministry of Defence, the Presidential Chapel, the National Congress, the Supreme Federal Tribunal, the National Theatre, the Praça dos Três Poderes (Square of the Three Powers), and more. Inaugurated on the city's birthday, April 21, 2000, all the visual art of the hotel is by Oscar Niemeyer, Japanese-Brazilian abstract painter and sculptor Tomie Ohtake, and her son Ruy Ohtake. I can't get enough of it: large bulbous red chairs, green fluid geometric counters, glowing white globe lights, amoeba-shaped swimming pools. Our hotel room overlooks the gigantic blue pool (no blue trees, but an abundance of blue water), which could hold at least a couple of hundred people in its swirling body, and Lake Paranoá. A towering bouquet of yellow lilies has been delivered to our room and I can smell their sweet fragrance from the balcony. I am feeling a little guilty because my mother, who is the oldest of the siblings, seems to be the worst off financially, and this is the most expensive hotel in Brasilia. So much for Marxism.

Today is the forty-third anniversary of Brasilia and the third of the Hotel Blue Tree. Riders on horseback follow the exact parade route as on the inaugural day of Brasilia in 1960. Brazilians are worried about the current president because he is not as vigilant about his personal security as previous presidents—part of his socialist politics and his self-stylization as Lulu, a man of the people. This lax security is at odds with the heightened security I've experienced in other Brazil venues, where many buildings are guarded by young male soldiers in their late teens or early twenties in green combat uniforms, machine guns strapped across their chests. I am informed that Brazil is considered by South Americans to be a peaceful nation: they fight with themselves, not with others. Like a dysfunctional family.

My mother is wearing her orange outfit again. She looks hideous, like a gigantic papaya, and she knows it. *I dress unfashionably on purpose,* she brags, adjusting her hat. *I will not follow the fashion of others. If I buy something and someone says, that is very stylish, I will not wear it again until it is out of style. And have I told you why I carry such a big purse?*

Because you're neurotic and require endless supplies for your multiple delusions? I shake my head even though she has told me, because her answers change like the weather and I like to gauge my mother's temperature several times per day.

Because no thief wants such a big purse. Thieves want light purses, heavy wallets. They don't want glasses and shoehorns and umbrellas and rubber boots and . . .

Lunch today is with immediate family only at Bargaço, a seafood restaurant specializing in Bahai cuisine with outdoor tables underneath straw umbrellas and thick white braided ropes for an entrance walkway. My family looks like a mix of Brazilian colonizers and European immigrants: Portuguese, Dutch, German, Italian. Blond and brown and black hair; blue and green and grey and brown eyes. Here I meet the infamous Uncle Fernando, who was away for the weekend with his partner's family and their daughter in the Amazon. I dreamt about him the night before—I was christening the TV Tower in honour of my grandmother and the entire family was present, including my unknown Uncle Fernando—and he looks nothing like what I imagined. I pictured him short and wiry, whereas he is large, stocky, and muscular. I have been told he is shy, but this, I soon learn, is far, far from the case. He is not shy; he simply despises chit-chat or socializing. He will only speak when he considers it important; he only listens for the same reason.

The family drama *The Myth of Fingerprints* begins with the main character, Warren, the eldest sibling in a ruptured family, telling his therapist, *I had a dream about my family. . . .* Warren hasn't been home in three years, but has agreed to visit, with his three other siblings and their various lovers, for Thanksgiving. He's not sure why he's going, only that he can't remember why he should stay away. As I sit eating shrimp and sipping coconut juice, I sympathize. I'm no longer sure what I'm doing here, a family tourist. And I appreciate the title of the film, the word "myth" rather than "lie" or "illusion" or "fable." A myth is a story but not a lie, a foundational story believed to be true by a group of people, a community or nation, to give them an understanding of who they are and what their purpose is on earth. It's up to the group to adapt the story over time to suit the new needs and goals of its people; here a family story, the story of fingerprints, what it means to share DNA, to share spaces where fingerprints linger.

Before I finish my appetizer, Uncle Fernando, who has not yet spoken to me directly, has convinced the rest of the family that as a professor I would want to see the university where he teaches. *We'll be quick and I promise to bring her back safe and sound.* I laugh, but soon discover why everyone seemed a little worried. Even by Brazilian standards, my Uncle Fernando drives like a lunatic.

Car Chase

He locks the doors of his little silver car and speeds us along the curved roads of the main highway to the University of Brasilia— not a destination, but a target. The only male in the family not in the air force, my uncle nevertheless proceeds like a military man on the offensive. I have no time to change into suitably defensive attire.

I don't care about you, he begins harshly. He says everything harshly, because English is not a musical language and he is curt and over-enunciates each syllable, hurling his limited vocabulary. He has a buzz haircut, large limbs and large ears and, framed by enormous glasses, telescopic eyes. Wearing a half-sleeve buttoned dress shirt and blue jeans, he looks like a contractor, pen peeking out of his shirt pocket, and I'm nervous he's going to pull out a measuring tape and size me up, but he's already beyond that. He's way ahead of me and my panic, tearing down wall after wall, and only expects me to keep out of his way. *Who are you? I don't care. You are no one to me. I met you in Ottawa, long time ago. I know this car better and longer than you.*

Arrive alive, I say to myself as a mantra, as we whip past dozens of other cars, switching lanes at the blink of an eye. Arrive alive. That's all I can hope for. What am I doing in this car? It's bad enough, as *The Myth of Fingerprints* makes clear, to endure the awkward toasts, stilted conversations, veiled threats, and resentments of family reunion gatherings, but to do so alone—I know I asked Chris to stay home because I wanted no barriers between my mother and me, but no barriers also means no protection, no safety, no tension-relieving laughter or sex—then to trap one's self in a car with an unknown maniac just because he's the brother of your lunatic mother suddenly seems completely absurd, the stuff of bad action films.

I wish I could calm this uncle down, say a magic word and diffuse him of his superhuman energy, engage the breaks and slide safely to the side of the road. Why can't each family come with its own emergency kit? This one would need stomach cramp medication and mouth gags and Tasers. Yes, a Taser would be perfect just about now. I would love to see the look on everyone's faces at the restaurant if I were able to drag my uncle back inside by the scruff of his shirt because he'd been Tasered. Wouldn't that show them I am also a force to be reckoned with?

I want you to tell me about your father. How is he? I think sometimes it would be better if he died. Understand me, if I were like him I would want to die. Understand?

Yes, I understand. My father's quadriplegia is not something many people think they can cope with. And yes, I understand that my uncle has no reason to care for me or wish me well. He, like me, is not after affection but information. Still, I don't know what to tell him. And this will be the very first thing I say to him.

I think of myself as a man. Strong man. Your father is more a man than I am. He's so big. His feet—so big. I am big for a Brazilian, but your father. So big. And happy all the time. I have very fond memories of your father. It has never mattered to me to see you or Amerjit, but your father . . . I would like to see your father again!

As intensely uncomfortable as his driving and harsh manner make me feel, the way he speaks so admirably about my father— something I know is straight from his heart, wherever this man's heart is located—instantly endears him to me. No one else will talk kindly of my father to me; I already sense this. Whether or not they blame him for my mother's estrangement or her hysteria, they won't utter his name or make mention of him for fear his shadow will hang over the proceedings like a ghost. But my uncle obviously cares less for their superstitions. He knew my father when he was happy, when he was a walking, working, running, swimming man. When he was six foot two, lean, muscular, and beaming. And he loved him. Perhaps loves him still.

And I'm reminded of a mother-daughter conversation between Mia, played by Julianne Moore, and Lena, played by the ethereal yet stoic Blythe Danner:

Mia: *There's no point to good memories.*
Lena: *They remind you of who you are, Mia.*
Mia: *No, they remind you of who you were.*

I have no memories of who my father was, so by opening his mouth my uncle opens up a magical cave of the past, a cave my father has kept blocked off. As scared as I am about what's inside the darkness, my greed for treasure is stronger: *Open Sesame!*

He used to tell so many jokes, your father. I'd never met a man who laughed so much. People called him the Indian Bob Hope, but Bob Hope wasn't funny to me. Your father was. When he would finish a swim and rise from the water, he'd still be laughing. He was the biggest man I'd ever seen, and his skin, it glowed and he laughed more. I was sorry to leave Canada. I'm not sure why I went. I went because everyone else was going. I worked construction and I loved it. I love snow. Snowshoeing. Snow shovelling. I loved being cold to the bone. Ooooohh. I loved ice. Ice made by clouds. Brazil is too hot. It's also too big. I'd love to live in a small town. A cold small town. I don't like people.

My father is a war god, I think, a line I will use later in a poem. My Uncle Fernando knows my father is no ordinary man. Neither is my Uncle Fernando. What kind of unearthly figure he might be, though, is still up for debate.

The car screeches into the university parking lot. The locks disengage. Uncle Fernando's door opens. He will not condescend to open mine. The main campus buildings, called the Central Institute of Science, also designed by Oscar Niemeyer, constitute two skinny parallel winding structures, two long hallways shaped into waves.

We call these buildings Minhocão, Giant Worm. Uncle Fernando's disdain is palpable. *Crazy to set up a campus like this. Brazilians are crazy. They only care about cars and carnival. My children are crazy. My daughters try to kill themselves.* He shrugs. *Here, students get a practical education. I teach math. Economics. When I'm lucky, waste management. I love teaching the subject of garbage. I love garbage, more than people. Teaching about garbage is important. Not if the angels are male or female. My chemist colleague is the one who started calling me Fernando Garbage, then Doctor Garbage. I like my name: Doctor Garbage. I wish everyone would call me that.*

Okay, Doctor Garbage. Sounds like a superhero. Ordinary man or trash-seeking missile? He can find a crying baby in a stack of recycled bottles! He can crush villains into square cubes with his bare hands! He can fuel a rocket out of a barrel of banana peels! Ta da! Doctor Garbage is in the dump! Just don't get too close to take a whiff!

In contrast to the majority of Brazilian buildings, which are either colourful or glossy white, these are prison grey—is the idea that students are distracted enough? Sections are splashed with graffiti, and some of the metal doors to the classrooms and labs shut like garages. Few students cross campus today; those who do are lounging about outside, eating, sleeping, and kissing rather than studying. I follow Doctor Garbage, who is walking briskly to I don't know where.

I attempt an answer to his question. *My father is well, considering. He still lives at home. With my brother. He is pleased that we are grown up and have careers. He'll be happier when my brother marries and gives him grandchildren.*

Doctor Garbage keeps up the pace, staring ahead, not once glancing in my direction. He must have another set of eyes on the back of his head. *You look like your mother did when she was young. Mostly. Except your nose. It's big. But it's not our nose.*

We speed past a woman in an "I fucked your boyfriend" T-shirt. *They'll wear anything English. They don't even know what it means*, he spits. *I hate English. It's a dumb language. Just a famous language. Why should everyone speak English to make money? I refuse to speak to my students in English. The only reason I am speaking in English to you is because it's your first language. But I hate your first language. Understand? Here, this is my office.*

Metal garage door. Shut tight. He doesn't lift it, open it, offer to let me peek inside. Am I supposed to stand here until I give the correct answer to a riddle? I don't know how to pass this test, and

I'm sure Doctor Garbage is testing me. The situation unnerves me so much that I am tempted to laugh but bite my tongue, although I am fairly sure now that with a cast of characters like these my tale must be a comedy not a tragedy.

Can I take a picture?

Sure, he says and steps out of my way.

No, of you.

Eyeing me suspiciously at first, he waves me over to a green patch beside the grey columns and straightens up, posing stiffly but with determination; I quickly take the shot. I have already been told he refuses to have his picture taken. I wonder why he's letting me take it so easily. He's not the sort to do so out of politeness. Then it hits me:

I will send this to my father.

My uncle Fernando smiles. When he smiles, I feel like I've been let in on an important secret. That I'm not a total waste of groceries.

You must have come here to learn about yourself. So, let me tell you two things you need to know about yourself: one, you will die of cancer; two, you will go crazy.

Faced with my death sentence and the deterioration of my mental faculties, I can't help it, I laugh.

You see, you laugh too much. My uncle makes only deliberate motions; he unbuttons his shirt to reveal three nasty surgery scars. *Cancer. Cancer. Cancer. Until six years ago I used to smoke five packs a day and a pipe and run ten kilometres per day. Now I only run. No more cigarettes. We have strong hearts in this family. Your heart will never attack itself. But cancer will come for you. It will find you eventually. You should know this.*

While I'm charmed by the image of our hearts refusing to attack, I can't say I'm convinced by his words. Our hearts are damaged. Some of them don't seem strong at all. Isn't that where the second dictum comes in?

But the women in the family live a very long time. Too long. They go crazy and drive everyone around them crazy. The men all die at fifty or sixty. None of them can learn languages. Only the women. I've always wanted to learn more languages, but I'm a man, so there's nothing I can do about it. You're a woman, so you'll live until you're ninety and then you'll die of cancer, but you'll be so crazy by then you won't care.

My uncle continues to smile as he relays these unhappy predictions, so I release another chuckle. It seems everyone in this family smiles or laughs at inappropriate moments, so I might as well give in to my genetic heritage. Plus, it's a lot of information to take in; it's like he keeps throwing jellybeans at me and I'm trying to snatch them from the air and store them in my pockets but I'm running out of pockets.

Here, look at this. He extracts a card from his wallet, larger than a business card but smaller than a photo, like a logo sticker for a car or an iron-on patch for a backpack. A cartoon. A cartoon character I know well: Daffy Duck. An image I recognize: Daffy Duck in hobo mode, red kerchief sack tied to a long wooden branch. But this Daffy's heart is outside his body, floating behind as he charges off to his adventures. And one of his wings is actually flipping the viewer off. Across his chest, like a garish tattoo, in vulgar English is written: *Fuck off!*

Patinho. Small duck. Peregrino. Traveller. Pilgrim. Alone. Warner Brothers would shit their pants. Roll over in the grave and shit their pants again. Though I feel a tide of laughter welling up inside me, I crush it down with shock. *He thinks only with his eyes, not with his heart. His heart is not inside his body.* I nod, very slowly; this is a lesson in a subject I am not familiar with so I must pay close attention. *This is me. I wish I had no heart, no family, no children. I wish to be left alone, you understand? This image is on my airplane—yes, I am not in the Air Force but I know how to fly and I own an airplane so I can take pictures of landfills. I*

*jump out of airplanes not for fun, you understand, not for fun, that
would be stupid, or for war, which is also stupid, but only to take
photographs of garbage. This is on my airplane, my motorcycles,
my skydiving jackets, everything. This is me, you understand? I
don't know what you are but I am a Peregrino.*

Suddenly, I'm jealous of my uncle's surety and his pictorial
avatar. It's rather wonderful, I say to myself, and then the laughter erupts, quickly but violently. Before I can pocket the card, it
disappears again in my uncle's wallet.

You see, you laugh too much, he repeats, concluding our tour.
*But you listen. I can see that. People who talk all the time under-
stand nothing.*

I laugh again, and add: *I quite agree.*

He laughs too. We have an understanding about whom we
speak.

On the way back to the restaurant, for a man who could not care
less if he ever saw me again, he offers up soliloquy after soliloquy just as quickly as he pops mint after mint to deal with his
nicotine cravings, which have not subsided in six years: *I am frequently mistaken for Anglo-Saxon because I have blue eyes. Victoria has green eyes. Wilhelm's mother is black and he really wanted
a dark child with green eyes. No luck. Wilhelm and I have gone
parachuting and deep-sea diving. My daughters are crazy. My wife
too. No luck. We do things because they are there to do. I went to
the Amazon and thought, I need a wife. So I got myself a wife. And
another baby girl. This girl was born white and then turned black
later on. I would trade all my girls for boys. Since my father died,
I am the only male in the family. This is very lonely. My wife laughs
too much. Like you. I have two daughters in Rio. One is a lawyer;
she's the one who keeps trying to kill herself. I don't know what the
other one does except hate me. Their mother hates me. The lawyer
wants a father so bad she's willing to pretend I'm a good father. I'm*

not. I'm a good father when children are small, very small, play-ing with blocks and balls, after that I'm useless. I'd rather be alone with my garbage. Your mother doesn't want you to visit Wilhelm and Victoria's house because she's jealous. But your grandmother insists. She's also crazy, but we all do everything your grandmother insists. Don't ask me why. We do things because they are there to do. Even your mother, who is the craziest of them all, will not go against our mother. So that's where we're going next. Look into your cousin Elizabeth's eyes and you'll see she's also crazy. Walter is her first boyfriend. Elizabeth is so nervous that she could never look at a boy, and now she has a first boyfriend at twenty-seven. She'll marry him and she won't know why. We do things because they are there to do. Your grandmother prays too much. She goes to church every day in the morning and sometimes even in the afternoon. She prays for things she did and then she prays for things she didn't do. She keeps photographs of your mother on her prayer table. I think she prays to apologize for your mother most of all. She thinks she'll have to answer to God one day about your mother. There's no such thing as God, but Brazilians are crazy. They'll believe in anything, the crazier the better. They'd rather be on their knees all morning instead of living. Crazy. But nothing can be done about your mother. She fights all the time with our mother. She thinks you need to wear a steel dress to survive in this world. She won't negotiate. She is always right, everyone else is always wrong. She's always in São Paulo. Then she comes back for two or three weeks, fights with everyone and leaves again. Your mother lives to fight, then realizes she is a coward and a weakling, and so she runs away. Then she forgets she is a coward and a weakling, and she returns to do it all over again. She couldn't face your father after he became a cripple. His sickness let out all her crazy. At once. She's never been able to put it back inside. Now she unleashes her crazy everywhere. At everyone. She's so used to being crazy she doesn't think anyone else is real. She fights with us to fight herself, you understand? I'm sure she's said some stupid things to you, very stupid, very crazy. She's not saying them to you, she's saying them to herself. You don't exist. Not for years. None of us exist anymore. She's happier in São Paulo. But I don't know if your mother is happy. I don't think so, but I don't know anything important about your mother at all. Only that she's the craziest of them all. She takes the cake. You'll go crazy too, in your own way, but I wouldn't plan on outdoing your mother, that would be too high a bar for you to reach. Goodbye! Goodbye!

Uncle Fernando/Doctor Garbage yells goodbye to all the drivers he cuts off on the highway until we're back at the restaurant parking lot. Before we get out of the car, staring out the windshield at the huge Brazilian sky, my uncle sighs, then brightens up: *I have no souvenir to give you. What will you take back of Brazil? I don't know. I don't care. But you care. You came to learn. Your mother does not want to learn anything, you understand? Remember she is a coward. Since you like to laugh, I will teach you a joke as a souvenir to take back with you. This is a Brazilian joke, you understand?*

God was creating the Earth and the angel Gabriel was invited to watch. God looked at Japan: Here some earthquakes! Then he looked at Africa: Here I will put the biggest desert on the planet and a host of diseases! He looked at North America: Here go some tornados and hurricanes. Then he looked at Brazil: Here I will put beautiful beaches, the biggest and most fertile lands of the Earth, bright sunshine and a big blue sky. Gabriel objected: But God, this place can't be that good. God replied: Wait until the sixth day, Gabriel, you will see the kind of people I will put here. Ha!

Once again, my uncle jumps out of his side of the silver vehicle and makes no motion toward mine. Hesitantly, I test my land legs, and we walk down the pathway uncle and niece: an uncle with a lead foot and a nervous condition that made him lose all his teeth but who thinks all the women are crazy, and a niece who is going to go lie down under a grotesque painting of herself tonight and write down every single word she can remember.

Before we cross the threshold, I risk a question: *So, do you think I'm already crazy?*

Like a real uncle, Fernando soothingly pats my arm. *Not yet. Take your time.*

The deal with my psyche is sealed.

True to Uncle Fernando's word, and regardless of my mother's objections, Grandmother's wishes are the family's command and our next stop is Uncle Wilhelm and Aunt Victoria's home on Embassy Row, across from Lake Paranoá in the western top of the city. Two frowning men with bullet belts and machine guns stand guard outside the house gates in the heat. Now I understand what it means to be head of the Brazilian Air Force. You are supplied with a gorgeous solar-heated house and spacious backyard with an outdoor pool, a high salary, the respect of your family members, and bodyguards. The small mansion boasts several balconies and outdoor lounging and eating areas perfect for a hot climate, as well as lush avocado and banana trees.

And monkeys for free, Uncle Wilhelm jokes, as we watch two Capuchin swing through the backyard. *Everyone who buys land in Brasilia must keep at least fifty percent green. This is law.* Aunt Victoria claims she'd like an apartment better—less work since Wilhelm is at the office all day and Elizabeth and Guilherme live in their other home in Recife in the north of Brazil. I'm not sure what "work" Victoria is referring to, since we've been greeted by a team of servants whisking away our coats and shoes and pouring out tea, never once uttering a single word. The house, it probably goes without saying, is spotless; the furniture tastefully modern; the visual art all watercolours of Brazilian beaches and architecture in matching frames.

At her sister's home, whenever I am asked a question, even if my mother is across the room, she quickly waddles over to answer it for me—amazingly, she does this even when she hasn't heard the question. Fear drips off her like sweat. It's evident my mother does not blend into the family unit—she is the outcast, and my rejection of her might be the last nail in her coffin. Or, more accurately, nail in her mouth. No one need listen to my mother if I don't need her as an intermediary.

She lives in a house. No, I live in an apartment.

She lives with a man named Chris who is a newspaper editor. No, he's a freelance editor for literary publishers. And a poet. And he's training to be an archivist.

She swims all the time. Actually, I'm not an active swimmer. I take springboard and tower-diving lessons. I'm afraid of heights and figured the lessons would help me get over my fears. They didn't, but I can block the fear out long enough to get up on my tippy-toes and fall backward from the three-metre tower or to swan dive headfirst from the five-metre tower—there's nothing quite like the rush of slicing through water in a perfect line, you don't even feel wet.

Victoria peppers me with questions about my neighbour-hood, the university where I teach, what I like to eat, where I have travelled. She's collected more information about me in fifteen minutes than my mother has managed to extract in over ten days. Victoria even asks me what I like to read.

I read the last pages of a book first to see if I will enjoy the end-ing. I don't want to read unhappy books, my mother says, clapping her hands decisively. Aunt Victoria chuckles. I've already noticed that Aunt Victoria chuckles a lot. And keeps her distance from my mother. Doctor Garbage is nowhere to be seen.

My mother's reading practices are more in line with Harle-quin Romance addicts, not literary enthusiasts. *That's no way to choose a book,* I say, losing my battle to curb my growing impatience.

My mother smirks. *Oh yes,* she says, *it's a good thing I do. I don't care that you don't like it.*

Any writer would say this.

I don't care.

I try to process the lessons Uncle Fernando has taught me. I don't exist. She's fighting to fight with herself. She's a coward and cannot face real people. But I can't help defending my vocation.

Then you don't care about art. I turn to Aunt Victoria. *Please,* I say with a chuckle, *do not read the last page of my novel first. Do not be like my . . . like her.*

And it hits me, like an avocado falling off a tree and striking me on the head: *I hate my mother. I hate her.* I've hated her for most of my life because she abandoned us, which I always took to mean she didn't care what happened to us. But I was willing to leave most of that hatred in the past and shake hands with the woman who exists today. And I am only too painfully aware that she does exist. However, the woman who exists today is just as hateful, if not more so, than the woman of the past. And she could still not care less about me, or my brother, or my father for that matter—it's just now she doesn't care for different reasons. If she cared, she'd have to face the ugliness of who she is. The wasted talents. The wasted time. The wasted opportunities. Her wasted life. My mother surrounds herself with movies and artworks and music so she never has to look inside her own heart. Discover if it's still beating.

I'll lend my copy to you, my mother blurts out before bustling off to the other side of the room. *But I don't think you'll like it.*

I'm glad she's escaped to the other side of the house, because now that I've admitted the truth to myself, my unfettered hatred is growing at an astonishing rate. I'm worried I will lose control of my emotions, even in these elegant surroundings, and stick out my foot to trip her, or pull her hair, or punch her smack in the gut. I'd love for this story to turn slapstick. For a pie to land on her face. For a monkey to jump on her back.

Elizabeth arrives, sheepish as ever, joining her mother and father and our grandmother on the couch as Uncle Wilhelm explains the Brazilian mania for soap operas, which air in the evenings, only four months each and then change again. Plot updates are published in the daily newspapers with weekly updates offered in weekend editions. Friends frequently make plans for "after soap opera." If a soap opera is overly melodramatic (I'm not sure how they define this) or poorly researched or contains extremely weak dialogue, they label it a "Mexican soap opera." *Brazilians are leaders in the soap opera business,* he jokes. *Also in the soccer business, the model business, and the plastic surgery business.* Elizabeth confirms that most young girls dream of growing up to become models, young boys soccer stars. Plastic surgery trends rotate with fashion seasons—a woman might sign up for breast reduction one year, breast augmentation the next. There is no stigma for plastic surgery, only the barrier of money. Liposuction is not an uncommon solution to holiday bingeing.

I went to the Alanis Morissette concert last year, Elizabeth offers. *I'm a big fan. Are you?*

Yes, I'm a big fan, I reply with amusement. All over the world, no matter what island you land on or backwater town you find, no matter how little English people possess, Canadians will always run into Bryan Adams and Alanis Morissette. Both from Ottawa, like me. But my connection to Alanis runs deeper. *Alanis was one of my best friends when I was in grade seven and eight. We went to the same Catholic school.* Elizabeth looks so mesmerized by this coincidence, I consider elaborating—how I would spend days at her house dancing and swimming while she sang; how, like silly girls, we decided to wear dollar-store rings and "get married"; and how her mother, one of my surrogates, kept trying to coax my father into writing a book about his life which she was convinced would end up a best-seller and turn our financial circumstances around—but decide my mother might misinterpret my story as name-dropping so I leave it at that.

Do you go to concerts a lot?

No. Not a lot. I'm a little nervous in large groups, Elizabeth admits, and I hear Doctor Garbage whispering in my ear, *Look at her eyes, she's crazy, like all the women, except Victoria. Victoria is the one exception. She missed the crazy. How you say, fluke?*

Do you go to the movies a lot?

No. Not a lot, mother and daughter reply in unison. *Once a week,* Aunt Victoria clarifies. *Not too much.* Everything is relative. In every sense of the word.

And then Uncle Fernando actually appears, a pile of ripe yellow bananas like a large child in his arms; he has taken them from the trees outside. *You can have a lot of money, but never too much. A lot of happiness, but never too much.*

Are you tired, Grandmother? I ask, since she's remained silent for most of this visit, fiddling with her house keys like beads on a rosary.

She's just dying! Uncle Fernando booms. *You're so old, die already, Mamma!*

My grandmother shakes her head at the insolence of her little boy. Aunt Victoria and Elizabeth giggle. Uncle Fernando delivers the bananas out to his car.

I wonder where things went wrong for the Campos family. Uncle Fernando has two estranged children. How is it my grandmother, in a land that valorizes mothers and families above all else, except Jesus—although here the Virgin is worshipped far more than Jesus or the disciples—has managed to produce two out of three offspring who have had no contact with their children, her grandchildren, for decades? No wonder she fawns over Guilherme and Elizabeth—what other option does she have?

I will answer the question that is on everyone's mind, Uncle Wilhelm announces. Oh shit, I think. Because the question on my mind is how I'm going to be able to withstand even another minute in my mother's presence. How I'm going to be able to stop myself from choking her fat face in the middle of the night. Standing up as straight as a military officer, he clarifies: *Yes, we can repeat!*

Good—I love second helpings. And thirds. No wonder family occasions always include lots of food. The ultimate distraction. We can stuff our faces rather than empty our hearts and minds of all the resentments and unhappiness. We can get through the next few hours with sugar and fat and passing dishes and licking spoons. So this is what it means to belong to a family that celebrates holidays together. Pile plate upon plate and we might all forget just how hungry we are for acceptance, for attention, for support, for love.

My mother's mental flashlight is set on me until we finish two helpings of coconut cake and pineapple jelly and can return to the mother-daughter retreat mirage of the Hotel Blue Tree. But before we do, Doctor Garbage slips the tabs from the four beers he's downed in an hour and a half into my hand, shrugging when I ask him what he wants me to do with them, and insists on taking a photograph of all the Campos women. *The only sure way of knowing how crazy you are,* he whispers while I explain how to use my digital camera, *is to have a daughter of your own. If you fight all the time, you'll learn how crazy you are.* Another good reason not to reproduce, to add to my ever-growing list. Check.

Winking at us crowded together, arms wrapped around each other, on the couch—Elizabeth, Victoria, Grandmother, me, and my mother, who refuses to sit anywhere except beside me—Uncle Fernando smirks gleefully, as if to say, *Wait until the sixth day, Gabriel, you will see the kind of people I will put here. Ha!*

Oh, Uncle Fernando, it's one of my favourite photographs of the trip. I'm smiling right back at you.

After a swim in the glittering pools of the hotel, I ask my mother if she'd like to take a walk with me on the grounds. *Since this space is so beautiful and we are only here for one night.* All I know now is that I will probably never like my mother, I might even hate her for the rest of my life, but I suppose I would like to take a stab at that grand cliché of the family-movie genre: making peace.

My words please her and we stroll for a good hour, in almost pleasant silence, watching the other guests swim and read and play cards under the garden lights.

Either you love someone or you don't, she finally risks, *it's immediate.*

So my mother knows I don't love her. That can't be easy for her to face. *I think love needs time to develop,* I reply, as gently as possible.

Some people don't have time. Time is taken away from them. Blood ties are everything in life.

Not all families are the same.

Families are generic, have laws. You are the mother. You are the father. She points to a couple lounging on bright red towels as their children wrestle with their floatation devices.

We were never such a family. *There are different kinds of families.*

You liked Soares right away. Me too.

But sometimes I like people right away and they turn out not to be nice people.

Almost pleasant silence. And would you believe we actually witnessed a shooting star? Neither of us spoke of wishes. Hidden messages crouch in our silence. Wounds. Threats. Regrets. Unrequited love.

As I change for bed, my mother places a pale-green plastic jewellery box on my pillow, and disappears. When you open the lid, a ballerina spins to Tchaikovsky's *Swan Lake*. A child's jewellery box. Did she go out and buy this before I arrived, or has she been saving this gift for years? Did I once ask for such a jewellery box? Did she own a similar one as a little girl?

Your father likes to tell me that it's only a mother who's allowed to love that way, unconditionally, the matriarch Lena says. But don't we all love conditionally, even if we haven't been able to articulate what those conditions actually are? I picture my mother slouched over the car wheel, angry because that is her primary physical response to the void inside that can't be fulfilled, not by a mother's love or a daughter's love, not by anything but her dead dreams, and I'm positive we all love each other conditionally.

There have been moments on this trip when I've also wondered about my mother's medications, whether they might be partly responsible for her erratic mood swings. But I don't think so. As Doctor Garbage also confessed on our high-speed car chase with the past: *Your mother is a coward. So am I. Some of us are not prepared to deal with life. Not when bad things happen. Better to run away. It was good my father died before my mother. He was not as strong and he was afraid she would die first. My mother is crazy, but she's also strong. Strong people are always crazy. You seem very strong. Most people don't know why you've come. Your mother is afraid of why you've come; the others are just confused. They think you seem nice, have a nice life in Canada, they know your mother is crazy, why would Priscila want to spend time with her? But I say, Priscila wants to know about herself.*

This, to me, is the myth of fingerprints. *I already am who I am*, I said. Firmly.

*Yes, I can see that. It's your mother that is not a full person.
I have no idea what goes on in her head. But she doesn't live here.
She doesn't live anywhere you can visit, you understand?*

Yes, I understand. She doesn't live in Brazil. Maybe that's why
it's taken me so long to discover her whereabouts; I've always
known, deep down, that my mother stopped living the day she
walked out on us. The best part of her died that day. It's what
an abandoned child is probably desperate to believe, so I've
attempted to suppress the thought, but it's true, fundamentally
true: my mother's life, like lost luggage, went astray, with very little hope of recovery. My voice message probably shocked her to
the core. She must want something, something huge, she must
have thought. Maybe money, maybe revenge, maybe the secret
to why she's so screwed up (I believe my mother would have
been infinitely happier if I'd arrived a washed-up heroin addict
or gambling fiend or an abused wife—then her absence would
have been more meaningful. If your daughter became a well-
adjusted, kind, and successful woman without your influence,
what does that say about your usefulness?). My pound of flesh is
different than what she expected. Knife and scales concealed in
my computer. *I'm here for the full story. I want to see who she is.*

You won't be happy.

I don't expect to be.

Your mother expected to be.

The full story. Because the final pages of the novel are torn out
(used by the father as kindling), Mia's childhood friend Cezanne
must recount the ending of the fictional novel *The Scream of the
Rabbits*. The main character of the novel has a memory of his
mother, not a grand memory, just a simple, unshakable memory
of her touching his back. *He couldn't understand why some memories were so vivid like a painting and others were as though they
hadn't even happened.* I have no idea what memories my mother
has of me as a child, and how these will now forever be affected

by my visit here. My presence might have ruined them all. My presence might escalate her growing madness. I wanted, on this trip, to be a detective, but to my mother I am likely a destroyer. A saboteur of memories.

According to Cezanne, you can improve your memory by standing on your head twice a day for two minutes. I consider this. It's horrifying for me to think that, as gapped and faulty and unreliable as it is, I am most likely the one in the family with the best memory. I decide to try.

I choose the wall that separates the washroom from the bedroom, put down my pillow, bend my chin to my neck, and roll up. Blood rushes to my forehead. I'm dizzy, but lean my back and legs against the wall. Remember. Remember. A ballerina in a jewellery box?

Two minutes. Five. Ten. I remember only the frustration of being inflexible in gymnastics class.

My mother's gift to me was accepting me to come; my gift to her now is staying. She can, at least, save face that I did not bolt and catch an early flight home. I already am who I am. A fellow writer once told me that under "occupation" on custom forms she writes "observer." A fitting title. I'm an observer, not a judge. I might hate her, but she's still my subject. And I still have a few things left to learn.

When my mother returns, she smiles widely, red lipstick still flush and bright on her bedtime lips, *I ran away. Did you notice?*

She doesn't mention the jewellery box, as if the hotel staff left me an apple for breakfast or a notecard of tomorrow's temperature.

Uncle Fernando at the University of Brasilia

11

the purple
rose of cairo

*Man (at the cinema): The real ones want their lives fiction
and the fictional ones want their lives real.*

I'M NERVOUS about the flight home. And about my mother.
The time in Brasilia has zapped her powers somehow. Bul-
wark armour exposed, she's sinking. The weight of the past
slowing down her movements like pounds of extra fat. Better to
hold on to an imaginary person rather than me. She knows I'm
not her life preserver.

Today, I can't get *The Purple Rose of Cairo* out of my head.
Unlike the majority of movie lovers I know, I'm not a Woody
Allen fan. I find the bulk of his characters unlikable, shallow,
uninteresting people who orchestrate their own misery by caring
so little about anything real, who talk and talk and talk and talk
and say nothing of interest. In *The Purple Rose of Cairo*, a work of
cinematic genius, Allen's brilliance is to deliberately fashion his
shallow characters into two-dimensional stock characters from

film, and to centre the plot around a character whose escape
from reality is her actual quest. Its self-reflexive subject matter
explores why we need movies to counter reality, why we project ourselves into the movies we watch. It also explores the costs
of projection. Unlike any other Allen film, I can watch this one
over and over again. And my heart always goes out to Cecilia,
played by the fragile blond flower Mia Farrow.

In the movie, which is set during the Great Depression, Cecilia is the abused wife of a deadbeat husband. Her only happiness, and her only coping mechanism, is watching escapist films
to forget her troubles. Jeff Daniels plays Tom Baxter (and the
actor who plays Tom Baxter, Gil Shepherd) in the movie-within-
a-movie, *The Purple Rose of Cairo*, which Cecilia goes to see
alone in the theatre again and again. The character Tom Baxter, noticing the same woman in the audience night after night,
finally addresses Cecilia from inside the screen and then physically leaves the film reel, stepping into "the real world" where he
desires to *live and be free to make my own choices*. Of course, he
soon discovers how few choices actually exist in the real world,
and how ill-equipped he is to fend for himself, even with the
adoring Cecilia on his side. For Cecilia, escorting Tom Baxter
about her city and then joining him for a night on the town in
the fictional black-and-white screen world constitutes a dream-
come-true welcome escape from her dreary life with an ungrateful, freeloading, boorish husband in an impoverished society.
My favourite line in the film is delivered by Cecilia: *I just met a
wonderful new man. He's fictional, but you can't have everything.*
No, you can't have everything. But even Cecilia, faced with the
choice of living inside the screen with the character Tom Baxter or in the physical reality of 1930s United States, eventually
chooses her home (admittedly, she is tricked by Gil Shepherd
into believing he will whisk her away to Hollywood). *No matter
how tempted I am,* she explains, *I have to choose the real world.*

Why won't my mother choose the real world? Does she suspect I am tricking her?

One of the paradoxes of art is how we can turn to it for solutions to our problems. We believe we can learn from the mistakes the characters make. We can recognize the parallels between the fictional plot and the arcs of our own lives. We can even explore our own relationships, test our emotional limits within a safe environment, draw conclusions, and return again at a later date for further discovery. A book can be reread countless times. A movie can be paused, rewound, reviewed again. And yet, art is not life, and it is sometimes painfully ill-equipped to prepare us for actual life. We can watch a character make the same wrong decision we're about to make, we can understand the terrible repercussions of that decision, we can identify the exact cause-and-effect relationship and chart out the line from beginning to end, but how is it we so rarely as a species put that learning into practice? Is art actually useful, or just a sophisticated distraction? Why are we so desperate to make our own mistakes? And why, after a couple of hours, don't they fade to black?

Today as we drive about the city—the Dream City of Juscelino Kubitschek, the Cidade de Fe or city of faith, which he hoped would gloriously reflect God's city—I think of two things: one, the famous photograph of him weeping inside the cathedral during the city's inauguration, overwhelmed by his dream transformed into reality; and two, how when I was researching the history of Brasilia, I came across a professor who talked about how the poor workers whose hands and sweat actually built the dream—thousands of workers in three and a half years, who wanted to remain in the city they had just built—were told to get on buses in the middle of the night. Those who refused were shot on the spot. Those who did were driven to the middle of nowhere and told never to return. This city of faith, like all cities, betrayed its people. Its soil, like all earthly soil, is not magical, but steeped in blood.

We make a quick stop at a shopping mall—I suppose this family does possess a shopping gene—as my mother assumes I'd like to purchase some final souvenirs. I stroll about aimlessly, my barely conscious mother following diligently behind me like an exhausted security guard, fondling a scarf here and stacks of postcards there. I buy Chris a T-shirt of Brasilia with cartoon sketches of the city's architectural highlights. My mother doesn't offer to pay, and I'm relieved. Briefly, I toy with buying my father a gift, but experience has taught me he doesn't want gifts. What he wants is for me to visit him more often. What he wants is for me to forgive him for those awful teenage years that drove me out of our house. What I want is for him to say he's proud of me. What I want is for him to read one of my books. Not this one—I would never put him through such torture—but one of them. As I unload the last of my Brazilian currency, my mother paces outside the souvenir shop, fists limp at her sides like a washed-up boxer. Uncle Fernando says she likes to fight, but I don't quite believe him. She fights because she doesn't know how else to get attention. And she wants attention. Because attention might lead to love. My mother is sick for love. Like Cecilia, she might even be dying for lack of love.

Back at the condominium, my mother orders me to pack. *Take your time,* she says in the same tone of voice my uncle used when instructing me on how to go crazy. She obviously wants some time to herself. Fair enough. While she retreats to her bedroom, I take the opportunity to snap photographs of her apartment—evidence or research, I'm not entirely sure which—from her clothes drying in the kitchen to her pyramids of paper to her pitiful prayer table. Several of the hideous painting. I feel guilty for this subterfuge—I know my mother wouldn't approve—but

I justify the betrayal this way: no one will believe me otherwise. Even with detailed journal notes. Some things need to be seen for full effect. This is the power of a genre like film.

I pack. Taking my time. Folding each shirt. Rolling each dress. Isolating my damp swimsuit in a plastic bag. Wrapping my jewellery box inside a sweater. (I have not asked her about the ballerina as I'm wary to unleash further sadness.)

But after twenty years apart and barely two weeks together, there is still too much time. I risk typing my journal notes of the last few days—I've been neglecting my journal due to all the family activities—but before I do, I decide to make another one of my lists, this time about what I think has been passed down to me from my direct ancestors, as I want to be clear on who we are.

Ten Things I Have Inherited From the Campos Clan

1. Wild hand gestures
2. The artistic gene
3. The shopping gene
4. The gene responsible for my grandmother and me wearing nylons under skirts and pants no matter how hot it is outside and even if we are wearing sandals
5. A very healthy appetite
6. Terrible driving skills
7. Lots of hair
8. The competitive gene
9. A love of movies
10. The crazy gene?

And I wonder how many of these are related. For instance, is No. 1 related to No. 6? I've always known I'd be a terrible driver—

I spend too much time in my own head, I rarely register street names or routes—so I've never learned. Are erratic hand gestures an indication of poor motor skills? Is No. 5 related to No. 8? Could a healthy appetite be the physical manifestation of the emotional desire for reaching one's full potential? Most importantly, do No. 2 and/or No. 9 lead directly to No. 10? Does an overreliance on art as a coping mechanism for life inevitably result in madness? Does such a person always end up living more and more in a fantasy land with which the real world can no longer compete?

We are both repelled and attracted by such a condition, as the continued popularity of the novel *Don Quixote* makes clear, hailed by many, including myself, as the greatest novel ever written. I've taught an entire course on the novel and at first the students laugh at the wiry old man, a virgin no less, who sports a barber's basin for a helmet and ventures out into the countryside spouting romantic gibberish learned from tales of knights rescuing princesses and fighting giants and dispensing justice, which results, in the real world, in Don Quixote's constant humiliation in the form of ridicule and physical punishments. But once the students get past the initial comedy of the situation and the slapstick humour, the tragedy begins to take root. And ambiguity rises. Is Don Quixote's madness the classical character flaw that instigates his downfall, or is it an honourable strategy for dealing with a cruel, uncompassionate world? At which point is indulging in imaginative fancy no longer an opportunity for transformation—of self or world—or even a satisfying coping mechanism, but a destructive force harming everyone in its path?

Time to go! my mother calls, waving her hands in front of me like a giant windmill. Instinctively, I shut the laptop lid. No need—she has her own narrative and hasn't the slightest interest in the characters on my screen.

I don't know what will become of my mother. Or me. I fear we might both be grotesque parodies of Don Quixote, locked in our individual cages after our failed adventures and forced to endure the long, humiliating ride home.

The last supper: Like every family I've ever met we take several photographs for no better reason than everyone is in the same place at the same time. Uncle Fernando insists on taking them so that he will not appear in any. *We should take photos of our cars. In Brasilia, there are more cars than people,* he informs me. My uncle has a way of eliciting real smiles from me, giving me reasons to remember.

Things I Want to Remember

1. My grandmother squeezing my arm over the metal tables at the airport. Her twinkling blue eyes.
2. Sneaking into the Oscar Niemeyer cathedral, my grandmother weaving between pews like a tired pilgrim.
3. The car ride from a *Dirty Harry* movie with my Uncle Fernando/Doctor Garbage.
4. Doctor Garbage stealing all those bananas and placing beer can tabs in my hand.
5. Elizabeth's quiet French offerings of friendship over Easter buffet breakfast.
6. My grandmother telling me all about the poets, musicians, and artists in the family—her carefully wrapping me a package of scores because yes, I am interested in these things.
7. The Capuchin monkeys swinging in Uncle Wilhelm and Aunt Victoria's luxurious backyard.
8. Uncle Garbage waxing poetically on the beauties of communing with garbage.

9. The warmth of my grandmother's hand in mine at Easter mass.
10. This last outing as a family. *A family.* An almost clear night— except for one heavy, black cloud.

It's because of the rest of the family that I will be able to look back on this trip with some fond memories. Although I'm under no illusion that my grandmother and Uncle Fernando are perfect people, free of blame in terms of how they've conducted their lives or even how they also chose to ignore our needs as children, they have offered me something my mother has not: an emotional connection to the Brazilian side of my family. When my mother, standing outside the movie marquee, reiterates, *Fantasies are good things. Magical things. It's better to go to the movies than to have bad memories,* I am actually sympathetic to her point of view. She would have made a perfect Cecilia. I'm sure she's fantasized about living on the other side of the black-and-white projections of many of her favourite films: running off with Harrison Ford through the wasteland of a deteriorating society or bravely diving without breathing apparatus into the dark depths of the ocean. Unlike Mia Farrow, however, my mother is not mousy and, notwithstanding her cancer treatments, she does not exude physical weakness. Faced with my mother, I'm not sure Tom Baxter or Gil Shepherd would have been able to get a word in edgewise. Likely, he would have begged to jump back into his cardboard sets and neon Copacabana lights. Another difference between the world of film and the real world: a woman who lives her emotional life through projection is not the kind of woman who will make you fall in love.

While my mother and I walk over to the salad buffet, she reveals that after my father's accident there was a plan afoot to build a house in Recife to accommodate them, a bungalow with low counters and shelves. *We would all have had a better life here.*

This is pure fantasy, of course, so I must tread carefully. *That's very nice of the family,* I offer, though I note my mother has brought this up while the rest of the family is out of earshot. *Just unrealistic.*

How, unrealistic?

Brazil is not a disability-friendly country. My father has no friends or family here of his own. He doesn't speak Portuguese. There were more opportunities for us in Canada. Lots of social services. Lots of rewards for scholastics. I've been able to fund my entire education with my brain.

My mother proudly presents me with a bowl. *You're so smart, Priscila. You see, you were better off in Canada without me, so you should not be upset by what I did. I am not to blame for anything.*

I should have known: my mother only invited me into this conversation as a trap. Nothing on this trip has transpired the way she expected it would. The entire family is aware of this; the grief is palpable, her disappointment like a black-lace widow's shawl. She wrote a full-length feature script and on the page mother and daughter were to shop themselves silly, taste culinary delicacies, between long and warm embraces. Every last resource at her disposal was funnelled into this production. I'm sure she's already watched this film over a hundred times.

There is comfort in predictability, scripted lines and actions, and happy endings. Woody Allen knows this intimately. In perhaps the most brilliant line from *The Purple Rose of Cairo,* an angry customer, faced with the unpredictability of the new circumstances of the film now that Tom Baxter has literally excised himself from the plot, yells at the abandoned characters on the screen: *I want what happened in the movie last week to happen this week. Otherwise, what's life all about anyway?*

As we rejoin the rest of the family at the table, my mother whispers: *I can't wait to return to my peaceful life, Priscila. You will have no effect on me. I will wipe you from my memory.*

This movie is not to her liking: too sad, too messy, too unpredictable; she will wait for the next movie to begin. I am a character who can disappear as easily as turning off the projector. *I will wipe you from my memory.* The standard coping mechanism in our family. As if our brains are computers and we can delete this or that file, this or that person, this decade or this failed marriage, with a single click. Has her life been peaceful? After this trip, and what I know about my past, my mother, my DNA, will I ever be? It's a strange thing to realize you don't exist for someone; you are an image in a mind, and when she cuts you, you don't bleed, when she washes you away, you don't drown, when she hugs you, you don't feel an ounce of love. Priscila is Theresa's daughter, who lives in Canada; that's it, that's all. No wonder she doesn't need additional information. At the close of the film, that's my credit line: Theresa's daughter, played by Priscila Uppal. A Brazil-Canada production with subtitles.

But there are bonus features. As my mother wanders off to the buffet line for a second time to feed her insatiable hunger, the others swarm me with urgent confessions.

Split-Screen in Four Parts

Uncle Fernando: *My daughter in Rio, the one who likes to try to kill herself, twice she took so many pills she ended up in comas. Her doctor told her next time you better hope to die because you will have serious brain damage. The doctors say she wanted attention. These were not serious attempts because her suicide notes speak of the future—"I would like to be a better person"—when actual suicides know it is over and write "I have been a horrible person." I gave up on her long ago, but how to tell her that so she doesn't cry for a father who will not be in her future, I don't know.*

Aunt Victoria and Uncle Wilhelm: *We can't wait to retire and travel for pleasure, not business. Just not to exotic countries. Only North America, western Europe, and other places in Brazil.*

Uncle Fernando: *My wife, Rosana, is one of eleven siblings. Her father tans fish skin—he is the last living person in Brazil to know this technique. He knows all kinds of old medicines from the plants and berries in the Amazon, but nobody cares. Only Rosana. But he doesn't trust her either. Knows our daughter isn't interested and so Rosana would be the last to know the secrets and he'd rather be the last of the line. This tanned fish is a present from Rosana to you: this tanned fish. Don't tell customs.*

Elizabeth: *Everyone knows your mother is difficult, but she's very good to me. She loves me. I just don't argue with her. I don't argue with anyone.*

Uncle Fernando: *The garbage in Toronto is famous. You have all kinds of plans to deal with garbage. Do you think you could ask the mayor of Toronto if I could study their garbage? Ask the mayor to invite me.*

Aunt Victoria and Uncle Wilhelm: *We will always take care of your grandmother. Do not worry about her. We used to think your mother might take care of her, since she has no children of her own—you understand, no children here—but she is not fit to take care of anyone.*

Uncle Fernando: *I am curious to see how much luggage you have. I bet a lot. Your grandmother's luggage was famous in the Air Force. You don't have to justify all your luggage. It's genetic.*

Elizabeth: *I have a nervous stomach. So does Grandmother. Nervous stomachs run in the family. Et vous?*

Grandmother Therezinha: *I always think of you, Priscila. And Amerjit too. I never forget to mark his birthday. It's a long time you did not look for your mother. Do you think she's unwell? . . . Yes, I too think she's unwell . . . Yes, it's hard to blame a sick person for being sick. There's nothing we can do. She can't be cured now. I'm so sorry. Do you think I will ever see Amerjit?*

Uncle Fernando: *The sun in Brazil is a liar. You don't mess with the Brazilian sun. It will kill you while you try to kiss it.*

Back to full screen

Have you been drinking? my grandmother suddenly asks her son. *You don't usually talk so much.*

Doctor Garbage shrugs. *I don't usually talk at all. But the girl is leaving, Mamma. I might die. You might die—you are very old, Mamma. She might die. These are things to say before we go.* Then, leaning into me, he flips open his cellphone to a series of numbers attached to his name. *Time to forget this. Understand?*

My mother is on her way back, her plate piled up to her nose. Like in a thriller, each step she takes echoes, and we rush to finish our intimate conversations.

Let us say, my grandmother whispers, her voice cracking, *that grandmother and granddaughter were wearing the same colour blue on their last day together.* She brings my hand up to her heart and then to her lips to kiss.

I am not wearing blue. This is when I recognize my grandmother is also a storyteller. Like me.

Before I slip under the red comforter and spend my last night in my mother's condominium, shadowed by the most upsetting image of myself I have ever encountered, she drops one last post-card on the coffee table:

AIR CANADA: I spoke to Camila. She confirmed Priscila Uppal leaves 9:10 p.m., Toronto 6:45 a.m.
check-in 2h30 antes = 6:40 p.m.

A bedtime story.

My mother must be anticipating the relief of tomorrow night, when she can sink into her theatre seat, wipe the useless tears from her eyes, and lose herself in the next Hollywood dream.

I'm not sure I ever had the chance to compete with that.

There is no name for my mother's condition, only hopeless survival.

When the characters in the film *The Purple Rose of Cairo* are left impotently waiting onscreen for Tom Baxter to return so they can continue with the plot of the movie, they beg their restless audience not to pull the plug: *No. Don't turn the projector off! It gets black and we disappear. . . . You don't understand what it's like to disappear, to be nothing, annihilated!*

My mother turns off the lights. I think I do.

The Painting of Mother Goddess and Her Two Children

END CREDITS

bye bye brasil

Gypsy Lord, Master of Dreams: Dreams can only offend those who don't dream.

ORGIVE ME, dear reader. Seven years after the event, only now do I discover to my surprise that I never kept notes in my journal about our parting. I'm sure I didn't want to remember it.

But I can't escape memory, so I will do my best to reconstruct our sad airport scene, our final moments, our final words to each other. This is not the stuff reunions ought to be made of, but there you are, life rarely conforms to art. I write this book for all those who have discovered, like me, that life rarely conforms to art. Even now, my hands shake as I type. I'm not acting, or pretending, or shaping this day into art. I'm simply reporting my pain. And I must do this as accurately as possible. For me. And for you. I would hate for you to come all this way with me and not be offered the "gift of truth."

My only journal entry reads: *Last day too heartbreaking to write about. Locked bathroom doors, sniffling, heads lolling on chairs, eyes pretending to be closed: counted, counted minutes.*

I must unpack these words. Reimagine:

The thin string clothesline in her apartment tugs at my heart. I'm reminded of when she used to hang the laundry out on the wire in our Ottawa backyard. This I remember, and helping her with the clothespins. I loved handing over the wooden pins into her open hands.

All night she screamed on the telephone. Actually screamed. I don't know to whom. Her mother? Her sister? That strange couple from the airport? Probably her mother—I'm told she likes to fight with her mother—but I don't ask. I can't. I don't want to, because maybe she'll tell me. Maybe she won't be able to help herself. They are probably arguing about me. About whether I'll ever return. About why no one else in the family is permitted to send me off at the airport—why my mother is keeping them out of this final scene. She screamed and cried, turned on lights, turned off lights, cried and screamed some more. My earplugs no match for her denouement. She's desperate to blame someone for her ruined dreams, and I know I fit the description of the suspect. I was the weak link in her plans. If I hadn't stayed home from school that day, hadn't observed the luggage being packed off into an unfamiliar car trunk, hadn't screamed my butt off at the handling of my brother, hadn't locked the front door and clung to our father's bed, her life might have been vastly different. Triumphant. She doesn't care about my life. Or Jit's. Which would have been vastly different too, but potentially more tragic. Hers certainly less so. *I* ruined her life. *I* crushed her dreams. *I* killed her. *Oh my god*, I now realize, *she hates me too.*

One thing I've learned on this trip is that when someone is scared of you, this person can't have a real relationship with you. This person can fawn over you, or put you up on a pedestal, or suspiciously watch your every muscle twitch, but this person can't approach you human being to human being. And I realize that one of the main reasons I've undertaken this journey, and will deem it a success, is that I am no longer scared of my mother. Whatever damage she has caused me, she can cause no more.

You can't kill me, she said. *No one can kill me.*

And she's right. I can't kill her. No matter how much I'd like to erase her from my memory bank, she's there, taunting me with her presence, her bulk, her phonograph mouth, her relentless dreams. But at least I am no longer afraid of my dreams.

Is Brazil built on dreams? *Bye Bye Brasil*, one of Carlos Diegues's iconic films, is dedicated to "the Brazilian people of the twenty-first century." The movie chronicles a travelling magic show, run by Gypsy Lord, Master of Dreams (played by José Wilker) and his exotic partner and lover, Salomé (played by Betty Faria), and all of the misadventures they encounter as their Caravana Rolidei is gradually supplanted by film and television. By the end of the movie, these once mesmerizing and mysterious characters, so enthralling that a young accordionist and his pregnant wife abandon their village to join their troupe, are reduced to selling sex instead of magic. In reality, the trip leads not to the stars, but to betrayal, heartbreak, disillusionment, to a tough and cruel future. No one wants to buy the dreams of the "Master of Clouds and Time," who can command the skies to snow in Brazil (using grated coconut), or engage in telepathy with dead relatives to comfort the many widows in small villages (he sees who in the audience is crying and directs his message to them). Instead, having struck it rich in smuggling, the Master of Dreams employs a harem and his Queen of Rhumba wears blinking Christmas lights in her hair. The Caravana Rolidei abandons mysticism and sensuality to deliver titillation with "commercial flair."

As I collect my luggage, my mother paces her living room, hands clenched into tight fists.

I resent wasted time. I've wasted so much time doing things for others. Now I do only for myself. Even God can't give you time back.

My mother isn't stupid. She doesn't say stupid things. She sometimes says wise things that are horrific when placed into her specific context, but frequently the things she says would be applicable to other sane situations. In her own way, my mother is a Master of Dreams, peddling her version of the world even in the face of brutal contradicting reality. Even in the face of her own sad and angry daughter. I have wasted her time. Dream time. She's right. Even God can't give you that time back.

Art is meant to create empathy. Art is ethical but it is not ethics. This has not happened for my mother. Art is either expressing something right or wrong. Art is an escapist addiction. Like heroin. Like the characters at the end of the film, she betrays her dreams. Did they (does she?) have any choice? Fair question. All of these dreams are understandable; all of these endings avoidable. Aren't they?

Or perhaps we need to face the fact that some dreams are meant to die.

In one of our last moments together we visit the airport washroom before I pass through security. I am standing in front of my mother in the line, arms crossed. I can feel her eyes on me like target sights, her frown covering the sinks. I am second in line. As the woman in front enters the recently vacated washroom, my mother points angrily at me.

You will be next.

I'm twenty-eight years old. I know how to use a washroom, I sigh.

I'm just being helpful, she announces to the line.

You're being bossy, I slap back before entering the sanctity of the stall.

When I re-emerge, my mother is outside the washrooms, hands glued to the handle of the steel luggage cart. One look at me and she propels the vehicle forward toward the security clearance area.

Thank you, I can push my own luggage.

She flashes a look that could smash bricks. *No, Priscila. I do the right thing. Until you leave, I will do the right thing, as I have this entire trip, no matter how you have treated me. Since I am so bossy, I will tell you to go now. I am not bossy. Americans and Canadians are bossy, not me. You wanted everything your way. And now you will see. You will never see or hear from me again. I will erase you from my mind. You can be in command in Canada. Here, I am in command. I wish nothing for you.*

These are our last moments. I must collect myself. She is physically ill, I tell myself, and very likely mentally ill as well. She is performing some script that makes sense to her. I suppose I must perform last lines from a script that makes sense to me.

Even though I feel like the cold, beautiful Salomé, who crushes her infatuated accordionist (*Don't think for a second that your love moves me. It makes me sick.*), I don't want my last words to be anger. There won't be another trip. I know this. She doesn't love me. And the truth is, while it hurts when people don't love you, it doesn't really hurt me more than when students or new acquaintances don't like me; nevertheless, how embarrassing it is that my mother is abandoning me for the second time. At least this time, I can say goodbye.

I can cue the bossa nova music and jump on my own travelling caravan. Even if, like the strongman, Swallow, who finally disappoints the Gypsy Lord by losing an arm-wrestling match on which he has gambled everything—their van, their equipment, their money, their monkey—I too have lost all my collateral on this risky bet. I can drop out, start over. As ugly as life gets, Carlos Diegues understands, there is still beauty in survival and happiness in small moments where dreams, old and new, almost seem possible. I can dream my own dreams. This is a basic human right no dictator, god, or bitter relative has ever been able to fully dismantle. I can dream my own dreams. My mother need not appear in any of them.

As my mother rolls the luggage cart, I remember that during one of her many sermons, she admitted the part of Catholicism she hates is confession. *I don't like telling a man my sins. My sins are between me and God. I do not need an intermediary.* Well, maybe God needs one, I think.

And I am reminded of the story of how I was kicked out of Catholic Sunday School when I was eight and we were living with my cousins in Michigan. The assignment: paint your favourite disciple. Around twenty kids pulled brown paper from a gigantic roll and traced each other's bodies in pencil to produce a proper human outline for our meagre painterly talents. We were then to fill in the outline on our own, adding a beard here, long hair there, robes, boots, belts. The nun on duty knew something was amiss when she found me drawing coins and a noose. *Judas! You're drawing Judas!* she cried. *Wicked girl! Wicked!* She tore my brown paper and yanked me into her office, ferociously scribbling a note to my aunt and uncle barring me from returning. I knew I was suffering an injustice. Though I lacked the eloquence to fully explain myself, I did manage to eke out, several times, the conviction: *Nothing happens without Judas.* Which was indeed why he was, and still is, my favourite disciple. From a literary point of view, the narrative has no meaning, no trigger to unleash the full depth of the crucifixion-resurrection experience that is central to Christianity, without Judas. Judas is as important as Jesus.

Nothing happens without Judas. I suppose nothing happened without my mother or my father. I arrived on her doorstep and she told me over and over again that she loves me, that she has always loved me. *One spends a lifetime waiting for these words. And when it happens, one's heart freezes,* admits Salomé. Was I ever willing to believe her? I think I was, but who knows for sure.

I recognize that for some, family ties are the only reason to live, work, make money, get up every day and do it again. But this dream is not for me. And I refuse to feel bad about this any longer. My goal was to find out who my mother is, who we are to each other. I've achieved my goal. We are strangers tied by blood and crushed dreams. We have damaged each other and now must simply live with that damage as best as we can. Some of us have just developed more excellent coping mechanisms than others.

I don't need a mother. And I no longer desire one. This doesn't need to be a tragedy. This can be comedy. This can be freedom.

Thank you for this opportunity to see where you live and who you are, and for bringing me to meet the rest of the family. I wish you a very healthy and happy rest of your life.

I've never been one for long goodbyes. Chris always teases me about it. When I make up my mind to leave a place—whether a bar or friend's house or a city I've just fallen in love with—I always want to get moving. Even if I'd like to stay, I am anxious at the thought of being left behind. That's worse than missing a place.

But my mother's short goodbye takes the cake. Like a delivery person, my mother backs away from the luggage cart. There will be no kisses, no hugs, not even the shaking of hands or a pat on the back, only that sickly half-smile on her face.

You too, she says. *Goodbye.*

I hear Maria Callas, the legendary opera singer, in her only non-singing film role, Pier Paolo Pasolini's haunting 1969 version of *Medea*, screaming out the last line of the movie as her dead children burn along with the city behind her: *Nothing is possible anymore!*

A home is a physical place. But more importantly, it is an imaginative concept. A place of shelter and support and comfort. My home is not here. My mother's home is not here either. But that's not my concern. It's her job to find hers, and my job to find mine. Perhaps hers really is in the movies.

Betrayals abound, especially in the form of kisses. I just hope I am able to do something creative with her betrayal. And with my own.

Isn't that what art is for?

Some dreams are meant to die. Without looking back, I walk through the security gates. Nothing blinks or buzzes. I am free to go.

I must rely on myself to create my own home. As I've always done.

The Women of the Family—(left to right) Fernanda, Victoria, Therezinha, Priscila, Theresa

blade runner,
the director's cut

Roy: It's not an easy thing to meet your maker.

AFTER being poked and prodded, I answer a series of questions from Dr. Iris Gorfinkel, my family physician. I adore Dr. Gorfinkel because even though she sees sick people all day long, she always looks distressed when you present her with physical complaints, like it's unusual, if not horrible.

"I just can't believe your mother rejected you," Dr. Gorfinkel says protectively. I know she's a mother of three.

"Wasn't enough to do it once," I laugh. "I don't think I'll be visiting Brazil again anytime soon."

"I just can't believe it," she repeats, shaking her head at me in my light-blue paper hospital robe perched on the steel examining table. "I would be so proud to be your mother." I know she is telling the truth. She's often told me that she finds my life story inspiring. She alludes to this again when she continues: "I still don't know how you've lived through all this and don't need a psychiatrist or medication. I would need extensive therapies. Are you sure . . . ?"

"I'm sure," I repeat for the third or fourth time in our history as doctor and patient. "What's a shrink going to tell me that I already don't know? I had a turbulent childhood. I know this. I experienced trauma. I know this. In fact, I think I function quite well despite everything. I just have to keep going." Suddenly, this sounds like something my mother would say. God wants me to live, so I live. I doubt my mother's ever set foot in a therapist's office.

"Priscila, in terms of your yearly physical, you're basically in excellent health," Dr. Gorfinkel informs me, after noting my height and weight on her chart. "But I'm going to prescribe antibiotics because your tests show that your stomach problems are not stress-related, as we first thought, but the result of a parasite." She makes one of her contorted faces when she says the word "parasite," as if she is picturing one crawling about my intestines.

I return the disgusted glance. Parasite? "You mean there's a foreign organism living in my system?"

"I'm afraid so. It's more common than you think. Considering all the stomach pain you experienced during your trip, I'd say you must have contracted the parasite right after you landed in Brazil. The antibiotics will wipe it out. Just rest and stay close to home if you can."

"I've been organizing my day according to where the toilets are for weeks now," I admit with embarrassment. And I think about how I could have felt better sooner if I'd known, how I could have enjoyed the holiday Chris and I took right after I returned home even more—*I've always wanted to visit Paris*, I told him, *and I need a beautiful trip after this horrible one*. Although we did have a glorious time, we also joked that it was my "bathroom tour of Paris," as I needed to utilize the facilities usually once an hour. Oh, well. If only I'd known a lot of things.

It's a test designed to provoke an emotional response . . .

I throw my hands up in the air. "A parasite. I just thought I hated my mother."

Dr. Gorfinkel giggles and then laughs. I join her. I'm sure those stuck in the waiting room must be wondering what's going on between us. We don't stop laughing for some time, as if I've told the funniest joke in the world.

True to Dr. Gorfinkel's word, in less than two weeks I am feeling like myself again, whoever that is. I continue teaching creative writing and writing poetry. I defend my dissertation and earn a Doctor of Philosophy. I try not to think about my mother. In order to accomplish this, Chris and I rent movies. Lots of movies.

Eventually, I stop thinking about my mother. The moral of our story is clear to me. Some relationships are not worth pursuing. But I can't help thinking about my grandmother, Uncle Fernando, and the cousins in Rio de Janeiro I haven't met, the estranged ones like me.

I've always preferred the 1992 Director's Cut ending of *Blade Runner*, the little origami unicorn left as both a threat and a message of hope in Deckard's apartment as he and his lover flee the city underneath these last elegiac words: *It's too bad she won't live, but then again, who does?* Not every movie should have a happy ending. Not every relationship either. And who says you can't go back and edit and cut, alter and transform the past. Or the future. We are mortal, yes, but we are also survivors.

What does it mean to have a mother? Is this the necessary condition of humanity? I have no idea. Overeducated as I am, this area of life was never properly covered to my satisfaction. Not then, and not now. Perhaps someday someone will enlighten me.

Before I know it, I am planning another trip, another visit half-way across the world to find out if there's life, real life out there, and perhaps another possible ending, one discarded on the director's cutting-room floor, one censored from public viewing, or one that hasn't yet been imagined.

I never thought I would return to Brazil, and I don't know if the decision to return for another adventure is evidence I am human or the opposite. What I do discover is that I am not a replicant. I'm a blade runner...

Fade to black.

Voice-Over

I can't wait to return to my peaceful life, Priscila. You will have no effect on me. I will wipe you from my memory. . . . You will never see or hear from me again.

In April 2005, Chris and I landed in São Paulo, Brazil, but quickly boarded a connecting flight to Brasilia, where we were greeted by my blue-eyed and white-haired seventy-something grandmother and my large-armed Uncle Fernando. When my grandmother squeezes my hand and asks why I've come back, I reply, *For you, Grandmother. Just for you!* Not only did my mother refuse to see us, she refused to be in the same city as us. Under these circumstances, we were surprised the rest of the family welcomed us so warmly, although we do hear about how she fought with all of them before we landed, deeming each and every one a *traitor*. We also travel to Rio de Janeiro where we are introduced to my cousin Diana, the eldest of Fernando's estranged daughters and the member of the family who most resembles me. Unfortunately, although my other cousin Juliana keeps promising to meet us for dinner or a walk on the beach, she never materializes.

When I ask Diana if it's true there's a crazy gene on the women's side of the family, she sighs heavily and nods.

I propose a toast: *To not going crazy.*

Firmly, she shakes her head. *No. It is easy to be the crazy one. It is not easy to have to take care of the crazy ones. So, we should drink to going crazy.*

Which we do.

Sometimes life is like the movies. Second chances. I'm glad that I decided to visit my family for the second time, and grateful that Chris was able to join me. If we hadn't gone then, we wouldn't have all our memories. We wouldn't have the privilege of knowing before it was too late.

Here is my list of what's important to know:

1. On June 18, 2007, my Uncle Fernando José Salvador Campos died of the cancer he always knew would take him down. He was sixty years old.
2. On June 14, 2008, my grandmother Therezinha, or Theresa Amélia de Góes Campos, died of cancer. She was eighty-two years old.
3. Aunt Victoria sent me a Catholic memory card prepared for my grandmother's funeral featuring the same portrait my mother displayed in her living room and photographs of her husband and her three children, but none of her grandchildren.
4. Elizabeth and Walter married in 2007.
5. I'm sure Guilherme and his fiancée married. I just don't know when.

6. I'm also sure Uncle Wilhelm and Aunt Victoria are enjoying retirement.
7. In 2006, Chris and I threw a "Ten Years and Tenure Party" to celebrate our tenth anniversary and my recent tenure and promotion. I designed matching T-shirts that read: TEN MORE YEARS! *Happily Unmarried since 1996.*
8. We are currently planning our eighteenth anniversary.
9. My brother, Jit, married Jennifer Hacking, a hockey doctor, on June 30, 2007. I was a bridesmaid. My father was lifted in his wheelchair to the reception by four men, including Chris, like the sultan he is.
10. Emmitt Uppal was born May 1, 2008, and Hunter Uppal on March 21, 2011. They love their crazy auntie who writes books.

True to my mother's word, I've never seen or heard from her again. Except in my dreams. And sometimes in films. But even these appearances are few and far between, and elicit little emotion. I'm simply encountering in two dimensions someone I used to think was real. So I say let them come, the deep-sea diving and the apple bombs. I've already seen this movie one hundred times.

Time to turn off the projector. Turn on the lights. And go home.

My Brother's Wedding Day: (left to right) Chris, Priscila, Avtar, Jit, Jennifer

ACKNOWLEDGEMENTS

the red carpet

This book has been years in the making, probably since I was eight years old. I might have a number of people to blame, but I have even more people to thank.

Thank you, first of all, to all of my role models growing up: teachers and coaches and friends of parents who supported me in my dream to become a writer. This book would never exist without you.

Thank you to my partner in crime, Christopher Doda, for believing I could handle the trip to Brazil on my own, and for believing in the importance of this book from the beginning. Thank you for all those nights with pizza and movies. And thank you, most of all, for understanding that spending all day thinking about your mother is unhealthy and requires lots of running (not running away, but literal running across the city).

Thank you to the many organizations that helped fund the research and writing of this book: Social Sciences and Humanities Research Council, Ontario Arts Council, Toronto Arts Council, and York University Faculty of Arts.

Thank you to my amazing agents, Hilary McMahon and Natasha Daneman.

Thank you to my insightful editor, Janice Zawerbny, and to everyone at Thomas Allen Publishers.

Thank you to the friends who provided an eager ear, a good meal, and good advice before and after my travels, especially Richard Teleky, Barry Callaghan and Claire Weissman Wilks, Tracy Carbert, Ann Peel, Toni Healey, and the Women Writers Salon.

Thank you to all the writers, journalists, editors, and publishers who have supported all the work that has resulted from this project in many forms: poetry, fiction, non-fiction, drama—including Rishma Dunlop and Michael Helm and the editors at *Brick* magazine; Helen Walsh and Disapora Dialogues; Iris Turcott and the Factory Wired Festival.

Thank you to the graduate assistants who have helped with this book, especially the thorough and calm David Sprague and the skeptical and enthusiastic Anthony Hicks. Thank you also to Christina Sacchetti, Tim Hanna, Tanya MacIntosh, and Jessica Abraham.

Also, thank you tons to Ricardo Sternberg and Vivian Ralickas for your contacts in Brazil and your generosity with all things Brazilian.

Thank you to my father, Avtar, and my brother, Jit, for supporting me despite their reservations and their own heartache.

Thanks to Grace Westcott for advice. Thanks to Dr. Iris Gorfinkel for excellent care.

Thanks to all those who sent movie recommendations. And to Queen Video and 2Q Video in Toronto.

movie credits

Blade Runner (1982), Director: Ridley Scott, Screenwriters: Hampton Fancher and David Webb Peoples (based on Philip K. Dick's novel *Do Androids Dream of Electric Sheep?*); *Maid in Manhattan* (2002), Director: Wayne Wang, Screenwriters: John Hughes and Kevin Wade; *The Big Blue (Le Grand Bleu)* (1988), Director: Luc Besson, Screenwriters: Luc Besson, Robert Garland, Marilyn Goldin, Jacques Mayol, and Marc Perrier; *God Is Brazilian (Deus É Brasileiro)* (2003), Director: Carlos Diegues, Screenwriters: João Emanuel Carneiro, Carlos Diegues, Renata Almeida Magalhães, and João Ubaldo Ribeiro (based on Ribeiro's short story "O Santo Que Não Acreditava em Deus" ["The Saint Who Did not Believe in God"]); *Ladyhawke* (1985), Director: Richard Donner, Screenwriters: Edward Khmara, Michael Thomas, Tom Mankiewicz, and David Webb Peoples; *Mommie Dearest* (1981), Director: Frank Perry, Screenwriters: Robert Getchell, Tracy Hotchner, Frank Perry, and Frank Yablans (based on Christina Crawford's memoir by the same name); *Stella Dallas* (1937), Director: King Vidor, Screenwriters: Harry Wagstaff Gribble, Gertrude Purcell, Sarah Y. Mason, and Victor Heerman (based on a novel by Olive Higgins Prouty by the same name); *Alien Resurrection* (1997), Director: Jean-Pierre

Jeunet, Screenwriters: Dan O'Bannon, Ronald Shusett, and Joss Whedon; *Freaky Friday* (2003), Director: Mark Waters, Screenwriters: Leslie Dixon and Heather Hach (based on Mary Rodgers's novel by the same name); *Throw Momma from the Train* (1987), Director: Danny DeVito, Screenwriter: Stu Silver; *The Myth of Fingerprints* (1997), Director: Bart Freundlich, Screenwriter: Bart Freundlich; *The Purple Rose of Cairo* (1985), Director: Woody Allen, Screenwriter: Woody Allen; *Bye Bye Brasil* (1980), Director: Carlos Diegues, Screenwriters: Carlos Diegues and Leopoldo Serran.